VOYAGES
that changed the world

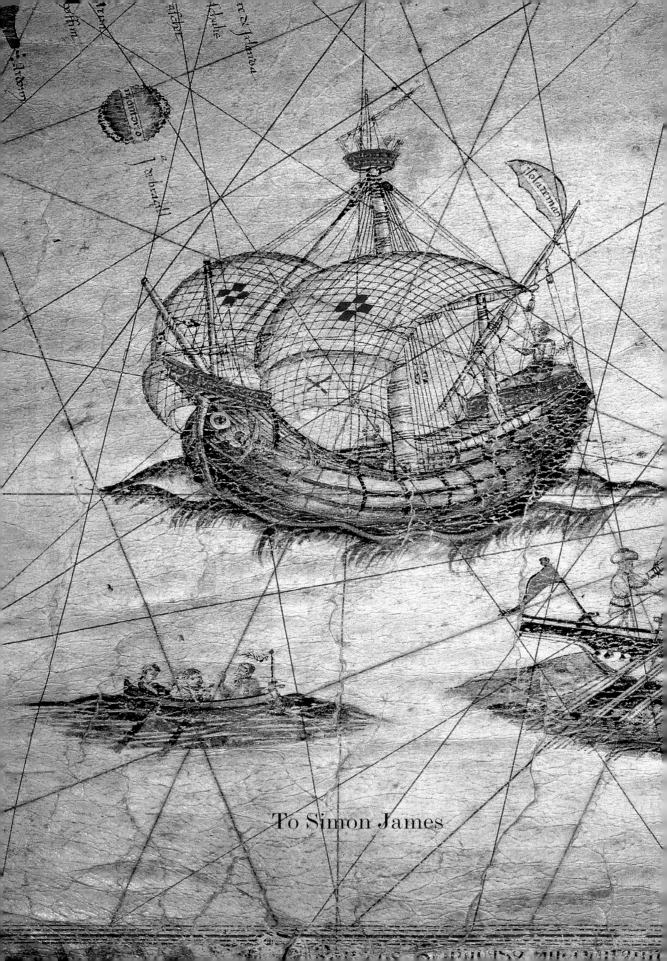

To Simon James

VOYAGES
that changed the world

PETER AUGHTON

Quercus

Contents

INTRODUCTION

Mankind has always wondered about the unknown world. We have always wanted to sail beyond the horizon, to find new settlements or simply for the sake of adventure.

Those of us who live in the Western world see the Mediterranean, at the time of the rise of Greece and Rome, as the starting point of world exploration. Many people in the eastern world would not agree with this starting point. Thousands of years before the rise of Rome there were movements of people across Asia and into Indonesia. These migrations were mostly land journeys covering thousands of miles and executed over several generations. Sometimes sea voyages were undertaken in primitive craft to reach and settle on uninhabited islands. In the centuries before Christ China was the largest and most advanced nation on Earth but the Chinese had competition from Japan, India and the ancient kingdoms of the east who also had a maritime coastal trade in these early centuries. These nations built seagoing ships, some built whole navies. They explored and colonized the offshore islands and they navigated parts of the Pacific Ocean.

The 'silk road' was the great trading route connecting the empires of Asia and it eventually reached the Mediterranean countries. It was a land route covered by caravans of mules or camels and it was run by the many merchants at the various trading points along the route. Nobody travelled the whole route, goods were exchanged at towns and trading points and by this method trade was opened up between east and west. The places along the Silk Road had very little knowledge of the different cultures in the distant lands with which they were trading. There was a 'spice route' that developed at much the same time. This was a sea route to the Spice Islands, it involved China and Japan and also Arabia, India, Southeast Asia and the Indonesian archipelago. In later centuries, when the Silk Road was well established, it was the goods from the exotic east, the silks and the spices, that motivated the European nations to sponsor great voyages. There were other reasons apart from trade. There was the search for new lands. There was the search for knowledge. There was colonization and exploration. The route to the Orient was always the greatest motivating factor however. Whether it was Columbus, or Cabot, or Magellan or whether it was the many who perished in the terrible search for the North West Passage, they all hoped to find a new and shorter route to get to the Orient.

This is the story of the great voyages that contributed towards the knowledge, the exploration and the mapping of the world. It is fortunate that we have journals and eye witness accounts of many great voyages and we can sometimes read for ourselves the words and thoughts of those who explored the seas where no ship had sailed before.

THE EARLY NAVIGATORS

THE PHOENICIANS CIRCUMNAVIGATE
AFRICA AND THE POLYNESIANS
MIGRATE ACROSS THE PACIFIC

c. 50,000 BC — 1150 AD

*'Phoenicians were the first great founders of the world, founders of cities
and of mighty states who showed a path through seas before unknown.
In the first ages, when the sons of men knew not which way to turn them…
and sent each wandering tribe far off to share a different soil and climate.
Hence arose the great diversity, so plainly seen,'mid nations widely severed.'*

DIONYSIUS OF SUSIANA, 3 AD

Voyages of settlement and colonization were made in the Pacific Ocean long before written records began. The exploration of the Far East was not confined to the offshore islands.

The Philippines were amongst the earliest discoveries. Exploration and settlement continued further south into Indonesia. Australia for example was colonized in about 50,000 BC when the Indo-Pacific peoples first crossed from the Indonesian archipelago into northern Australia. The sea level was about 100 metres lower at that time than it is at present, but this was not low enough to form a land bridge between New Guinea and Australia. The crossing of the Torres Straits must have been made by boats and those who made the crossing were the ancestors of the Australian Aborigines.

By 10,000 BC the Indonesian people had reached the Bismarck Islands and the Solomons, but for several thousand years these islands remained the limits of human settlement in the Pacific Ocean. It was not until about 1200 BC that the island groups of the Fijis and the Tongas became inhabited, together with Vanuatu and New Caledonia. These islands were settled by what we now call the Melanesian people. The migration continued slowly to the west but it was not until the first century after Christ that the Society Islands were discovered and settled; they were followed by settlements in the Tuamotus and the Marquesas. By this time the Polynesians can be identified as a separate race to the Melanesians and it was the former that were destined to make the most spectacular voyages across the Pacific.

The evidence suggests that Easter Island was settled in about 440 AD. There is little doubt from the culture and the language that it was settled by the Polynesians crossing either from the Australs or from the Society

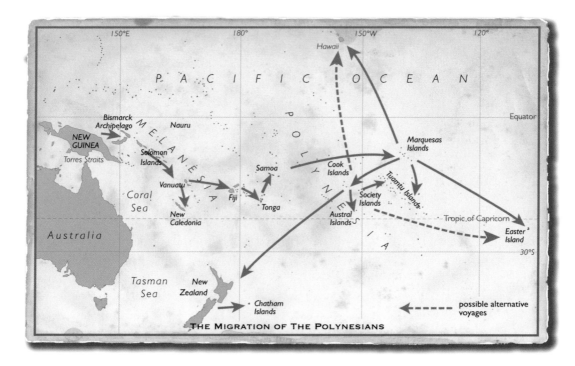

THE MIGRATION OF THE POLYNESIANS

Islands. This was a journey of about two thousand miles made in open canoes, probably by pure accident but perhaps through systematic exploration. Many years later, when the Society Islands were first discovered by the Europeans it was found that the Polynesians had an excellent navigational system, they had maps showing their neighbouring islands and they could use the stars to work out their position at sea. It is still remarkable that they could cross the Pacific as far as Easter Island and form a stable community there.

New Zealand There are two further important migrations in the Pacific, both of which are credited to the Polynesians. One is the discovery of the Hawaiian island group. It is thought that Hawaii may have first been reached from the Marquesas but it is also possible that the island may have been settled from the Society Islands. Either way the amount of ocean covered by the open canoes is staggering, yet the culture and language of the Hawaiian islands leave no doubt that the native peoples have Polynesian ancestry.

The other important migration came much later, probably in about 1150 AD. This was the discovery of New Zealand, also by the Polynesians. The distance is again of the order of two thousand miles and although New Zealand is a far greater landmass than Easter Island or Hawaii it still required good navigation to find it. When James Cook first landed in New Zealand in 1769 he carried with him a resident of Tahiti called Tupia who was able to converse well with the Maoris. The speech of the Maoris had evidently not developed significantly from that of the original settlers several centuries earlier.

The Polynesian and Melanesian voyages were made very early in the history of exploration. These peoples solved some of the problems of navigation and they created successful colonies on islands many miles away from their native island groups. The very earliest voyages, to the Tonga Isles and the Fiji group, predate the earliest voyages in the western world. Unfortunately what we lack is written evidence, or traditional sagas and stories, describing the voyages themselves and the names of the people who made them.

In the western world we do not start with an ocean as vast as the Pacific but we are lucky enough to have a written record of many early voyages. The Mediterranean in ancient times was exactly what its name implies – it was seen as the sea in the middle of the world. The many countries bordering on the Mediterranean coast could trade with each other by sea. They could also trade with lands outside the Mediterranean. Exotic goods, such as the silks and spices from the east, were exchanged through the overland trade along the silk road. It was well known that these luxuries were carried for many miles and for several years before reaching the market but how far they had travelled and for how long was no more than mere conjecture.

Ancient philosophers naturally wondered about the nature of the world beyond their horizons, about where it ended and where it began. Their flat world could not be infinite, and since everything by its nature fell to the ground then it followed that any voyage undertaken far

THE PILLARS OF HERCULES

The Greeks had a far more romantic name for the Straits of Gibraltar, they were known as the Pillars of Hercules with the rock of Gibraltar as one of the pillars. In early Greek times the seas beyond were considered stormy and un-navigable. Plato tells the story of the fabled lost city of Atlantis which lay beyond the Pillars of Hercules, but he gives no credible details to enable Atlantis to be identified.

enough in any direction would eventually reach the edge of the Earth at a point where it would be impossible to go any further. Greek philosophy was developed by thought and discourse rather than by practical methods. It was assumed that, just as the land surrounded the Mediterranean Sea, so the land in its turn was surrounded by a vast ocean. The ocean was assumed to lie outside the Pillars of Hercules but it enclosed the whole of the three known continents of Europe, Africa and Asia. In the long centuries before Christ there were a few practical astronomers who speculated that the true shape of the Earth was not a disc but a sphere. Their theories were not tolerated for long and the common-sense theory of the flat earth prevailed.

The early Greeks thought it unlucky to sail by night and even when travelling by day they did not recommend sailing out of sight of land. A passage from Hesiod reflects the general consensus about travel by sea:

If you are afflicted with the desire for uncomfortable travelling over the sea, then remember that the blasts of all the winds rage when the Pleiades flee before the mighty strength of Orion and set in the misty deep... The right season for mortals to sail is fifty days after the solstice, when the burdensome days of summer come to an end. At that time you will not wreck your ship, nor will the sea destroy the men, unless the earth shaker Poseidon desires it or Zeus, king of the immortals wishes to destroy them.

To the Greek mind the art of navigation was simply a question of knowing and following the coastline or hopping from one to another of the many islands that dotted the Mediterranean. Beyond the Pillars of Hercules lay the Atlantic, this was a part of the great ocean that enclosed the whole world. The Atlantic was a much heavier and hardier sea than the Mediterranean. It had huge waves and ferocious storms to toss the greatest of ships and it had winds that could tear the strongest of sails to shreds. The sea pounded hard with its great white breakers against the rocks and cliffs of the distant coastlines and gradually wore them away. The weather was invariably wet, windy and foggy and the tides were enormous compared to those in the Mediterranean.

Yet trade through the Straits of Gibraltar did exist before the time of Christ, certainly to the north along the Iberian Peninsula and into Northern Europe. Tin from the Cornish mines of Britain found its way to Athens and Rome. There was trade too with the settlements around the coast of Africa. Even the Canary Islands were known to the Romans and were named after the local inhabitants, the canine beasts that dominated the islands.

Those who ventured out into the Atlantic, and those who were brave enough to sail by night across the Mediterranean, came to know the constellations in the night sky. They knew that all the stars appeared to revolve about the Pole Star. They knew therefore that the Pole Star gave them direction at night just as the position of the sun gave them direction during the day. The sun was in the east at sunrise, it lay due south at noon and it appeared in the west at sunset. To those who could measure the angles the sun could be used to determine direction at any time of the day. The ancients knew also that the height of the Pole Star against the mast varied little throughout the Mediterranean. The height of the noonday sun in the sky varied with the seasons but they knew that this variation was predictable through the annual cycle of the seasons and it was possible to allow for it in their navigational calculations. There is a passage in Homer where Odysseus navigates his way across the sea guided by the goddess Calypso:

It was with a happy heart that the good Odysseus spread his sail to catch the wind and used his seamanship to keep his boat straight with the steering-oar. There he sat and never closed his eyes in sleep, but kept them on the Pleiades, or watched Bootes slowly set, or the Great Bear, nicknamed the Wain, which always wheels round in the same place and looks across at Orion the hunter with a wary eye. It was this constellation, the only one that never bathes in the ocean's stream, that the wise goddess Calypso had told him to keep on his left hand as he made across the sea. For the seventeen days he sailed on his course, and on the eighteenth there hove into sight the shadowy mountains of the Phaeacians' country, which jutted out to meet him there. The land looked like a shield lying on the misty sea.

The Best Seafaring Race In the second millennium before Christ a people arose who gained a reputation as the best seafaring race in the known world. They were the Phoenicians. They quickly became a dominant trading force throughout the Mediterranean. The chief cities of Phoenicia were Sidon, Tyre, Berot (modern Beirut) and also, from an early date, the island of Cyprus. Several Phoenician settlements were founded as stepping stones along the westerly and northerly coastal route to Spain with its mineral wealth. In their excursions to the west and south the Phoenicians colonized areas on the coast of North Africa such as Carthage and Anatolia. Carthage became the chief maritime and commercial power in the western Mediterranean. Trade developed to the Atlantic coast and Phoenician exports included cedar and pine wood, fine linen, cloths coloured with the famous Tyrian purple dye made from snails, wine, embroideries, metal and glass work, salt, and dried fish.

THE PHOENICIANS

The Phoenicians are remembered as the finest navigators of the ancient world, they traded along the Atlantic coast of Africa and as far north as the British Isles.

Navigation is not their only claim to fame. According to the Roman historian Pliny, the Phoenicians were the first to discover how to make glass from sand and saltpetre. Their most enduring claim to fame however, was their new 'phoenetic' system of writing, the first alphabet of the western world.

The Phoenicians carefully guarded the secrets of their trade routes and discoveries and their knowledge of winds and currents. They were bold navigators and they had no hesitation about trading beyond the Pillars of Hercules. Their ships were built primarily for trade but they could also be used as warships if this became necessary. According to pictorial evidence from murals, pottery and other sources the ships were galleys but they were also wind powered, they carried a single mast with a square sail with steering oars on both sides of the hull. The war galleys were low in the bow but high in the stern, and they had a heavy ram just below the waterline; the ram was the principal weapon in war when

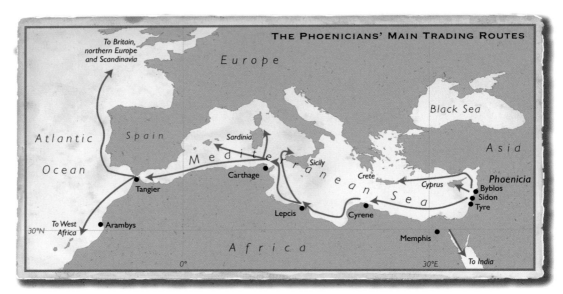

speed and manoeuvrability could be decisive in battle. Usually the galleys carried only one bank of oars, but sometimes two banks of oars were shown to both port and starboard.

A few geographers of the ancient world were convinced that there existed a sea passage around Africa. They also thought that Europe and Asia could be circumnavigated by sea. To describe the attempts at the circumnavigation of these continents we have no less an authority than the Greek historian Herodotus. He records at least two attempts by the Phoenicians to sail round Africa. One resulted in success and the other in failure. Herodotus tells the story of the successful voyage before telling us about the failure but it seems more logical for us to look at the failure before the success. He tells us that an Achaemenian called Sataspes had incurred the wrath of a high ranking local family by raping their daughter. The ruler Xerxes found Sataspes guilty of rape and the sentence was a painful death by impalement. Sataspes' mother pleaded with Xerxes to give her son a punishment other than death. Xerxes relented and Sataspes was called upon instead to try and make the dangerous voyage around Libya or the continent of Africa:

His mother begged him off by promising to inflict upon him a punishment even more severe; this was to force him to circumnavigate Libya, returning by way of the Arabian Gulf. Xerxes agreed; and Sataspes, on his arrival in Egypt, procured a vessel and crew and sailed to the Straits of Gibraltar. Passing through the Straits, he doubled Cape Soloeis and continued on a southerly course for many months; but when he found that far though he had sailed, there was always need to sail further yet, he put about and returned to Egypt. From Egypt he went to Xerxes' court where he reported that at the most southerly point they had reached they found the coast occupied by small men, who wore clothes made from palm leaves. When they landed, the pygmies used to abandon their settlement and escape to the hills. Sataspes' men had done them no harm, beyond entering their villages and taking some of their cattle. As to his failure to complete the circumnavigation, Sataspes declared that the reason was that his ship was brought to a standstill and was unable to make headway. Xerxes however, refused to pardon him, and, on the grounds that he had failed to accomplish his set task exacted the original penalty and had him impaled. A eunuch in Sataspes' service when he learned of his master's death, escaped to Samos with a great deal of money. It was all seized however by a certain Samian, whose name I willingly forget – though I know it well.

The details given and the meeting with the pygmies seem to confirm the truth of the account. Even the claim by Sataspes that his ship was brought to a standstill could be true. At the wrong time of the year adverse winds and heavy weather at the Cape of Good Hope could make it impossible to make any headway with the oars. The primitive sail was of no use whatsoever when sailing directly into the wind.

Herodotus goes on to tell us that Libya (Africa), Asia and Europe did in fact vary greatly in size but he was convinced that all three were surrounded by water. He states erroneously that Europe was as long as the other two continents put together, but he recognized that the other continents were, in his opinion, much broader than Europe. His length seems to be longitude, his breadth latitude. The belief that Europe was surrounded by sea was a natural conclusion, the sea journey northwards around Portugal, Spain and France took the ships through the English Channel and through the Straits of Dover where some traded as far away as Scandinavia. They reached as far as the Baltic Sea but the icy waters and jagged promontories prevented them from sailing further to the north or the east. It seemed reasonable however, to assume that a sea passage existed through the Baltic which would somehow bring them to the Black Sea and hence through the Hellespont and back to the Mediterranean.

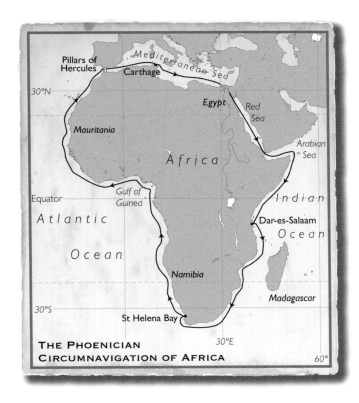

THE PHOENICIAN CIRCUMNAVIGATION OF AFRICA

Herodotus then tells us an exaggerated story that the greater part of Asia was discovered by Darius. He had heard of the River Indus which, like the Nile, had crocodiles living in its waters. Darius sent a party under the leadership of a man called Scylax and the expedition followed the course of the Indus east and south until it reached the sea. Scylax managed to buy or build a ship or ships. Turning westward, his ships followed the coast and after a voyage of some thirty months reached a point in the Red Sea near Suez. Darius was able to use the sea route along the Indian Ocean to trade with India. Darius thought that by using the River Indus he had proved that the whole of Asia was surrounded by sea, a very fanciful deduction which takes no account of the great lands to the east of the Indus.

Students of Greek history will note some resemblances between the expedition of Scylax and the great mission of Alexander the Great several centuries later. It is obvious that Alexander was motivated by the writings of Herodotus and he took his all-conquering army eastwards as far as the Indus. He also reached the shores of the Caspian Sea and he concluded wrongly but, quite reasonably, that he had found a vast ocean bordering the north and east coast of Asia. When the eastern limits of his great campaign brought him to the River Indus he too followed the river to the estuary and he too returned by the coastal route, or at least his fleet sailed along the coast whilst he took his army on the terrible waterless return journey by land.

We can now study Herodotus' account of the successful circumnavigation of Africa, which he calls Libya, undertaken by the Phoenicians. The expedition was in the opposite direction to the one that failed, that is sailing clockwise around the continent and east to west around the Cape of Good Hope. The description is brief but it is one of the most fascinating passages in an amazing history:

As for Libya, we know that it is washed on all sides by the sea except where it joins Asia, as was first demonstrated so far as our knowledge goes, by the Pharaoh Necho II who, after calling off the construction of the canal between the Nile and the Arabian Gulf, sent out a fleet manned by a Phoenician crew with orders to sail round and return to Egypt. And to the Mediterranean by way of the Pillars of Hercules. The Phoenicians sailed from the Red Sea into the southern Ocean, and every autumn put in where they were on the Libyan coast, sowed a patch of ground, and waited for next year's harvest. Then, having got their grain, they would put to sea again, and after two full years rounded the Pillars of Hercules in the course of the third, and returned to Egypt. These men made a statement which I do not myself believe, though others may, to the effect that as they sailed on a westerly course round the southern end of Libya, they had the sun on their right – to northward of them.

Firstly, from the genealogy of the Egyptian Pharaohs we can calculate the date of the circumnavigation to within a few years. The reign of Necho II was from 610 to 595 BC. A second point of interest is that at this very early date Necho was obviously considering cutting a canal through the isthmus of Suez, technically from the Red Sea to a point on the River Nile rather than a direct route to the Mediterranean. The scheme was not beyond the reach of Egyptian technology but it was presumably far too costly to execute at this time. Regarding the voyage itself, the account tells a remarkable story of the mariners planting and reaping their own crops to feed themselves on their long journey. For the first part of the journey there were settlements along the Red Sea and they may have been able to

'These men made a statement which I do not myself believe, though others may, to the effect that as they sailed on a westerly course round the southern end of Libya, they had the sun on their right – to northward of them.'

purchase food and provisions until they entered the Indian Ocean but once they were out beyond the Red Sea they had to be self sufficient. The voyage took more than two full years and therefore two harvests had to be sown and reaped. It is possible to guess roughly the location of the stopping places on the journey, the first was probably far to the south on the east coast of Africa before the Cape and the second somewhere in the Gulf of Guinea.

Yet the most fascinating part of the account is Herodotus' words 'These men made a statement which I do not myself believe, though others may, to the effect that as they sailed on a westerly course round the southern end of Libya, they had the sun on their right – to northward of them'. Here we have the professionalism of the greatest of all the Greek historians. He does not believe the claim about the sun in the northern sky but he chooses to publish it because the Phoenicians told him the strange story. Herodotus knew nothing about a spherical Earth, yet his honesty in repeating the story told by the Phoenicians proves the truth of the circumnavigation beyond any shadow of doubt.

Is. S. Brandano
Cabo finis ter
Insulæ Fortunato
Cabo de No
Mauritania
M. A
Africa

Saint Brendan's Miraculous Voyage

An Irish monk crosses the Atlantic in a tiny leather boat

c. 530 AD

'It was only the monks of Hibernia in their monasteries who wrote and read, read and wrote, and illuminated, and then jumped into little boats made of animal hide and navigated… These were the great men. Saint Brendan reached the Isles of the Blest and sailed along the coasts of hell, where he saw Judas chained to a rock, and one day he landed on an island and went ashore there and found a sea monster.'

Umberto Eco, *The Name of the Rose*

Ireland, in the early centuries after Christ, became a centre of Christianity from where the word was passed to other parts of the British Isles and further afield. But none of the monks and friars carried the word as far as St Brendan who is reputed to have made a most fantastic voyage around the Atlantic Ocean in a primitive open boat – what we would now call a curragh.

Brendan was born in Ireland in about the year 489 AD near Tralee in the county of Kerry. He is an Irish saint with a feast day on 16 May who founded monasteries at Clare, Galway and Kerry and became the abbot of the monastery of Clonfert on the River Shannon. His voyage is usually dated to within about five years of 565 AD but, if his date of birth is correct, this puts Brendan in his late seventies. A date of about 530 AD therefore seems more likely.

The stories of St Brendan were initially told and retold from person to person in the market places, exactly like the stories attributed to Homer in ancient Greece. They were repeated in the monasteries from generation to generation by travelling minstrels and bards. The accounts grew with time to include fabulous and supernatural stories and these became entwined with the truth. Eventually the stories were written down and manuscripts were copied from monastery to monastery across the Christian world. The earliest written texts date from the ninth century, about three hundred years after the event. It is not surprising therefore to find that a great deal has been embellished over this very long period, but the account was probably circulating in a written form long before the earliest manuscripts that survive today. The Brendan script was copied so frequently that 120 or more texts of the voyage have been found. One of the earliest is by Ducil dating from circa 825 AD. More than six centuries later still, when the first printed books became available, Brendan's voyages went into print and the earliest and most quoted document is the *Navigatio Sancti Brendani* which was printed in 1450 from a text which goes back at least as far as that of Ducil.

The voyage was made by Brendan himself and a number of his brother monks. Their boat was made from a framework of oak or ash covered by ox-hides and it was open to the skies. It had a mast and a sail but it also needed a set of oars for otherwise it could make no headway against the wind. The first leg of the voyage was from Ireland to the Faeroe Isles lying north of Scotland. These islands were inhabited by crofters and Brendan called them the 'sheep islands'. He decided to sail further to the west in search of more land but he was forced back to the Faeroes by strong gales and heavy weather. On his second attempt he

BIOGRAPHIES OF THE SAINTS:

Anglo-Norman literature was rich in legends of the saints and Benedeit's *Voyage of St Brendan* was probably the first purely narrative French poem to be written in what became known as the octosyllabic couplet. It set a fashion for the writing of a saint's life in what became a standard form. In the twelfth century Anglo-Norman writers produced numerous biographies, many connecting religious houses with their patron saints.

He continued to the West Indies where he discovered a fruit with a yellow peel, inside it was white and red, it grew in twelve sections and it weighed about one pound. He had discovered the grapefruit which grew in abundance on the island of Great Inagua.

had better fortune and favourable winds took his boat thousands of miles south to another set of islands that can be identified as the Azores. It seems incredible that he could have covered this immense distance from the Faeroes to a very distant part of the Atlantic and be fortunate enough to find a landfall, yet the account of his landing and the subsequent events do lend support to this claim. His account describes two springs at the same place, one warm and the other cold, a very rare combination but one which does actually occur at Flores in the Azores. He founded a small religious order of twenty-four men and he sailed from Flores to visit the island of São Miguel.

From the Azores, Brendan sailed west with a following wind to reach an area where the sea was thick with weed in a 'thick curdled mass'. The Sargasso Sea answers well to this description. He continued to the West Indies where he discovered a fruit with a yellow peel, inside it was white and red, it grew in twelve sections and it weighed about one pound. He had discovered the grapefruit which grew in abundance on the island of Great Inagua. His journey took him on to the Bahamas chain where he sailed the Great Bahama Bank. At this point he described a sea so clear that the fish and the sea bed could be seen beneath the boat:

On a certain occasion, when St Brendan was celebrating the festival of St Peter, in the boat, they found the sea so clear that they could plainly see what was at the bottom. They therefore, saw beneath them various monsters of the deep, and so clear was the water, that it seemed as if they could touch with their hands its greatest depth; and the fishes were visible in great shoals, like flocks of sheep in the pastures, swimming round, heads to tails. The brethren entreated the man of God to say mass in a low

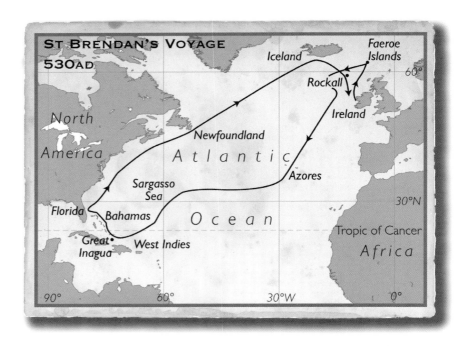

voice, less these monsters of the deep, hearing the strange voice, might be stirred up to attack them; but the saint said: 'I wonder much at your folly. Why do you dread these monsters?'. Having thus spoken, he proceeded to sing the mass in a louder voice, as the brethren were still gazing at the large fishes, and these, when they heard the voice of the man of God, rose up from the depth, and swam around the boat in such numbers, that the brethren could see nothing but the swimming fishes, which, however, came not close to the boat but swam around at some distance, until the mass was ended, when they swam away in divers directions, out of the view of the brethren. For eight days, even with a favourable wind and all sails set, they were scarcely able to pass out of this pellucid sea.

The Coast of Florida

The Coast of Florida When they were offshore from the coast of Florida they picked up the Gulf Stream which carried them to the north. They were never far from the American mainland but there is no record in the saga to indicate that they got a sighting of it. At one point on the journey they met with a huge creature that can only have been a whale:

The venerable father and his companions sailed out into the ocean and their boat was carried along for forty days. One day there appeared to them a beast of immense size following them at a distance. He spouted foam from his nostrils and ploughed through the waves at a great speed, as if he were about to devour them. When the brothers saw this they called upon the lord, saying: 'Deliver us lord, so that beast does not devour us'.

St Brendan comforted them, saying: 'Do not be afraid ye of little faith. God, who always defends us, will deliver us from the mouth of this beast and from other dangers.'

As the beast came near them he caused waves of extraordinary height to go before him right to the boat, so that the brothers were more and more afraid. The venerable elder also raised his hands to heaven and said: 'Lord, deliver your servants, as you delivered David from the hand of Goliath, the giant. Lord, deliver us, as you delivered Jonas from the belly of the whale.'

After these three pleas asking for deliverance, a mighty monster passed near them from the west going to encounter the beast. He immediately attacked him, emitting fire from his mouth. The leader spoke to his brothers: 'Look, my sons, at the great deeds of our Saviour! See how the beasts obey their creator. Wait presently for the outcome of this affair. This battle will do us no damage. It will rebound to the glory of God.'

When he had said this the wretched beast that pursued the servants of Christ was cut into three pieces before their eyes. The other returned after his victory to where he had come from.

It is possible to identify the huge spouting beast as a whale. It is impossible to identify the fiery beast that killed the whale and saved the explorers. But we all know that sailors have always told yarns about sea monsters and fire-breathing dragons. The sighting of the whale may be taken as a fact, but the sea monster was probably one of many fabrications added by later generations. These tales were included to improve the story but, at the same time, they can destroy the authenticity that we are seeking.

THE LIFE OF BRENDAN

Brendan is thought to have been born in about 484 to 489 AD at Tralee, now in County Kerry, Ireland. He is sometimes called Saint Brendan of Clonfert to distinguish him from other saints with the same name. He was reputedly raised and educated by the Abbess Saint Ita at her boys' school in Limerick. He then went on to study under Abbot St Jarlath of Tuam. His legendary voyages belong to the early sixth century.

Another claim that has been greatly embellished is the paradise of birds. Brendan's crew landed on an island to take on water. They found a spring where there was a great tree covered with white birds. The birds spoke with them and sang a song beating their wings: 'A hymn is due to thee O God, in Zion, and a vow shall be paid to you in Jerusalem.' They repeated the song for about an hour. Here is the sure touch of the over-creative copyist. Yet the idea of a tree full of chattering birds is probably based on a true experience. Brendan met with a migratory flock of birds that chose the tree for their resting place on their long journey to the south.

The Iceberg Cavern As the Gulf Stream carried the boat further north the sailors found themselves in the foggy seas off the coast of Newfoundland. Here they saw great white columns reaching right up into the clouds. They had encountered icebergs carried from the north and melting as they reached a warmer climate. As Brendan's ship approached, the monks saw a great cavern inside the iceberg with beautiful clear icicles hanging from the ceiling:

One day, on which three masses had been said, they saw a column in the sea, which seemed not far off, yet they could not reach it for three days. When they drew near it, St Brendan looked towards its summit, but could not see it, because of its great height, which seemed to pierce the skies. It was covered over with a rare canopy of a material of which they knew not; but it had the colour of silver, and was hard as marble, while the column itself was of the clearest crystal. St Brendan ordered the brethren to take in the oars, and to lower the sails and mast, and directed some of them to hold on by the fringes of the canopy, which extended about a mile from the column and about the same depth into the sea.

'...they saw the peak of the mountain unclouded, and shooting up flames into the sky, which it drew back again into itself, so that the mountain seemed like a burning pyre.'

The monks ran their boat in closer for a better view. The great iceberg shone in the sunshine and it was dripping pure water. The explorers sailed inside the great cavern where the sea was as placid and still as a millpond, beneath the water they could see that the ice pillars went down to a very great depth. Brendan took measurements and found the iceberg to be seven hundred yards in length and breadth.

This was not all. As the boat sailed back to the west on her homeward journey they encountered a very rare phenomenon. The sea itself seemed to be on fire. This was not a fantasy, they were passing the volcanic coast of Iceland and it happened that a volcano was erupting at the time:

On another day there came into view a large and high mountain in the ocean, not far off, towards the north, with misty clouds about it, and a great smoke issuing from its summit, when suddenly the wind drove the boat rapidly towards the island until it almost touched the shore. The cliffs were so high they could scarce see the top, they were as black as coal, and upright like a wall... Afterwards a favourable breeze caught the boat, and drove them southwards; and as they looked back they saw the peak of the mountain unclouded, and shooting up flames into the sky, which it drew back again into itself, so that the mountain seemed like a burning pyre.

Leaving Iceland behind him Brendan sailed to the east in search of Ireland. He sailed past Rockall where he encountered a hermit living off fish. A few days later he was back in Ireland.

We are therefore left with this gripping account of an Atlantic voyage nearly a thousand years before Columbus. Other evidence exists. Irish books and artefacts have been found in Iceland and there are stories of Irish-speaking races amongst the Eskimos of Greenland. The evidence is scanty but it is sufficient to prove the case.

The question has been raised as to whether it was possible for a man like Brendan to navigate the Atlantic Ocean in an open boat with a timber frame and leather hull. The answer to this was found in 1976 when Tim Severin and his companions built a boat by the traditional ancient methods. They constructed the hull from fifty-seven leather ox-hides tanned with the bark of oak, oiled with cod oil and stitched together with twenty-three miles of flax thread. Two miles of leather thong, treated with tallow and fish oil, were used to hold the oak and the ash frame of the boat *Brendan* firmly together. Severin, with his crew of four, sailed the *Brendan* on the latter part of St Brendan's journey through the North Atlantic. Severin proved that, with luck and favourable currents, the journey across the Atlantic could indeed have been made in the sixth century by such a boat as described by Brendan.

THE ICELANDIC SAGAS OF ERIC THE RED AND LEIF ERIKSSON

NORSEMEN LAND ON THE AMERICAN CONTINENT CENTURIES BEFORE COLUMBUS

982 – 1000 AD

'Ashore they (the Vikings) found self-sown fields of wheat where the ground was low lying, and vines wherever there was high ground… (the natives) were dark, ugly men who wore their hair in an unpleasant fashion. They had big eyes and were broad in the cheek.'

THE SAGA OF ERIC THE RED

The long ships of the Norsemen were, in their times, amongst the finest and fastest ships in the world. Their construction made them very sea-worthy. They were clinker built from the hardwood forests of Scandinavia with their external planks overlapping and probably finished with copper nails.

They carried a great square sail to maximize the favourable winds and, if the wind direction was against the ship, then the sail came down and there were oars to port and starboard so that only the very worst of weather could delay their progress. The ships were long with a high prow and stern. On the prow an ornate figurehead faced the seas ahead, it was carved in the fine and intricate interlaced style of the Celts to frighten away the evil spirits of the sea. At the rear was a steering board which gave the name 'starboard' to the right hand side of the ship. The Vikings were proud warriors and on the flanks of their ships they carried a colourful row of overlapping round shields. When they landed with their shields, broadswords and horned helmets they caused terror in coastal communities. The Norsemen, known also as the Vikings, sailed from Norway, Sweden and Denmark across the North Sea, sometimes to the east coast of England, sometimes to the English Channel where they raided and plundered to both north and south. Sometimes they took their ships to the north of Scotland, then round to the west coast of Scotland and on to Ireland and the west coast of England. No coastal community north of the Bay of Biscay was safe from their raids. The *Anglo-Saxon Chronicle* described a raid on Lindisfarne in the year 793:

In this year fierce foreboding omens came over the land of Northumbria, and wretchedly terrified the people. There were excessive whirlwinds, lightning storms, and fiery dragons were seen flying in the sky. These signs were followed by great famine, and shortly after in the same year, on January the 8th, the ravaging of heathen men destroyed God's church at Lindisfarne through brutal robbery and slaughter: and Sicga died on February 2nd.

Iceland The Norsemen knew that there was an uninhabited island several days sail towards the setting sun in the North Atlantic. They called it Iceland because most of the island was covered in ice and snow. But in parts of the south there was pasture, the island was heated by volcanic activity and hot springs that made it tolerably warm for much of the year. The land was green and fertile and it would support crops. In 874 a group of Norsemen and women, who had quarrelled with King Harald the Fairhaired of Norway, sailed under the leadership of Ingolfur Arnarson to Iceland where they planned to make a settlement. The story is told that Arnarson took with him two great posts from his house in Norway and he threw them into the sea saying he would build his house at the point where they floated ashore. He called the place where they landed Reykjavík, meaning 'smokey bay' after the steaming volcanic springs near the little inlet. Ingolfur Arnarson farmed with his wife Hallveig Fródadóttir and the *Viking Book of Settlements* enumerates more

*They called it Iceland because
most of the island was covered
in ice and snow. But in parts
of the south there was pasture,
the island was heated by
volcanic activity and hot
springs that made it tolerably
warm for much of the year.*

than 400 settlers who sailed with their families,
servants and slaves to Iceland and who staked a claim
to the land. Most of the settlers came from Norway, but
some came from other Scandinavian countries and a
few came from the scattered Norse settlements around
the British Isles.

The Icelandic settlement became a great success.
The population grew steadily and by the middle of the
tenth century it had reached several thousand. There
was trade with Scandinavia and other parts of Europe
and in the early generations of settlement there seemed
no point in exploring further to the west. This situation
changed towards the end of the tenth century when a man called
Thorvald arrived from Norway. He had been exiled for manslaughter
and he brought his son Erik with him, also known as Erik the Red. Like
father like son; for some unknown offence, Erik the Red was exiled from
Iceland for three years in about the year 982.

From the top of the mountains of western Iceland it was possible to
see that there was another land to the west. It lay across 180 miles of
water but it could easily be reached with a good crew and a Viking
longboat. Erik the Red decided to explore this land to the west. He sailed
in 982 with his household and livestock but he was unable to make a
landing because of drifting ice. He sailed to the south and rounded the
southern tip of land. Here he was able to make a successful landing and
he settled in an area near the present town of Julianehåb. During the
three years of Erik the Red's exile the new settlers encountered no other
people but they survived their first few years and they returned to
Iceland in 986. Erik exaggerated the merits of the new land, which he
called Greenland; he deliberately chose the name to make it sound green
and fertile. His descriptions convinced many people that to the west
there existed a land more habitable than Iceland.

Twenty-five ships sailed from Iceland to create the Greenland colony
but only fourteen ships and 350 colonists are believed to have landed at
an area later known as Eystribygdh. By the year 1000 it is estimated that
the population of the Greenland
settlement had grown to a
thousand, but an epidemic in
the year 1002 considerably
reduced the population. The
Greenland colony, which was
commemorated in the Icelandic
saga of Erik the Red, gradually
died out; but other Norse
settlements in Greenland
continued and they maintained
contact with Norway until the
fifteenth century.

Two Norse sagas, namely
the *Saga of the Greenlanders* and

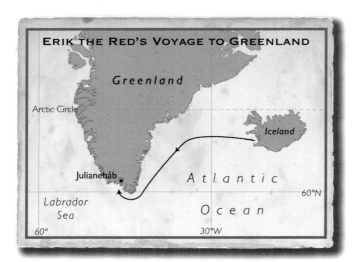

ERIK THE RED'S VOYAGE TO GREENLAND

Greenland

Arctic Circle

Iceland

Julianehåb

Labrador
Sea

Atlantic

Ocean

60°N

60°

30°W

the *Saga of Erik the Red* are the source of the Norse claim to the discovery of the American mainland. According to the Greenlanders' saga, a Norseman called Bjarni Herjulfsson arrived in Iceland in the year 985. He was related to Erik the Red and he wanted to sail on to Greenland to meet his kinsman.

The First European on the American Mainland He found a crew to help him on his way but not one of them had sailed to Greenland before. No sooner had they left Iceland behind than the skies clouded over, they were unable to see land and they were at the mercy of the elements. Bjarni Herjulfsson lost his way and as a result he accidentally became the first European to set foot on the American mainland. He realized that his landfall was too far to the south to be Greenland so he followed the Atlantic coast of Canada northwards. The ship sailed past a well-wooded country with low hills that he knew could not be Greenland. Then they came to a high and mountainous island but the land was very bare. Again he knew it was not Greenland. Four days later another land appeared and he knew from the valleys and the glaciers that it must be the land he sought. His reasoning was correct and he had little trouble finding the settlement of his kinsman Erik the Red.

The Greenlanders were very interested to hear of the lands to the south. They wanted to sail there themselves to explore and perhaps to settle but they took no immediate action. It was fifteen years before they got around to doing anything about it and, by this time, Erik the Red felt he was getting too old to undertake what he knew could be a long and arduous journey. His son Leif Eriksson was chosen to lead the expedition. In the year 1000 a crew of thirty-five men led by Leif Eriksson set out to try to find the land that had accidentally been discovered by Bjarni Herjulfsson.

The islands were rediscovered in the reverse order to that of Herjulfsson. Eriksson's expedition came first to an icy, barren land which they called Helluland or 'Flat-Stone Land'. It was Baffin Island. It was so bare and empty that there was little point in stopping to explore. Sailing southward, they encountered the flat, wooded land which they named Markland meaning 'Wood Land'. It had white sandy beaches and the land sloped gently down to the sea. They did not stay many days before they took to sea again and continued their voyage to the south.

After only two days they came to a warmer and greener land where they went ashore again. There was dew on the grass and after the salty rigours of the Atlantic it seemed to them to be the sweetest water they had ever tasted. They went back to the ship and sailed into a sound between the islands where there was a headland to the north. They steered around the headland and they made another landing near a river estuary. They liked the place so much that they decided to winter there and to build some houses. The approximate latitude can be calculated

from the fact that on the shortest day of the year there were about six hours of daylight. The sun was up at nine and set again at three in the afternoon.

Eriksson wanted to explore the land further but he gave his men instructions not to wander far from their houses. One member of the expedition was a man named Tryker who was described as a 'Southerner'. To a Norwegian or a Greenlander this could mean that Tryker came from practically anywhere in the world, but the evidence indicates that he was a German. Tryker struck off on his own and he penetrated further south than the rest of the expedition. Eriksson was not too pleased about losing one of his party but it was not long before Tryker returned to rejoin them. When he was questioned about his absence Tryker rolled his eyes and made faces, he spoke in German and nobody could understand him. Then he changed his language to Norwegian.

'I did not go much further than you, but I have news to tell. I have found grapes and vines.'
'Is it true foster father?' said Leif Eriksson.
'Certainly,' he replied, 'I was born where there is no lack of vines or grapes.'

Vinland This is the most difficult event to explain in the story. The expedition was much too far north to find wild grape vines. There were berries which could have been mistaken for grapes but, as Tryker said, he was familiar with the grape vine and he would not be likely to make a mistake. The reports of grapes growing wild in Vinland caused the Greenlanders to leave behind a colonizing expedition of about 130 people (or possibly only half this number, according to which saga is taken as correct). But by the time the party had wintered there for three years the local Indians were complaining that the Greenlanders were living off their resources and the trade with the Indians was in danger of turning into mutual warfare. The colonists therefore gave up their settlement and returned to Greenland.

Modern researchers have suggested that 'Vinland' did not mean 'wine land' but rather 'grassland' or 'grazing land'. The remains of house sites and other artefacts of a Norse settlement have been discovered at L'Anse aux Meadows, at the northernmost tip of Newfoundland and dating techniques have conclusively proved that the remains date from about 1000 AD. In 1965 Yale University Press published a medieval map showing the outlines of continental Europe, Iceland, Greenland and Vinland, the latter being described in a notation on the map as 'Island of Vinland, discovered by Bjarni and Leif in company'. The authenticity of this map has been sharply debated but the early discovery of North America by Leif Eriksson is beyond dispute. The American mainland was undoubtedly discovered before the end of the first millennium. A settlement was definitely made on the American mainland but it survived for only a few years.

ARCHAEOLOGICAL EVIDENCE

- In the 1960s a Viking settlement was discovered and excavated at L'Anse aux Meadows in Newfoundland in Canada
- There were remains of eight buildings on the site including a forge and a timberyard
- Artefacts found included a ring-headed pin of Norse design and wood carvings

Madoc ab Owen Gwynedd's voyage across the Atlantic

A Welsh prince lays his claim to America

c. 1170

'Silent and thoughtful, and apart from all,
Stood Madoc; now his noble enterprise
Proudly remembering, now in dreams of hope,
Anon of bodings full, and doubt and fear.
Fair smiled the evening, and the favouring gale
Sung in the shrouds, and swift the steady bark
Rushed roaring through the waves.'

ROBERT SOUTHEY

In the 1580s when Richard Hakluyt, the geographer, was collecting information on English voyages he discovered a strange and very interesting story which was not English at all but a Welsh tradition of a voyage across the Atlantic from four centuries before his time. The story was based on the account of a Welsh bard who came across it in the chronicles at Conway Abbey and Strata Florida Abbey where the stories of Welsh life and history were traditionally recorded.

The account originated in the twelfth century, with the death of the king, Owen Gwynedd, in 1169. The king left nineteen sons and possibly as many daughters - but the majority of them were illegitimate. The result was that the kingdom of Gwynedd degenerated into a bloody civil war as the sons of the deceased king fought each other over their right to rule. One of the claimants, Madoc ab Gwynedd, very wisely kept out of the fighting as he was illegitimate and his claim was therefore a very poor one, but, in any case, he saw himself as a man of peace rather than a man of war. Madoc and his brother Riryd decided to leave the fighting in Wales and sail to the west to seek out new and more peaceful realms. The brothers took two ships on their venture, called the *Gorn Gwynant* and the *Pedr Sant*. Apart from the names we have no details of these ships but they were probably similar in construction to the open ships of the Vikings, carrying a single square sail and powered by banks of oars to port and starboard. Madoc landed in Ireland. He then decided to venture further to the west and he struck out into the Atlantic taking advantage of the favourable currents that carried him to the south. After a crossing of unknown duration he rounded the peninsula of Florida and his ships sailed into the Gulf of Mexico. He landed at a river estuary, a place that became Mobile in Alabama, in the deep south of North America.

The traveller and historian, Thomas Herbert, writing in 1638, gave a description of the voyage and of the country discovered by Madoc. This account was written in the short period when it became fashionable to date events from the origin of the world as described in Genesis. He calculates the year 5140 from Adam as 1170 from Christ, which gives the date of 3970 BC for the creation. This differs by thirty-four years from the year 4004 BC calculated by Archbishop Usher and widely accepted at about this time, but we need not be concerned by this discrepancy if we accept 1170 as the date of the voyage:

After a crossing of unknown duration he rounded the peninsula of Florida and his ships sailed into the Gulf of Mexico. He landed at a river estuary, a place that became Mobile in Alabama, in the deep south of North America.

The yeere he set forth in was from Adam 5140, from Christ 1170, the wind and sea seemed to favour him (omens of good fortune) so as, after some patience and weeks saile due west, hee descried land, a land where he found store of good victuals, sweet water, fresh ayre, gold, (and which was best) where they were a good whiles healthfull, such as over-whelmed him with joy, but moderated when he considered how Almighty God was alike powerful and gratious in all places; his exile now turned into comfort...

THE LEGEND OF PRINCE MADOC

When Owen Gwynedd died in 1169 Wales degenerated into a state of civil war. Madoc was an illegitimate son of Gwynedd and his claim to the throne was therefore very weak. He decided to avoid the fighting and to try and create a peaceful colony across the seas to the west. Legend has it that he created a successful settlement in Mobile in modern Alabama.

A Land Unknown The land he had discovered was fruitful but uninhabited. Herbert's account states that on his first voyage Madoc left 120 men in America and that he raised fortifications for the defence of his colony. We do not know if women were included on this first voyage, but if the figures are correct then, allowing for sufficient men to man and row the boats on the return journey, the two boats must have carried at least 150 men between them when they left Wales. An earlier account, taken from Richard Hakluyt's findings, was published in 1584 by a Dr David Powel. It describes Madoc returning to Wales to encourage others to sail back with him to the newly discovered land. The civil war that followed the death of Owen Gwynedd created a great deal of bad feeling and the opportunity to sail to a new land where the combatants could live in peace and harmony was very appealing:

He came to land unknown where he saw many strange things… Of the voyage and return of this Madoc there may be many fables faimed… And after he had returned home, and declared the pleasant and fruitful countries that he has seen without inhabitants, and upon the contrarie part, for what barren and wilde grounde (in Wales) his brethren and nephues did murther one another, he prepared a number of shippes, and got with him such men and women as were desirous to live in quietnesse, and taking leave of his friends took his journie thitherwards againe… This Madoc arriving in the countrie into which he came in the yeare 1170, left most of his people there, and returning back for more of his own nation, acquaintence, and friends, to inhabit that fayre and large countrie, went thither again.

Madoc must have needed some time to recruit the volunteers he needed to sail back with him to the colony in America. This time the colonists included women. In the year 1170 ten boats assembled at Lundy Island in the Bristol Channel. This meeting place implies that the whole of Wales was involved rather than just the area around Gwynedd alone. The Pole Star is mentioned as Madoc's means of navigation. It was a long voyage across the Atlantic but, presumably, if the navigators knew their latitude from the Pole Star and if they arrived off the coast of Florida it would not be too difficult to follow the land round to the Gulf of Mexico and on to Mobile. Madoc successfully crossed the Atlantic a second time and, fortunately for all concerned, he managed to find his original landing place at

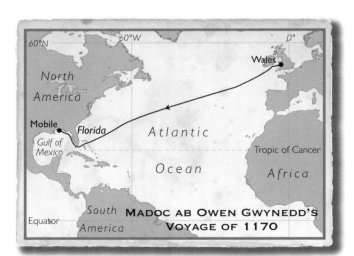

MADOC AB OWEN GWYNEDD'S VOYAGE OF 1170

Mobile, but when the fleet arrived it was to discover that many of those they left behind had not survived. Thomas Herbert gives an account of Madoc's findings:

Great rejoycing was among them at that their happinesse, but no lesse sorrow followed: for, being come to the Plantation, they found few of those they left there, living: caused by too much eating, the indisposition of Novelty of that ayre and climate, (which though never so excellent, yet causes sicknesse and alteration in new inhabitants) by some trechorie of the Barbarians. Madoc digested it with a Christian fortitude and patience, and forth-with bettered the Colony, by help of Eneon and Edwall his brothers contriving every thing with so good order, that they were secure from any enemie, and had all things conducing to ease, plenty, and contentednesse: they threw away the too indulgent thoughts of their native homes, by this reason, that if they died there, they were in the same distance from heaven, and had as easy a journey thither... so that Madoc and his Company returned (to Wales) no more, nor did the Welsh sail thither afterward, whereby one of another in small time were in some sort forgotten and never remembered.

New Settlers When the new party of settlers had arrived the colony spent the next few years exploring the rivers of Georgia, Tennessee and Kentucky. They penetrated deep into the interior, sometimes building stone fortifications, and they eventually made a settlement on the banks of the Missouri where they were welcomed by the local Indians. The accounts claim that they intermarried and integrated into the Mandan tribe.

Further evidence has been put forward to support the truth of Madoc's expedition. In the sixteenth century, when the Spanish were exploring the area around Mobile, Cortes discovered that the Indians thereabouts had some ceremonies that seemed to be European. The Indians claimed that many years ago a strange nation landed on their shores but they did not know the names of the ceremonies or the land from

> **THE WELSH BARDS**
> The English poet Robert Southey wrote an epic poem 'Madoc', published in 1805 recounting the story of Prince Madoc. This was many centuries after the event but it indicated that the story of Madoc had been kept alive for more than six centuries by the Welsh tradition of travelling bards and minstrels.

whence the strange peoples had come. Another story to support the case tells that in 1666 a Welsh missionary, the Reverend Morgan Jones, was captured by an Indian tribe and was about to be executed. He prayed loudly in Welsh for deliverance. Hearing his plea the Indians suddenly changed their attitude and treated him as an honoured guest. He found that he was able to converse freely with them in the Welsh language. There are similar reports from the seventeenth and eighteenth centuries of Welsh-speaking Indians and also of tribes with fair features and even fair hair.

George Catlin, a nineteenth-century painter who spent eight years living among various Indian tribes, was among those who were impressed by the Mandan's remarkable traits. The opening picture on page 30 shows a Mandan archery competition in which some of the men appear to have pale skin. Catlin wrote: 'A stranger in the Mandan village is first struck with the different shades of complexion, and various colors of hair which he sees in a crowd about him, and is almost disposed to

The Indians claimed that many years ago a strange nation landed on their shores but they did not know the names of the ceremonies or the land from whence the strange peoples had come.

exclaim that these are not Indians.' The artist also noted 'a most pleasing symmetry and proportion of features, with hazel, gray and blue eyes'. During his long stay which lasted for years among the Mandan tribe, Catlin made paintings of almost every aspect of their daily lives as well as written observations. Catlin was the only white man to make a written and pictorial history of these rituals and customs. He finally came to the conclusion that the Mandan's were the descendents of Madoc's people based partially on these factors.

Some of the anecdotes in the story of Madoc ab Owen Gwynedd, such as the navigation by the Pole Star and the hardship of the first settlers, seem to be authentic. The great weakness is that there is no direct evidence prior to the sixteenth century to support the story. The voyage of Brendan, by comparison, was kept alive by the monks who copied manuscript versions of the story for hundreds of years until such time as the printing press became available. By the time the story of Madoc came to be printed, a great deal had been discovered about America and this made it possible for the storytellers to add more details and to make the narrative sound more authentic. If the story is true then it can only have been kept alive by minstrels and bards who passed it on by word of mouth from generation to generation. This means that the original is probably greatly altered over the four hundred years which elapsed from the actual event to the first written records. It is not impossible however, that the basis of the story is true, for we know that the Icelandic Sagas survived for centuries without a written record and that the classical Greek stories of the *Iliad* and the *Odyssey* were perpetuated far longer by very similar means. In the case of the story of Madoc ab Owen Gwynedd there is no reason why the Welsh bards should not have kept their story alive by the same method as the Icelanders and the ancient Greeks.

THE EPIC JOURNEYS OF
THE MING DYNASTY

FOUR GREAT CHINESE ARMADAS
NAVIGATE THE WORLD'S OCEANS

1415 — 1421

'By the time of their sixth voyage Zheng He's fleets had inherited expertise gained from six centuries of charting the stars in the night sky and had predicted and noted the return of Halley's comet on every pass since the second century. They were aware that the earth was a globe and they had divided it into 365 and a quarter degrees of latitude and longitude.'

In 2001 a Chinese lawyer called Liu Gang bought an antique map from a book dealer in Shanghai. The map was dated 1418 and it gave a very accurate picture of the whole world, including both North and South America.

It showed a large island in the southern hemisphere which could only be Australia. If the map is genuine then it would prove beyond reasonable doubt that early in the fifteenth century virtually the whole world had been explored and mapped by the Chinese. It is well known that Admiral Zheng He made a great voyage from Beijing in the years 1415-1418, and the map can safely be assumed to be a record of the world as discovered by Zheng He and his fleet.

In 2002 Gavin Menzies published his book, *The Year China Discovered the World*, describing the later voyages of 1421 that set off in Admiral Zheng He's trail. The map had not been discovered when Menzies was writing his book. But the Zheng He voyage must have greatly influenced the 1421 voyages. Menzies' book also reveals a lot of evidence to show that the story of the discovery of the globe needs to be rewritten, or at least it needs to be modified to accommodate the claims of the Chinese. The book describes in detail four great voyages, all of which began in the year 1421. These voyages were very different from the conventional voyages of discovery made from Europe later in the same century. Each one was made by a great fleet of several hundred ships under the command of a grand admiral. Their instructions were to explore the world, to map their findings but also to create colonies wherever suitable sites were found to make a settlement. The great expeditions were an attempt by the Ming Emperor Zhu Di to discover and conquer the world. As well as finding new lands the fleets were expected to discover unknown peoples and civilizations and to create new markets for trade. The inhabitants of all the new lands discovered by the Chinese fleets would be required to pay tribute to the Ming Emperor. The new Chinese colonies were also expected to send taxes to increase the wealth of the mighty Ming Empire.

Each one was made by a great fleet of several hundred ships under the command of a grand admiral. Their instructions were to explore the world, to map their findings but also to create colonies wherever suitable sites were found to make a settlement.

There is no doubt that in the early fifteenth century the Chinese were great ship builders. They knew how to build a large hull and they knew how to make it watertight. Their largest ships measured as much as 100 metres in length and fifty across the beam. The great ships were of the type commonly called junks and they were rigged with as many as ten red silk sails on each of nine masts. A large junk could therefore carry nearly a hundred sails. They were known as 'treasure ships' because of the great value of the cargoes they could carry.

Great Armadas The findings claimed in Menzies' book are truly astonishing. The great armadas all sailed from Beijing across the Indian Ocean to the east coast of Africa. One fleet, under Admiral Yang Qing, returned from there by the coastal route back to China but the other three continued to the west by rounding the Cape of Good Hope. Then, by following the circulatory currents in the Atlantic and the Pacific, the fleets went on to explore the whole of the world. A second fleet, under Admiral Hong Bao, crossed the Atlantic and followed the coast of South America right down to the Straits of Magellan. The fleet passed through the Straits of Magellan to enter the Pacific Ocean but turned immediately to the south to reach the icy coast of Antarctica at the South Shetland Islands. From there Hong Bao sailed east at a latitude of 52° and took his fleet across the cold waters of the South Atlantic and South Indian Ocean to Western Australia. From there, after a brief landing on Australian soil, he took his fleet north and returned to China.

A third fleet, commanded by Admiral Zhou Man, also sailed through the Straits of Magellan but then turned to the north and followed the coastlines of Chile and Peru. The Chinese made contact with the Inca civilization. The fleet then sailed onwards to the north as far as the coast of California but they went by way of a rather lengthy detour to the west, exploring the east coast of Australia and also New Zealand. After mapping most of the Australian coastline Zhou Man took his fleet to the North Pacific and crossed the ocean to make a landing at a point in California. He then mapped the American coast southwards as far as Panama before crossing the Pacific a third time and heading back to Beijing.

If these feats have not already left the reader gasping for breath, there is still more to come. A fourth fleet under Admiral Zhou Wen made an even more amazing journey. Parting company with the other two fleets at the Cape Verde Islands, the fleet crossed the Atlantic and sailed along the north-east coast of America. From there the armada reached the south tip of Greenland and the ships proceeded northwards along the east coast. They followed the coastline, sailing through miraculously clear seas at incredible latitudes, to the north of Greenland. They touched on Iceland and returned from there to China. The fleet did not return the obvious way via the Cape of Good Hope but the hard way. The great armada sailed the North East Passage, powered by wind alone across the ice-bound seas to the north of Asia and Siberia. They returned to the North Pacific through the Bering Straits.

Questions to Answer There is more. But this summary should be sufficient to leave the reader totally dumbfounded and reeling in disbelief. There are so many questions to answer that it is difficult to know where to start. Could the Chinese have built ships capable of making these voyages? How did they cope with the problems of fresh food and that scourge of all the early voyages – the dreaded onset of scurvy? How did they find the latitude and the longitude? How did they navigate the ice and freezing temperatures of the polar regions? Perhaps the most puzzling question of all is why there seem to be no records of the voyages in the Chinese archives. Why are the Chinese scholars reluctant to acknowledge this great achievement of the past?

With regard to the first question, were the Chinese ships of this early

EVIDENCE IN FAVOUR OF THE 1421 VOYAGES:

The world map discovered by Liu Gang in 2001.

The high standards and volume of Chinese shipping.

Chinese knowledge of astronomy and navigation.

The maps showing accurate coastlines but with a shift in longitude.

Genetic fingerprints.

EVIDENCE AGAINST THE 1421 VOYAGES:

There is no Chinese claim to support the discoveries.

The Chinese junk was not capable of sailing into the wind.

It was not possible to provide fresh food and water for so many ships and their crews.

The ravages of scurvy could not have been avoided.

Navigation was good, but not good enough to cross the Atlantic and Pacific and to map every coastline as claimed.

Navigation of the seas north of Greenland and north of Asia under sail has never been possible.

There was no colonization, trade or follow up of any kind.

HONG BAO

YANG QING

period capable of making the voyages around the world, the answer is 'yes' but there are certain limitations. The large sea-going junks were quite capable of crossing the great oceans of the world. During the wars against Japan in the early fifteenth century, the Chinese built a fleet of ships believed to be the biggest navy ever assembled up to that point in time. Shipbuilding activity at the shipyards at Nanjing became a mania. As it gained momentum and as expertise accumulated in the expeditions against Japan, the knowledge was used to create the fleet for the epic voyage of Admiral Zheng He. The same expertise was used to build the armadas of Zhu Di. The junks were not capable of sailing into the wind so it would appear that they could only cross the Atlantic and Pacific in one direction. The Chinese, however, had a good knowledge of the winds and ocean currents. They could not always avoid a situation where they encountered a contrary wind, but by reefing all the sails they could always utilize the prevailing currents and make progress in the required direction. This method was extensively used by the European ships in later centuries.

What would be the amount of food and fresh water needed for voyages of such magnitude with so many ships? We need to know the number of people involved to answer this question. The Chinese may well have been able to carry foods that did not deteriorate with time, and in sufficient quantities to make a voyage around the world with the minimum of replenishment. But the fleets were so large, with each one comprising hundreds of ships and tens of thousands of people, that no settlement could possibly provide enough food to feed so many hungry mouths and to replenish the stocks for another ocean crossing. Even the provision of fresh water seems an almost impossible problem to solve at all but the largest islands and landing places. It has to be accepted that the Chinese were not immune from scurvy. There is no way in which this disease could have been contained over the long periods required to make the voyages. The death toll from scurvy must have been very high. One theory put forward is that there were indeed deaths by the thousand from scurvy and other causes, but that the numbers who sailed in the expedition were so large that only a fraction of them needed to survive for the voyages to achieve their objectives.

The Chinese were excellent astronomers and they had records of the movement of the stars and the planets dating from long before the observations in the west.

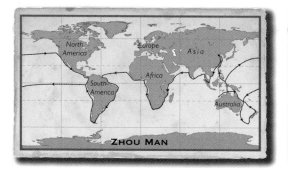

ZHOU MAN

ZHOU WEN

Excellent Astronomers On the positive side, the Chinese were excellent astronomers and they had records of the movement of the stars and the planets dating from long before the observations in the west. They knew how to find the latitude from the Pole Star and, in the Southern Hemisphere, they eventually worked out how to use the star Canopus to determine latitude even though the star was some distance away from the South Pole. Longitude was another matter. They knew how to use a lunar eclipse to find it but this was a relatively rare event and, consequently, many of the maps they produced show substantial errors in the longitude. The coastlines they depict are still recognizable however, and the fact that the longitudes were in error actually helps to support the truth behind the theory.

It took centuries for the Europeans to find a passage from the Atlantic to the Pacific Ocean. It took them even more centuries to find a way through the North East Passage across the north of Asia. It was the twentieth century before this feat was achieved, in an age of icebreakers and powered vessels. For a whole Chinese fleet to sail those frigid waters in a fleet of open sailing vessels, at the mercy of the ice and the bitter cold and unable to tack into the wind was an impossible undertaking. For the Chinese to attempt the passage would be no less than a horrific form of mass suicide. There is no way that a fleet of several hundred sailing ships could have made their way through the North East Passage.

> ## THE MING DYNASTY
> The Ming Dynasty lasted from 1368 to 1644, it provided an interval of native rule between the eras of Mongol and Manchu dominance. It was founded by Chu Yüan-chang, a man of humble origins who later assumed the title of Hung-wu. The Ming became one of the most stable but also one of the most autocratic of all Chinese dynasties.

The Vinland map seems to give a very good delineation of the northern coastline of Greenland and it has been argued that the coastline was copied from earlier maps produced by the Chinese. The sea north of Greenland has never been free of ice in recorded history and the passage through it has never been attempted even by the people of Greenland and Iceland. This is not to say that all the voyages described by Gavin Menzies are impossible, simply that the extent of the Chinese exploration is far too optimistic and has been grossly exaggerated.

Convincing Evidence The whole world is strewn with the wreckage of ships from many eras and there are many wrecks that have never been positively identified. Gavin Menzies has discovered many wrecks which he claims are from the Chinese voyages of 1421. Some of these are disputed and some may be genuine, but a lot more research needs to be done before the full picture emerges. Much of the conjecture is inconclusive, but this leads us to the most convincing evidence for the voyages. These are the maps of countries and coastlines that survive from this time and which soon afterwards seem to have made their way to Europe. The evidence of the maps is hard to refute. The Chinese can only have put the maps together by making the voyages – there was no other way to compile them. Fragments of coastline can be identified with the correct latitudes but with the wrong longitude. As said above, without some error in the longitude, however, the maps would not be as authentic.

There is a sad ending to the story of the great Chinese voyages. When the fleets reached home at long last after their magnificent achievements there was nobody waiting to welcome them. The Empire of Zhu Di had fallen into disgrace and his entire regime was discredited. Official accounts of the voyage were never published. For a few fortunate travellers it was a welcome homecoming, but so many died on the expedition that in nine cases out of ten the return of the ships simply brought tragedy and bad news of missing and lost relatives. The whole enterprise was ignored and it was never recorded in the history of the Ming Dynasty. All the evidence for the great exploration was forgotten and it did not resurface until centuries later when the maps of the voyages were rediscovered and came to be studied by later historians.

It is probable that the Chinese brought back exotic animals from their great voyages, perhaps never seen before in China. This painting is by Shen Tu and it dates from the early fifteenth century. The giraffe could have been brought back to the Ming court from Africa.

Henry the Navigator's colonization of Atlantic islands

Portuguese captains cross the equator and map the coast of Africa

1394 – 1460

*'Of a surety I doubt, if since the great power of Alexander and Caesar there has ever been any prince
in the world that had set up the marks of his conquest so far from his land.'*

Gomes Eannes de Azurara

Prince Henry the Navigator was born in 1394. The Portuguese make much of him as the man who initiated some of the greatest voyages of discovery in the fifteenth century.

Henry never actually took command of a ship but he was the main force behind new ventures in seafaring and it was through his efforts that Portugal came to the forefront of exploration in his times and for several generations after him.

Henry was the third son of King John I of Portugal and his mother was an Englishwoman, Philippa of Lancaster. She was the daughter of John of Gaunt and therefore the granddaughter of Edward III. This is the reason why the English as well as the Portuguese are great advocates of Prince Henry the Navigator. The contemporary royal chronicler Azurara described Philippa glowingly as 'a woman, most acceptable to God who would never espouse the interest of the Infidels, nor do anything in their favour, the more so as she was English, and England is one of those nations that hate the Infidels'. Even as late as the twentieth century one Portuguese historian wrote the compliment that 'She found the court a sink of immorality; she left it as chaste as a nunnery.'

Famous school of Navigation Henry was brought up and educated at court with his brothers Duarte and Pedro. He became the Duke of Viseu and Lord of Covilha. In his early years he fought for his country against the Muslims in North Africa but, in 1419, he retired from the court to become governor of the Algarve, the southernmost province of Portugal. It was there, on the rocky promontory of Sagres, at the extreme south west cape of Portugal where the Atlantic breakers beat ceaselessly against the rocks below, that Henry founded a famous school of navigation. He attracted the leading cartographers, astronomers, geographers, instrument makers and seamen of his time who came from all the known world to study under Henry the Navigator. In 1420, at the age of twenty-six, Henry was made grand master of the Order of Christ, a supreme order sponsored by the Pope that had replaced the crusading order of the Knights Templar in Portugal. This honour did not oblige Henry to take a formal vow of chastity but he was still expected to uphold the standards of a chaste and holy life. In Henry's case it was just a little too late for chastity, he had already sown a few wild oats and he was the father of an illegitimate daughter. The

TERRITORY EXPLORED BY THE PORTUGUESE

Portugal
Azores
Madeira
Cape Nun
30°N
Canary Islands
Cape Bojador
Tropic of Cancer
Rio de Ouro
Cape Blanco
Cape Verde Islands
Cape Verde
River Gambia
Africa
Atlantic
Ocean
Gulf of Guinea
Equator
30°W
0°

matter was not held against him and funds made available through the Order of Christ helped to finance Henry's great enterprises of discovery. This was on the condition that he agreed to convert the pagan people he discovered to Christianity.

Madeira and the Azores Portuguese exploration of the world began with the Atlantic. In 1418 the navigator João Goncalves Zarco was driven off course by a storm and the accident led him to rediscover Madeira. The island had been discovered in the previous century but it had never been inhabited. Henry immediately started a colony so that he could claim Madeira for Portugal. In the next decade the Azores were discovered by Diogo de Sevilha and the first Portuguese settlement was made there in 1432. This discovery involved a journey of 800 miles into the Atlantic with no coastline to guide them. The next find was the Canary Islands. These islands were known to the Romans but in Henry's time they had still not been settled and he was therefore at liberty to use them as a valuable offshore base for his explorations of the African coast. In the 1450s, Henry's captains encountered the Cape Verde Islands and this gave the Portuguese a sequence of provisioning stations from where they could explore the west coast of Africa. The islands were better suited than the mainland for this purpose, partly because of the climate but also because of the ease with which they could be defended.

In 1433 Henry's brother Duarte became king. Duarte supported Henry's plans and the latter was able to persuade his captains to venture further to the south along the unknown coast of Africa. There followed several decades of exploration. Every year ships returned with new discoveries as Henry's captains took their vessels further and further towards the south. In the early voyages Cape Nun was the most southerly headland to which the seamen were prepared to sail. They would go no further. There was a legend that nobody could return if they ventured beyond the cape and hence the name which was a corruption of 'Cape None'. At the tropics a vertical sun was believed to boil the sea and to scorch every man until he was black. A 'fact' which was easily proved by the colour of the indigenous population.

Cape Nun was duly rounded and in 1434 Gil Eanes reached Cape Bojadar at a latitude of 29°. In 1441 an expedition reached Rio de Ouro which lay on the Tropic of Cancer. Then came Cape Blanco at a latitude of 21°, named from the dazzling white of the beaches. The next significant cape was Cape Verde at less than 15° from the Equator; it was discovered by Dinis Dias and was rightly claimed as the most westerly cape in Africa. This was the time when the Cape Verde Islands were discovered, giving the Portuguese their staging post off the African coast. The exploration continued with new expeditions at regular intervals. In 1456 Alvise de Cadamosto and Nuno Tristão reached the River Gambia and their journals describe the explorers eating the flesh of an elephant. Stone columns called padrões were erected at the key capes and headlands of Henry's discoveries; each one carried inscriptions showing his claim to the west coast of Africa.

PORTUGUESE DISCOVERIES ON THE ATLANTIC COAST OF AFRICA

Some islands were rediscoveries, the Canaries for example were known to the Romans, but the Portuguese were the first to colonize the islands to help with their exploration of the African coast.

1418	Madeira
1427	The Azores
1450	The Canary Islands
1456	Cape Verde Islands
1430	Cape Nun
1434	Cape Bojador
1441	Rio de Ouro
1445	Cape Blanco
1445	Cape Verde
1456	Alvise de Cadamosto reached the River Gambia
1473	Lopo Goncalves crossed the Equator

THE MYTH OF PRESTER JOHN

Prester John was a legendary Christian ruler who was said to control much of central Africa and who would support the Christians against the Muslims. The legend goes back as far as the eleventh century in the early years of the Crusades. It was so persistent that Prester John was still thought to be alive and a real person 500 years later, in the sixteenth century.

Gold and Spices Henry was seeking knowledge but, like all explorers of his time, one of his main quests was for gold and spices. Gold was the commercial incentive yet Henry took his sponsor's wishes seriously and he was very keen to spread the gospel of Christ to the people of Africa. All Christendom at that time believed that there was a great Christian ruler called Prester John who held sway over most of Africa. The mythical figure of Prester John had been around from before the time of Marco Polo, two centuries earlier, but for generations the belief still held that he was alive and he ruled the African interior. The evangelical motive was the reason why all of Henry's ships bore a red cross on their sails; the explorers saw themselves as crusaders carrying the word of Christ to the undiscovered world. It has to be said, however, that Henry's laudable religious intentions were lessened by the fact that he was also running a slave trade. Much of his profit came from capturing the African natives and bringing them back to Europe to be sold off at the quayside of Seville and other slave markets in the Mediterranean. It is difficult to realize at this distance in time that slavery was seen as a necessary factor in a 'civilized' society. It did not raise any eyebrows and the morality of the trade was never questioned by the church or any other authority.

A fifteenth-century map depicts Portuguese galleons with rounded hulls and swelling sails, alongside a galleon with a single square sail and many oarsmen.

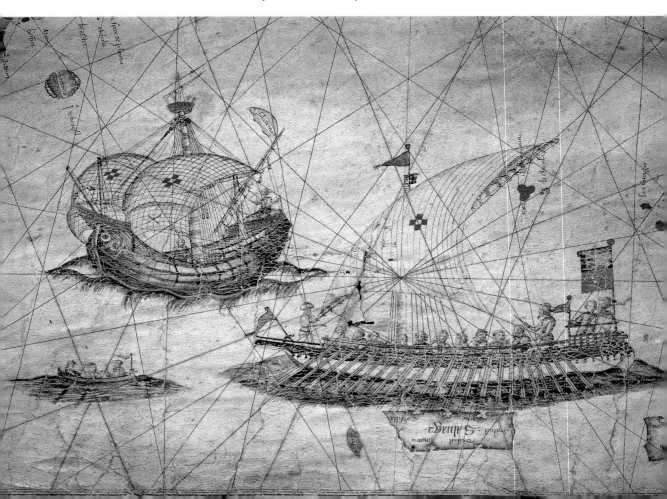

Henry the Navigator died in 1460. On the 500th anniversary of his death in 1960, the 'Monument to the Discoveries'(see page 41) was inaugurated commemorating Portugal's maritime empire. His achievements look small compared to those who followed him, but his contribution was very valuable. He had opened up trade along the African coast and he had set the scene for the great Portuguese expeditions in the generations to come. The exploration of the African coast was continued by private ventures after his death but it was not carried out with the same enthusiasm as when it had royal support.

It was the English who awarded him the title of Henry the Navigator. Henry had sown the seeds of great voyages in the future. It was not until a generation after his death that the most important of the Portuguese discoveries were made, when it was proved that there existed a sea passage around Africa to the shores of India and eventually on to the Orient. It was also suggested by more advanced thinkers that a sea passage to the Orient might be discovered from Europe by exploring to the west as well as to the east, and some thought that the western passage might turn out to be the shorter route.

THE JOURNEYS OF BARTHOLOMEW DIAS AND VASCO DA GAMA

TWO GREAT PORTUGUESE NAVIGATORS TRAVEL EAST AND DISCOVER THE VITAL SEA ROUTE TO INDIA

1487 – 1497

'*Late on Saturday (18 Nov. 1497) we beheld the Cape (of Good Hope). On that same day we again stood out to sea, returning to the land in the course of the night. On Sunday morning (19 Nov.) we once more made for the Cape, but were unable to round it… At last on Wednesday (22 Nov.) at noon, having the wind astern, we succeeded in doubling the Cape and then ran along the coast.*'

ANON. *JOURNEY OF THE FIRST VOYAGE*

In 1481 the Pope issued a bull to the effect that any new discoveries south of the latitude of the Canary Isles should belong to Portugal, but north of the line all new discoveries would belong to Spain. This was one of the main factors that caused the revival of exploration by the Portuguese in the 1480s. Countries such as England, France, Germany and the Netherlands were simply ignored. The major splits between Catholic and Protestant countries still lay in the future, but the Pope seemed to think that Spain and Portugal were the only two powers that mattered when it came to finding new lands.

Henry the Navigator had opened up the West Coast of Africa for trade and exploitation but his expeditions fell a long way short of discovering the southernmost cape of Africa. In 1483 Diogo Cão was despatched by King John II of Portugal to try and discover a sea route around Africa to India. He was supplied with the same stone pillars called padrões carved with inscriptions in Latin, Portuguese and Arabic that Henry the Navigator's ships had used. These were to be set up on all the prominent capes and headlands along the coast. When Cão reached the mouth of the Congo in 1483 he set up a padrõe there and another at Cape Cross which was nearly 22° south of the Equator. He opened up a further 1500 miles of the African coast but still the land seemed to continue further and further to the south. Cão never found an end to the land. He never found a passage to the east. He and many others became convinced that the African continent went all the way to the South Pole and that there was no sea passage around Africa to sail to the east.

About four years later, in 1487, Bartholomew Dias set off on another expedition which like all the previous ones was veiled in secrecy. Dias had a convoy of three ships and he followed the coastline beyond the point reached by Cão four years before him until he had crossed the Tropic of Capricorn. A violent gale took his ships well out to sea and out of sight of land. Dias persevered by sailing southwards for many days until the wind and currents drove him back again towards the east. There was still no sign of land but Dias decided to turn his ships back to the north again. Soon afterwards land was sighted again and he was able to make a landing at a place which became known as Mossell Bay now in Cape Province, South Africa. When he followed the coast from Mossell Bay he discovered to his surprise that soon he was travelling to the north east. It was a wonderful moment for Bartholomew Dias when he realized that the storm

BARTHOLOMEW DIAS AND VASCO DA GAMA

Lisbon
Asia
Tropic of Cancer
Africa
Calicut
Malindi
Equator
Mombasa
South America
Indian
St Helena Bay
Tropic of Capricorn
Atlantic
Ocean
Mossell Bay
Ocean
60°S
Spain
Portugal
40°W
0°

- - - - Vasco Da Gama
———— Bartholomew Dias
- · - · - Treaty of Tordesillas, 1494

must have taken him around the final cape of Africa. He knew that his ship was sailing along the East Coast and into the Indian Ocean.

Dias was greatly elated by his achievement, but his crew did not share his joy. They were totally exhausted by their exertions and they were very uneasy about being so far from home sailing in such strange and stormy waters that they were afraid of going further. The superstitions about boiling seas and great sea monsters began to arise again and there were many mutterings below deck. Dias had to justify his next decision to his sponsors:

An engraving of Bartholomew Dias.

Dias was the first European to take his ship around the southernmost point of the African continent. His men refused to sail any further. The distinction of being the first to reach India by the sea route fell to Vasco da Gama.

As the people were much fatigued from the terrible weather they had gone through, they all began to complain, and begged they might not proceed, as their provisions would all be expended, and before they got back to the store ships, they should perish for want: that it was sufficient to have discovered so much coast in one voyage: and that they must have doubled some great cape, which on their return they might discover. Bartholomew Dias, to satisfy the murmurs of his people, went on shore with his officers, and required them solemnly to declare what they thought was best to be done for the honour of their king. All agreeing to sail back, he made them sign a paper: yet he begged they would indulge him with sailing a day or two more along the coast, and if they found nothing remarkable, he would immediately return, which they agreed to. In these two or three days they discovered nothing but a river, about twenty five leagues beyond the island of the Cross in latitude thirty two degrees and two-thirds: as Juan Infante, captain of the vessel St Pantelam, *was the first that put foot onshore, it took its name from him, and continues the name of Rio de Infant. He then returned to the island of the Cross and with great regret left it, remembering with pleasure the asylum it had afforded him after the great danger they had escaped.*

Cape Bon Esperança The crew was still on the verge of mutiny. They were afraid of the unknown ahead of them and they declared that they would sail no further. Dias was forced to turn his ships at the very gateway to the Indian Ocean and to sail back home again. On their return journey the southernmost cape of Africa was seen by Dias and his men. He called it the Cape of Storms but when he returned home the king renamed it the 'Cape Bon Esperança' – the 'Cape of Good

Hope', for everybody knew that it was a significant discovery and it was the key to the long sought for passage to India.

It was not until nearly ten years after Bartholomew Dias that another voyage was launched, and those who are aware of the dates will know that momentous discoveries were made to the west during this decade of the 1490s. There had been other significant developments. The Pope had issued a bull in 1493 when he had carefully chosen a line of longitude at 38° west and he decreed that discoveries to the west of this line should belong to Spain, discoveries to the east were in the province of Portugal. If Spain and Portugal had been the only countries involved then this would have been a very fair division. After the voyages of Christopher Columbus however, the Pope decided to move the line to the west, at 46° 37'. The establishment of the new line in 1494 was called the Treaty of Tordesillas. The extent of South America was not known at this time, but the new treaty proved to be a very fortunate move for it gave the Portuguese a legitimate claim on Brazil.

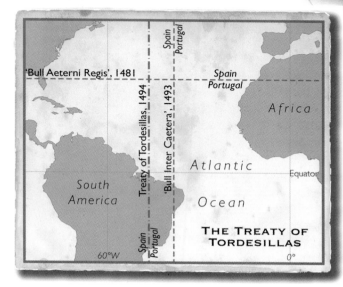

THE TREATY OF TORDESILLAS

It was 1497 when the next expedition set off to round the Cape of Good Hope, to follow in the wake of Bartholomew Dias and to discover the hoped for passage to India. This time the commander was Vasco Da Gama (pictured opposite page 47, meeting 'Christians' at Sâo Tomé – now part of Madras). Four ships sailed from Lisbon, they were the flagship *San Raphael* captained by Da Gama himself, the *San Gabriel* captained by his brother Paulo Da Gama, the *San Miguel* captained by Nicolas Coelho and a store ship whose name we do not know. Bartholomew Dias piloted the expedition on the first leg. He left the ships at the Cape Verde Islands with instructions to sail due south into the Atlantic right down to the latitude of the Cape of Good Hope where westerly winds would bring the ships back again to the land. It was a dangerous policy to sail so far from land for so long but it was the wind and the coastal currents that had made the journey so difficult for the previous explorers who insisted on clinging to the coast. Dias' advice proved to be sound and after a good passage Vasco Da Gama made a landfall on what is now St Helena Bay not far from Cape Town. After resting his men and preparing his ship for the voyage ahead Da Gama took to sea again and he successfully rounded the Cape of Good Hope. He rediscovered Mossell Bay where Dias had landed. It was here that he experienced exactly the same

It was a dangerous policy to sail so far from land for so long but it was the wind and the coastal currents that had made the journey so difficult for the previous explorers who insisted on clinging to the coast.

THE TREATY OF TORDESILLAS

In 1481 the Pope issued the *Bull Aeterni Regis*, awarding all new lands south of the Canary Islands to Portugal, north of the line to Spain. In 1493, following the voyages of Christopher Columbus, he amended the boundary from a line of latitude to a line of longitude at 38° west, *Bull Inter Caetera*. Discoveries west of the line belonged to Spain, discoveries east of the line to Portugal. By the Treaty of Tordesillas in 1494, the line was moved to longitude 46° 37' west. The world was divided between Spain and Portugal. Other countries were ignored.

problem as Dias before him. The convoy hit a ferocious storm and the ships lost contact with each other. When they eventually came together again within hailing distance Nicolas Coelho, the captain of the *San Miguel*, addressed the sailors:

'Brothers, let us strive to save ourselves from this storm, for I promise you that as soon as I can get speech with the captain-major, I will require him to put back, and you will see how I will require it of him.' With this they remained satisfied. Some days having passed thus with heavy storms, the Lord was pleased to assuage the tempest a little and the sea grew calm so that the ships could speak to another: and Nicolas Coelho coming up to speak shouted to the captain major that: 'It would be well to put about, since every moment they had death before their eyes, and if they who were captains did not choose to do so, and some many men who went in their company were so piteously begging with tears and cries to put back the ships, and they did not choose to do so, it would be well if they should kill or arrest us, and then they would put back or go where it was convenient to save their lives; which we also ought to do, and if we do not do it, let each one look out for himself, for this I do for my part, and for my conscience sake, for I would not have to give an account of it to the Lord.'

Sailing on to India Da Gama would have nothing to do with the suggestion of turning back. He had rounded the Cape of Good Hope and this was the occasion when he made his famous assertion that nothing would stop him from sailing on to India. He declared that he would not turn back from his course by even the breadth of a spar.

The coast was well populated by the African peoples and the ships were able to stop and replenish some of their supplies. The first place of any consequence they came to was Mozambique – it was the first sign of civilization since they left the west coast at the Cape Verde islands. The Portuguese ships looked strange and foreign when they arrived amongst the Arab merchantmen from the East. They found themselves in a Muslim community and they did not get a very friendly reception. Centuries of crusades and warfare between Muslim and Christian had taken their toll and news of the recent expulsion of the Moors from southern Spain had travelled quickly throughout the Muslim world. The sultan of Mozambique refused the trinkets presented for trade and asked instead for scarlet cloth which the Portuguese did not have. Da Gama was dismayed by his reception but he did manage to find a local pilot to guide him on to the north. Again he met with a hostile reception, this time at Mombasa where the Portuguese were once more treated with suspicion. It was obvious to the Arab traders that if the strange ships had sailed all the way from a Christian country as they had claimed, then the newcomers were in danger of stealing much of their trade with India and further east. It was not something the Arabs wished to encourage.

The Sultan of Malindi At Mombasa an attempt was made to steal the ships. Luckily the Portuguese were given notice of the plan and they were able to thwart it. Then Da Gama heard a rumour that by sailing only a short distance northwards up the coast he would probably get a much better reception at Malindi. He took the advice and his information proved to be correct. The Sultan of Malindi welcomed the newcomers with open arms and with such warmth that Da Gama became convinced that the people must be Christians. The belief in the mythical Prester John still held and at Malindi Da Gama was sure that they would hear of him or even meet up with him soon. The other good news was that he was able to take on board an Arab pilot who could take the ship across the ocean all the way to the Indian coast.

The Portuguese ships looked strange and foreign when they arrived amongst the Arab merchantmen from the East. They found themselves in a Muslim community and they did not get a very friendly reception.

It may look a simple enough matter to sail on a north-easterly bearing from Malindi to India but Da Gama knew that there were problems with the great variation of currents and winds between the different seasons. At this time the latitudes of the Indian ports were not reliably known and the longitudes could certainly not be relied upon. The pilot hired by Vasco Da Gama was Ahmed Ibn Majid. He knew about the monsoon winds and that the ships would have to wait for the right season to sail, he also knew the optimum route to take full advantage of wind and current. Once the land was behind them it took Da Gama's ships only twenty-three days to sail from Africa to the coast of India. On 20 May 1498 Vasco Da Gama arrived at Calicut (not to be confused with Calcutta), a main centre of trade on the Malabar Coast. Once again the Europeans got a welcome reception, this time from Zaromin, the governor of the Indian port.

Local Arabs and Indians

In Vasco Da Gama's time visitors from the West to India were very few. The few travelled through the Mediterranean and overland to Suez where they could find a ship to take them to the Indian Ocean via the Red Sea. There were not enough of these western traders to threaten the established trade of the local Arabs and Indians. A large ship arriving from the south however, such those which Vasco Da Gama commanded, could carry large and valuable cargoes and this was the reason why some of the Arab traders, like those on the African coast, reacted with jealousy and resistance to the appearance of the sea-going ships. For these and other reasons Da Gama had problems in disposing of his goods in Calicut.

THE LATEEN SAIL
By the time of Dias and Da Gama the ships had improved considerably over the previous century and they could sail to within 55° of the wind. The lateen sail made this possible. It was a triangular sail, mounted on the rearmost mast, known as the mizzen mast. With a lateen sail a ship could achieve in three tacks what would take five tacks for a square rigger. This made a great difference when rounding a promontory such as the Cape of Good Hope against the wind.

His initial reception was tempered by a plot against his life but luckily the assassins did not succeed. The Portuguese however, once they became accepted, were convinced that the Indians they had landed amongst were Christians. They even persuaded themselves that one of the Hindu temples was a Christian church. The temple contained a statue of the goddess Devaki which Da Gama thought was a Madonna.

They threw holy water over us and gave us some white earth, which the Christians of this country are in the habit of putting on their foreheads, breasts, around the neck, and on the forearms... many other saints were painted on the walls of the church, wearing crowns. They were painted variously, with teeth protruding an inch from the mouth and four or five arms.

The Portuguese however, once they became accepted, were convinced that the Indians they had landed amongst were Christians. They even persuaded themselves that one of the Hindu temples was a Christian church.

It seems amazing that the Indian temples could be mistaken for Christian churches, but the Portuguese had made a similar mistake in Malindi. They were so keen to establish the Christian religion everywhere they landed that they assumed that any other religion they encountered was simply a variation of their own. Their language skills and communication were obviously very poor and not good enough to convey the more abstract ideas of religious differences between the two cultures.

The ships remained in Calicut until the end of August. They then set sail back to Africa to take advantage of the easterly winds. The winds were not so favourable as on the easterly crossing and it took three months to reach the African coast. This was the most terrible part of the voyage. Men fell sick and some died from scurvy. Every day more and more bodies had to be committed to the deep. By the time they sighted the African coast, there were so few still alive that Da Gama had to abandon one of his ships. He did not have enough crew left to man all three of them.

It was many months later that the expedition staggered back to Lisbon. Only forty-four out of the original complement of 170 men returned. But in spite of his losses Vasco Da Gama was seen as a great explorer and navigator who had made the passage around the Cape of Good Hope and persevered in his ambition to reach India. Da Gama had proved that it was possible to reach the Orient by a sea route and his feat puts him amongst the greatest explorers of all time. The total distance covered by his voyage was equivalent to the circumference of the Earth. He mastered the difficulty of making a landfall beyond the Cape and he navigated the fierce currents off Mozambique. His skills as a captain were shown by the way in which he handled the problems of a near mutiny and survived more than one plot against his life. And despite all he brought two of his ships back home to Lisbon. He returned with many Indian artefacts and with new knowledge and understanding of the East. His voyage had opened up the first sea route to the Orient, but it was still only a beginning.

AMERICA IS DISCOVERED BY CHRISTOPHER COLUMBUS

IN HIS QUEST FOR THE INDIES, THE FAMOUS EXPLORER
REACHES THE NEW WORLD

1492

*'Sunday 9 Sept (1492). He made 15 leagues (about 45 miles) that day and
decided to report less than those actually travelled so that in case the voyage proved
long the men would not be frightened and lose courage.'*

BARTOLOMÉ DE LAS CASAS

Christopher Columbus was born in 1451 in the Italian city of Genoa. Little is known about his youth apart from the fact that his father was a weaver. His son Fernando said that he studied at Pavia University but the records do not confirm this claim.

He must have received some education however, as he was obviously literate and when he went to sea at the age of about fourteen he soon mastered the techniques of navigation. He worked for several years with his brother Bartholomew as a chart maker and it was during this part of his career that he began to wonder about the geography of the world. His son Fernando gives a description of Christopher Columbus at this time:

A well built man of average height; his face was long, with rather high cheekbones, and his body was neither fat nor lean. His nose was aquiline, his eyes light in colour, and his complexion fresh and ruddy. His hair was fair when he was young but turned grey when he was thirty. He was very restrained and modest in his dress, and temperate in matters of food and drink. He had an easy way with strangers, and was very pleasant with his household, though rather serious.

Columbus was fascinated by the travels of the Venetian merchant Marco Polo who, in the thirteenth century, had travelled by land from Venice to the Far East. It was obvious to Columbus, from Marco Polo's account of his journey, that he had travelled a very great distance to the east. Columbus knew that if the Earth was a sphere then it must be possible to reach Asia by sailing to the west, the opposite direction to Marco Polo.

MARCO POLO

Marco Polo was a Venetian and he knew of the valuable silks, spices and exotic goods that were carried on the silk road from the Far East. He decided to follow the trade route and to discover the East for himself. He stayed seventeen years in China. When he returned he was highly feted for his descriptions of lands and creatures which were no more than legend in Europe. His journeys took many years to accomplish and he tried to work out the distance to China but his estimates were far too long.

He became convinced that the sea route to the Orient would be much shorter than the overland journey made by Marco Polo. Where Columbus was in error however, was that he imagined Asia to reach much further round the globe than was actually the case. It was impossible in his times to measure longitudes with any degree of accuracy. Had he known the true longitudes of China and Japan then he would have known that the passage to Asia sailing to the west, if it existed, was at least as far as the passage to the east.

Christopher Columbus travelled extensively by sea over the known trade routes and he became a very experienced sailor and navigator. He researched his ideas thoroughly and at one stage he travelled to Iceland where he gossiped to Bristol sea captains who traded there. They claimed to know of strange lands such as the Isle of Seven Cities and the Isle of Brasil that lay further to the west in the Atlantic Ocean.

Columbus became so convinced by his ideas, that he made approaches to royalty in the hope of getting sponsorship for a voyage to the west. When King John II of Portugal turned down his approaches Columbus went on to approach Ferdinand and Isabella of Spain. In a long feud, fought over many centuries, the Spanish had managed to drive the last of the Moors out of the Granada region of Spain. The wars in Granada were all part of the long and depressing struggle between the Christian and Muslim religions in which neither party showed any sympathy for the views of the other side. But Ferdinand and Isabella were feeling confident enough after their success to be interested in new discoveries and colonial settlements. They agreed to sponsor Columbus for his venture to sail to the west in search of the east.

Misconceptions Many misconceptions have arisen about Christopher Columbus. One of which is that he was one of very few people to believe in a spherical earth and that his contemporaries and the men who sailed with him believed the Earth to be flat. In fact the flat Earth theory had been disposed of long before Columbus came on the scene. The instruments of navigation, the quadrant and the astrolabe, both of which were carried and utilized by Columbus, had been in use for centuries and the methods were based on the assumption of a spherical Earth; globes were certainly available in the Middle Ages. Any navigator measuring the latitude with these instruments knew perfectly well the theory behind the instruments and that they measured angles north or south of the equator. The primitive world maps of the time included lines of latitude and longitude. The only advocates of the flat Earth theory were the uneducated, a sector that admittedly constituted the great majority of people, and a few philosophers and theorists who never ventured out to sea.

He travelled to Iceland where he gossiped to Bristol sea captains who traded there. They claimed to know of strange lands such as the Isle of Seven Cities and the Isle of Brasil that lay further to the west in the Atlantic Ocean.

Another misconception was the idea that Columbus thought the world was far smaller than it really was. In fact he knew the circumference of the Earth to an accuracy of less than one per cent. It is true that he thought the distance westward by sea to the Orient was far less than the true distance, but this error was not based on his opinion of the size of the Earth. He, and others with him, thought the overland distance to the far eastern countries of China and Japan was much further than it was in reality and therefore the distance to reach them by sailing west was far less than was generally supposed. Columbus certainly did not consider that there could be room for another continent between Europe and the far east of Asia.

A third misconception is that Columbus was not allowed to recruit qualified seamen for his ships and that he had to accept a ship manned by convicts. This is easily dismissed by the list of the ships' crew that luckily still survives. Certainly there were convicts amongst the crew, but every ship bound for a long voyage had a quota of convicted men. It was so difficult to find men prepared to endure the hardships of a long voyage that prisoners were allowed to volunteer as part of their sentences. It would have been very difficult for Columbus to man his ships for such a dangerous voyage without offering places to some convicts.

Columbus was supplied with three ships. His flagship was a carabela called the *Santa Maria* with a crew of thirty-nine. In support were two

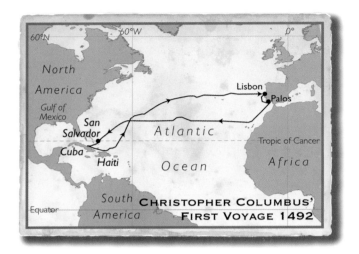

smaller vessels called the *Pinta* and the *Nina* (all pictured in the opening illustration). Both the latter names appear to be affectionate nicknames. 'Pinta' is a word for a piebald pony. 'Nina' means 'little girl' but it could also be a play on the name of the owner and ship's master Juan Nino. The *Pinta* and the *Nina* were manned by crews of twenty-seven and twenty-two men respectively – this gives us some idea of the relative sizes of the three ships. All the ships carried three masts and they were all three built with high castles both fore and aft. The mainmast carried a mainsail and a topsail, the foremast carried a square sail and probably a topsail, and the mizzen mast carried a triangular lateen sail on a sloping yard. It was also common usage for the carabelas to carry a sail below the bowsprit.

As the leader of the expedition Christopher Columbus was awarded the title of admiral. Juan de Cosa, the owner of the *Santa Maria*, was the ship's master and his pilot was Peralonso Nino. The captain of the *Pinta*, and second-in-command of the expedition, was Martin Alonso Pinzon. The master of his ship was Francisco Martin Pinzon. Vincente Yanez Pinzon was the captain of the *Nina* and the master was Juan Nino who was also the owner of the vessel. The Pinzons were brothers and they obviously had a large stake in the expedition as also did the Nino family.

It seems that seamens' superstitions about sailing on a Friday did not hold in Columbus' time. His fleet sailed from the tiny Spanish port of Palos de Frontera on Friday 3 August 1492. After passing through the straits of Gibraltar the ships made directly for the Canary Islands where they arrived on 8 August with no major incidents except for some damage to the rudder of the *Pinta*. They stopped to take on provisions for the long voyage ahead and had the *Pinta's* rudder repaired in the dockyard.

The Sargasso Sea Columbus set sail again on 6 September and he headed due west along a line of constant latitude. He kept a journal in which he entered the distance covered every day and the compass bearing, but in the ship's log he entered a different set of figures which implied that the distances covered were less than the true distances. His reason for the deception seems to have been twofold. He did not want any rival powers to follow his tracks into the Atlantic and to claim his discoveries as their own, but he was also concerned that the seamen would revolt if they knew how far from home they had travelled. The early part of the voyage was long and uneventful. By 16 September the convoy had reached the Sargasso Sea and they saw bright green weed around the boat. On the 17th a tropical bird was sighted. The 21st

Portrait of Christopher Columbus by Sebastiano del Piombo, 1519.

Columbus never set foot on the mainland of North America, but he discovered the Caribbean islands and he made four voyages across the Atlantic Ocean.

showed other signs of land but nothing could be seen from the lookout. It was on the 25th that Martin Alonso gave a great shout from the masthead of the *Pinta*, he thought he could see land ahead. There was a great scurry of activity and prayers were given to the Almighty. The sighting was a false alarm and the next day showed that Alonso had seen only a cloud formation.

September turned into October. There was another call of land from the *Nina* but again it was a false alarm. Columbus became a little worried for his crew were growing restless at having travelled so far from land. He knew from his true log that he had sailed considerably further than his men thought they had sailed from the figures in his false log. The men were on the brink of mutiny.They were afraid of venturing any further to the west with no signs of land to reassure them. It is certain that some of them must have known about the voyage of Bartholomew Dias when the mutinous crew insisted on turning the ship back home from the Indian Ocean. It is even possible that some of Columbus' crew had sailed with Dias five years earlier. After some coercion from Columbus the men agreed to sail westwards for another four days. After that time they

*At ten o'clock Columbus thought he could
see a light on the horizon, it seemed to be a
fire and it flickered like a candle... At
about two hours after midnight there was
no doubt about the fires... This time it
was not a false alarm. On the Friday
morning the little convoy found that it was
approaching an island. They sailed closer.
The island was inhabited.*

insisted that the ships must turn back to whence they came.

Columbus was fortunate. He did not after all have to face a mutiny. On Thursday, 11 October the ships were sailing WSW in a heavy sea with the roughest weather that had so far been encountered on the voyage. There were petrels near the ship and there was a green reed growing in the sea. A thorn branch was fished out of the sea with red berries which appeared to have been newly cut. It seemed that land was near but the darkness was coming on with tropical rapidity and soon the convoy was sailing through the night. At ten o'clock Columbus thought he could see a light on the horizon, it seemed to be a fire and it flickered like a candle. He called one of his officers, Pedro Gutierrez, and he too claimed to be able to see the light. The *Pinta*, the fastest of the three ships, sailed ahead of them. At about two hours after midnight there was no doubt about the fires. Rodrigo de Triana claimed to have sighted land and the *Pinta* gave the signal to those following behind. This time it was not a false alarm. On the Friday morning the little convoy found that it was approaching an island. They sailed closer. The island was inhabited.

We saw naked people, and I went ashore with a boat with armed men, taking Martin Alonso Pinzon and his brother Vicente Yanez, captain of the NINA. I took the Royal standard, and the captains each took a banner with the green cross which each of my ships carries as a device, with the letters F and Y (Ferdinand and Ysabella), surmounted by a crown, at each end of the cross. When we stepped ashore we saw fine green trees, streams everywhere and different kinds of fruits. I called the two captains to jump ashore with the rest, who included Rodrigo de Escobedo, secretary of the fleet, and Rodrigo Sanchez de Segovia, asking them to bear solemn witness that in the presence of them all I was taking possession of this island for their Lord and Lady the King and Queen, and I made the necessary declarations which are set down at greater length in the written testimonies.

It was an historic moment. They had landed on the island of San Salvador. The little fleet had crossed the Atlantic Ocean. The islanders gathered around chattering excitedly at the curious new arrivals. Columbus gave out red bonnets, glass beads and necklaces. The islanders swarmed around the boats giving balls of cotton thread, darts and brightly coloured parrots in exchange.

The island was lush with tropical vegetation, there were green trees, some laden with fruit, and there were streams of fresh water. The local people had primitive canoes made from hollowed-out tree trunks in which they were able to cross to the neighbouring islands. They had simple huts and villages and the parrots seemed to be the only wildlife on the island. The Europeans wanted to find gold above anything else and they noticed that one of the women had a small piece set in her nose. Christopher

Columbus decided to take one of his small boats and to sail round the island which he named San Salvador. He was amazed by how fertile it was:

Near the islet I have described there are groves of the most beautiful trees I ever saw; so green with their leaves like those of Castile in April and May. There is also plenty of water. I explored the whole harbour, and then returned to the ship and set sail. I saw so many islands that I could not decide which to go to first.

Communication was good in spite of the language problem. The newcomers were able to trade for food and to discover the whereabouts of islands beyond the horizon. It was evident that San Salvador was only a small island but the native people indicated that there were other much larger islands not very far away. The large island they called Juana lay to the south west; it was the island now known as Cuba. Columbus set sail from San Salvador for Cuba. The ships passed the island of Rum Cay (Saint Maria de la Conception), then Long Island and Crooked Island which he named 'Ferdinand and Isabella' after his patrons. Columbus was in no great hurry and the ships stopped to take on fresh water and to explore the islands. They sailed past a group they called Ragged Islands and then they headed to the south west. On 28 October the little fleet reached the mainland of Cuba. Columbus was again very taken with what he found:

It was an historic moment. They had landed on the island of San Salvador. The little fleet had crossed the Atlantic Ocean. The islanders gathered around chattering excitedly at the curious new arrivals.

I never saw a lovelier sight: trees everywhere, lining the river, green and beautiful. They are not like our own, and each has its own flowers and fruit. Numerous birds, large and small, singing away sweetly. There are large numbers of palm trees, different from our own and those in Guinea; they are of medium height, without the skirt round the base; the leaves are very large, and are used to thatch the houses. The land is very level.

The Most Beautiful Isle He took a boat and went ashore. He found the houses of two fishermen but they fled in fear at his approach. There was a dog but it did not bark. In the houses were nets, ropes, fishhooks and other fishing equipment. Columbus continued to praise the beauty he saw around him:

I returned to the ship and sailed a good way upriver. It is a joy to see all the woods and greenery, and it is difficult to give up watching all the birds come away. It is the most beautiful isle I have ever seen, full of fine harbours and deep rivers. It appears that the sea must never be rough, for the grass on the beach comes down almost to the shoreline, which is not the case where there are rough seas. So far I have encountered no heavy seas anywhere in these islands.

He made his way eastwards along the northern coast of Cuba, stopping and examining every place of interest. According to Columbus the local people thought the Europeans had arrived from heaven, certainly they

With a horrific crack the planking split open and the sea water rushed into the ship from below the water line. Columbus' flagship the SANTA MARIA was incapable of being re-floated and saved. She became a wreck.

thought the ships had come from another world. They would flock around and touch the newcomers, sometimes kissing them on the body to see if they were real. Columbus was very keen to convert the people to Christianity and wherever possible he would erect a cross for all to see. He found two large timbers on a spit of land and had them fashioned into a cross. He and his crew knelt before the cross and said their prayers. He wanted to take some of the Cubans back to Spain with him and he did not need to resort to kidnapping as there were plenty who were only too eager to undertake the journey:

A canoe came alongside us yesterday with six young men. Five of them came aboard, and I ordered them to be seized and have brought them away with me. I then sent men to a house on the west side of the river, and they brought back seven females, some young and some adult with three children. I did this because men behave better in Spain when they have women of their own with them than when they are deprived of them. Men have often been taken from Guinea to Portugal to learn the language, and given good treatment and gifts, and when they were taken back with a view to employing them in their own country they went ashore and were never seen again. Others behave differently. If they have their women they will be eager to take on whatever duties one asks of them, and the women themselves will be good for teaching our people their language, which is the same throughout these islands of India. They all understand each other, and go about from island to island in their canoes; quite differently from in Guinea, where there are a thousand different languages, incomprehensible to one another.

Last night a husband of one of these women, the father of the three children, a boy and two girls, came out to the ship in a canoe and asked me to take him with them, which I was very pleased to do. They are all happier now, so it appears they are all related. The man is about forty-five.

Ill Fortune At Tanomo Bay the three ships made a foray out to sea. Columbus returned with his flagship and the *Nina* but Alonso Pinzon in the *Pinta* made off on his own to the island of Babeque which was visible on the eastern horizon. Columbus reached the easternmost point of Cuba from where he could see across to the island of Haiti which he named Espanola. It was at Haiti on Christmas Day that the *Santa Maria* met with the worst possible ill fortune.

It was the Lord's will that at midnight, knowing that I had lain down to sleep, and seeing that the sea was like water in a bowl, a dead calm, everyone lay down to sleep and the helm was left to the boy, and the currents took the ship very gently onto one of the banks, which could be heard and seen a good league away even at night. The boy, feeling the rudder grounding and hearing the noise of the sea, cried out, and I heard him and got up before anyone else had realised that we were aground. Then the master, who was an officer of the watch, came on deck. I told him and the others to get into a boat we were towing, take an anchor and drop it astern. He jumped into the boat with a crowd of others, and

I thought they were obeying my orders, but all they did was row off to the caravel half a league to windward.

Columbus saw his men fleeing from the stricken vessel. The tide was receding to leave the *Santa Maria* stranded on a sandbank. The ship was in great danger and he had no alternative but to order the carpenters to cut away the mainmast and lighten the ship as much as possible. He tried to float her off the bank but the tide was ebbing lower all the time and the ship was firmly grounded. The *Santa Maria* listed to one side as the water level fell, then her seams began to open under the strain of the unsupported weight. With a horrific crack the planking split open and the sea water rushed into the ship from below the water line. Columbus' flagship, the *Santa Maria,* was incapable of being re-floated and saved. She became a wreck.

It was a terrible disaster to lose the flagship. The islanders came with their canoes and they worked hard to help unload the stores from the stricken ship. Christopher Columbus decided to make the most of the situation. It had always been his plan to leave behind a colony on one of the islands and there were volunteers amongst the crews who were prepared to stay and try to make a settlement. There was a minor piece of fortune in that the part of the island where the ship was wrecked happened to be very well suited for a colony. It was easy to defend, there was fresh water and a harbour, it seemed to be well supplied with food and it had good fertile land to farm.

Having lost the flagship, Columbus at this point was reduced to a single ship which was the smallest of the three. Alonso Pinzon, the captain of the *Pinta*, who had sailed off on his own to explore the island of Babeque later claimed that he had been accidentally lost but Columbus did not believe him. Both men had heard rumours of great quantities of gold on the island of Babeque and Columbus was convinced that Pinzon had gone to find the gold for his own profit. Columbus and all his men were obsessed by the search for gold over and above all other forms of trade. They were lucky, for the islands did in fact have gold and the Indians knew how to pan for it and how to work it into simple ornaments. They would willingly exchange gold artefacts for the mirrors and little bells that the expedition carried with them.

He never set foot on the mainland of North America, but he was the first European to discover the West Indies, South America and Central America. He returned to Spain and he died at Valladolid in 1505.

On 6 January Columbus met up again with Alonso Pinzon in the *Pinta*. The ships sailed together along the coast of Haiti until they reached Samana Bay. At last, on 16 January the *Nina* and the *Pinta* left the West Indies behind them to sail back home. There were stories of an island on the route called Matinino which was populated only by women. Men visited once a year and nine months later babies were born. The men came back the next year to claim the male children but the female children remained with the island community. Columbus never found the island so there is no description of this interesting sociological experiment.

Columbus headed for the Azores which he knew to be at a latitude of 39°. He made good progress until he reached the final approach but then his fleet was hit by the most ferocious storm of the voyage, with seas so rough that the hardened mariners claimed they had never known so terrifying a storm. His ships survived to replenish their stocks at Santa Maria and then to sail the final leg into Lisbon. Columbus called at Lisbon harbour but his was a Spanish voyage and he dared not stay long; he sailed from Lisbon back to Palos. He wrote up the account of his voyage and he made his way to Castile where he presented his findings to his sponsors Ferdinand and Isabella. All were amazed by the West Indian people they brought back with them and the wonderful objects and souvenirs from the Caribbean.

Three more voyages Columbus' first voyage of 1492 is the one that is remembered and which fired the imagination. But he made three more voyages to the West Indies. He set out in September 1493 with seventeen ships, leaving several hundred more people at his colony of Isabella on Haiti. He went on to discover Jamaica and Puerto Rico but later on in the voyage he became ill and nearly died. He recovered sufficiently to return to Spain about two years later.

He found it difficult to get sponsorship for a third voyage, but in 1498 he set out to the west again and discovered Trinidad. He eventually reached the coast of South America near the mouth of the Orinoco River. His enemies accused him of badly administering the new colony of San Domingo. The discoverer of America was brought home in chains and it was some time before he regained favour.

On his last voyage in 1502 Christopher Columbus reached the shores of Honduras in Central America. He followed the land as far as Panama but he could find no passage through to India. He never set foot on the mainland of North America, but he was the first European to discover the West Indies, South America and Central America. He returned to Spain and he died at Valladolid in 1505.

As he lay on his deathbed, Christopher Columbus still believed that the lands he had discovered were in Asia. He had no idea that his voyages had opened up a whole new continent. By this time there had been other discoveries to the north and other nations were staking their claims to the lands across the Atlantic.

JOHN CABOT'S SEARCH FOR THE NORTH WEST PASSAGE

A VENETIAN SAILS FROM BRISTOL TO NEWFOUNDLAND ON BOARD THE *MATTHEW*

1496 – 1499

*'The Venetian, our countryman, who went with a ship from Bristol in quest of new islands, is
returned, and says that 700 leagues (2100 miles) hence he discovered land… The king has
promised that in the spring our countryman will have ten ships, armed to his order… The
king has also given him money wherewith to amuse himself until then, and he is now at
Bristol… His name is (John Cabot) and he is styled "the great admiral"… The
discoverer of these places planted on his new-found land a large cross, with one flag of
England and another of St Mark, by reason of his being a Venetian.'*

LORENZO PASQUALIGO TO HIS BROTHERS

In the year 1481 the Pope first fixed a line of latitude through the Canary Islands as the boundary between Portuguese and Spanish discoveries. After the voyage of Columbus, which was sponsored by the Spanish Court, the Spanish were claiming land that lay south of the Canaries and which was therefore in Portuguese territory.

The Papal advisors soon realised that something must be done about the situation and in 1493 they came up with a new boundary line, this time a line of longitude at 38° west. This gave the West Indies to Spain and the African coast to Portugal. After the discoveries of Vasco Da Gama and Christopher Columbus, it seemed to be a reasonable division but the Portuguese objected and the following year, at the Treaty of Tordesillas, the Vatican moved the line to the longitude of 46°37′ to appease them. It proved to be a fortunate move. In 1500 Pedro Alvarez Cabral set sail from Portugal to follow in the wake of Vasco Da Gama. He headed southwards but he was carried too far to the west by contrary winds and currents. He discovered a new coastline but his instructions were to sail to India and the coast was so long that he did not have the time to explore and chart it. Cabral's accidental discovery was the coast of South America and it allowed Portugal to lay claim to Brazil.

It is pertinent to ask how the Pope came to be the authority for deciding which parts of the undiscovered world belonged to which country. It can be argued that somebody had to take on the responsibility for assigning new areas of exploration to different countries. To the Christian world, the Pope, whose authority covered the whole of Christendom, was the best possible person to make the decisions. The Pope was under the impression that the whole of the undiscovered world should be divided between Spain and Portugal. The reaction of other countries, such as England, France and Holland can easily be imagined. These expanding countries with strong maritime traditions were being told that they had no claim at all on any new discoveries they might make anywhere in the world. This exclusion was clearly nothing to do with the Protestant religion for the split with Rome still lay many years in the future. The Vatican simply did not consider that other countries had any claim to be involved in exploration. Consequently, in the last years of the fifteenth century, Spain and Portugal thought they had no competition in the search for new lands. But there was one country which was quickly rising to challenge their dominance.

London, the capital city of England, was not only the greatest centre of trade in the country, it was also a major port, but the London waterside faced to the east of England where there were no new discoveries to be made. In the fifteenth century, the three largest cities after London were Norwich,

BRISTOL IN THE FIFTEENTH CENTURY

Bristol began life as the Saxon settlement of Brig-stow, meaning the 'the bridge town'. It was situated where traffic from the south-west to the Midlands and north crossed the traffic from Southern England to South Wales and it became a great place of trade. It was situated on the River Avon about eight miles from the Severn Estuary and in the Middle Ages the sea-going vessels could easily sail upstream as far as Bristol Bridge. By the end of the fifteenth century Bristol had overtaken York and Norwich to become the second city in England in terms of population and trade although strictly speaking it did not become a city until the sixteenth century.

York and Bristol. Of these three only Bristol was a seaport and it was situated on the west coast of England. Bristol was an important trading hub and it was very well placed to explore the Atlantic Ocean and in the High Middle Ages Bristol rose to become the second city in England. In 1480 William Worcestre, the Bristol topographer, described the amazing volume of trade and shipping:

Black stones sited in the river Severn at Hollowbacks, 4 miles from Bristol (i.e. the Avon Estuary) beyond Hungroad, where ships and boats wait for the next incoming tide. And when the tide begins to rise from the Severn towards Bristol past King Road, Hung Road, and past Ghyston Cliff and, the said small rocks are covered by the sea; and, as I learned, thus on the turn of the tide, all the ships at the Hollowbacks (from Spain, Portugal, Bordeaux, Bayonne, Gascony, Aquitaine, Brittany, Iceland, Ireland, Wales, and other countries) weigh their anchors and set sail toward Bristol.

High tide at Bristol was a scene of great activity. There were only a few hours in the day when it was possible for the larger vessels to make their way along the River Avon and through the limestone gorge to the quaysides. When the merchant William Canynges died in 1474 he owned nine ocean going ships including the *Mary Redcliffe*, a vessel of 500 tons, and his largest ship the *Mary and John* of 900 tons. The Bristol merchants traded with all the coastal countries of Europe. We do not know whether or not Christopher Columbus ever visited Bristol but we do know that he travelled to Iceland where he picked the brains of the Bristol captains. His motivation was that he had heard of new discoveries in the seas beyond Iceland, made by the Bristol seamen.

Icelandic Trade Trade between Bristol and Iceland was well established at this time. The outward cargo consisted mainly of cloth and manufactured goods and the return cargo was 'stockfish', a name given to dried cod from the Icelandic shelf. The Bristol sailors believed that islands existed in the seas to the west of Iceland where they found many pieces of dark red wood floating on the Gulf Stream which they claimed was from a place they called the Isle of Brasil. They believed that there was another island called the Isle of the Seven Cities lying further west again.

Some of the Bristol merchants harboured romantic notions of a new route to the Indies, but they had a more down to earth problem in that the powerful Hanseatic League was challenging their right to trade with Iceland for the stockfish. If islands existed in the western seas then the Bristolians might be able to find new fishing grounds there and make their trade independent of the Hanseatic League. In July 1480 John Jay, a Bristol merchant who was related by marriage to William Worcestre, sponsored a ship of 80 tons to sail westwards into the Atlantic in search of the Isle of Brasil. William Worcestre was actually present in Bristol on the

THE HANSEATIC LEAGUE

The Hanseatic League was a powerful alliance of commercial towns dominating northern Europe. It was founded by a group of German towns in the thirteenth century and by the end of the fourteenth century it had more than a hundred members. Trade routes were jealously guarded and when the Bristol ships started to trade with Iceland the Hanseatic League looked upon them with suspicion. In later centuries the League declined and its last meeting took place in 1669.

day the ship returned. His notes are incomplete and partly illegible but the gist of the message is obvious:

On the 15th day of July (1480) the ship of (Joan?) and John Jay the younger, of the weight of 80 tons, began a voyage from Kingroad at the port of Bristol to the Island of Brasil to the west of Ireland, sailing over the sea by… (Blasket Island?)

And… Lloyd was master of the ship, the most knowledgeable mariner in all England. And news came to Bristol on Monday the 18th day of September that the said ship had sailed the seas for about 9 months (an error for 9 weeks), not finding the island, but had been forced back by storms at sea to the port of… in Ireland, for refitting the ship and (reorganising) the crew.

The Isle of Brasil The next year there is a mention of two small ships, the *Trinity* and the *George*, setting sail on the same quest of 'examining and finding a certain island called the Isle of Brasile'. They were loaded with salt, which seems to imply that they hoped to make a good catch of cod. The Bristol records are silent about their fate. Later events indicate that they might in fact have discovered land but the evidence for this claim will be given when more of the story has unfolded. There is no doubt that the Bristol merchants were searching for land in the western ocean in the decade before Columbus and there is little doubt that Columbus himself was well informed of their voyages.

In 1495 an Italian merchant called Giovanni Caboto arrived in Bristol. By chance he was born in Genoa like Columbus. He became known in England as John Cabot and he too had heard of the Bristol voyages into the Atlantic sponsored by John Jay in the 1480s. Cabot, like Columbus, was interested in finding land to the west and in March 1496 he obtained a royal assent from Henry VII of England (as pictured on page 63) 'to find, discover, and investigate whatsoever islands, countries, regions or provinces… which before this time were unknown to all Christians'. Cabot lost little time and, in the late summer of 1496 he made his first abortive venture into the Atlantic with a single ship. According to the English agent John Day 'his crew confused him, he was short of supplies and ran into bad weather, and he decided to turn back'.

Cabot, like Columbus, was interested in finding land to the west and in March 1496 he obtained a royal assent from Henry VII of England 'to find, discover, and investigate whatsoever islands, countries, regions or provinces… which before this time were unknown to all Christians'.

In the next year Cabot made a second attempt and on about 20 May he sailed west in a three-masted caravel called the *Matthew* with a crew of eighteen seamen. The voyage got off to a slow start, Cabot's ship met with heavy weather and he had to put in to the Welsh coast for shelter. After this short delay the ship headed out beyond Ireland and into the Atlantic. The days stretched to weeks as the *Matthew* beat ever westward into the setting sun and the Pole Star lay to starboard as she sailed through the Atlantic night. The voyage was in midsummer, the longest day came and went and there was still no sign of land. But on 24 June there was great rejoicing aboard the ship – to the great delight of the sailors the sea abounded with fish -

but far more significant was that a new coastline had appeared on the horizon. The *Matthew* approached the coast and searched for a place to land. John Cabot went ashore and planted the English flag on the new found land. The findings were described in a letter from John Day to Christopher Columbus:

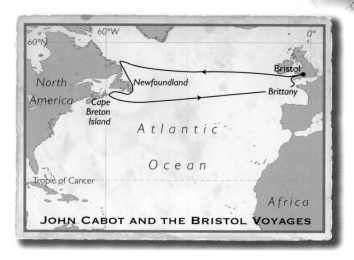

JOHN CABOT AND THE BRISTOL VOYAGES

... and they (i.e. Cabot's men) found tall trees of the kind masts are made, and other smaller trees and the country is very rich in grass. In that particular spot, as I told your Lordship, they found a trail which went inland, they saw a site where a fire had been made, they saw manure of animals which they thought to be farm animals, and they saw a stick half a yard long pierced at both ends, carved and painted with brazil, and by such signs as they believe the land to be inhabited. Since he was just with a few people he did not dare advance inland beyond the shooting distance of a cross-bow, and after taking in fresh water he returned to his ship. All along the coast they found many fish like those which in Iceland are dried in the open and sold in England and other countries, and these fish are called in England 'stockfish'; and thus following the shore they saw two forms running on land after the others, but they could not tell if they were human beings or animals; and it seemed to them that there were fields where they thought might also be villages, and they saw a forest whose foliage looked beautiful.

A shorter route to Asia The *Matthew* spent about two weeks exploring the coastline that ran southwards from the point where the landfall was made. The ship then headed back to the east and with the help of the prevailing winds she landed in Europe after a crossing of only fifteen days. Cabot's landfall was well to the south of Bristol , it wasn't even in England, for he found he was off the coast of Brittany. This implies either that the skies were never clear enough to measure the sun's altitude or that Cabot was not skilled at finding his latitude, but by 6 August Cabot was back in Bristol and by the 10th of the month he was in London telling the king of his new discoveries.

John Cabot, like Columbus, was convinced that he had found a shorter route to Asia, and he made another voyage in 1498, this time with five ships. Little is known of the fate of this expedition, only one ship returned to Ireland badly damaged. It is thought that Cabot died on the expedition. It was early in the same year (1498) that the Englishman called John Day wrote a letter to the Spanish 'Grand Admiral', who at that time was none other than Christopher Columbus, with details of the Cabot expedition as quoted above. The letter, written in Spanish, lay undiscovered in the castle of Simancas,

It was early in the same year (1498) that the Englishman called John Day wrote a letter to the Spanish 'Grand Admiral', who at that time was none other than Christopher Columbus, with details of the Cabot expedition...

central Spain, until 1955. The account adds a few fascinating details related to the story. It implies that a landfall was made in the Atlantic Ocean by the Bristol men before Cabot and before Columbus! Furthermore it implies that Columbus knew of this discovery:

It is considered certain that the cape of the said land was found and discovered in the past by the men from Bristol who found 'Brasil' as your Lordship well knows. It was called the Island of Brasil, and it is assumed and believed to be the mainland that the men from Bristol found.

Other adventurers followed Cabot, and in 1501 three Bristol merchants, Richard Warde, Thomas Assehurst and John Thomas, petitioned Henry VII to set off on a joint expedition with three Portuguese merchants to 'seek out and discover some islands lying in our sphere of influence'. In the same year the Bristol 'Company Adventurers into the New Found Lands' was formed and was granted letters patent for voyages of discovery and annexation.

THE NAMING OF AMERICA

In 1507 the German map maker Martin Waldseemuller published a new map of the world, showing the new discoveries to the west under the single name 'America'. The continent was thus named after the Florentine explorer Amerigo Vespucci and the name quickly became generally adopted. This was a great injustice to men like Columbus and Cabot who were the true discoverers of the new land. When John Cabot returned from his Newfoundland voyage to Bristol, his royal paymaster was called Richard Ameryke and this has been put forward as an alternative theory for the naming of America.

Sebastian Cabot John Cabot had a son, Sebastian, who was also an explorer. Sebastian left Bristol in 1509 with two ships and 300 men bound for America. His objective was to try and find a passage to Cathay by exploring beyond the lands discovered by his father. The voyage of Sebastian Cabot is very poorly documented but there is evidence that he entered Hudson Bay in what was the first of many attempts to find the North West Passage from the Atlantic to the Pacific. Cabot did not find a passage, but after exploring to the north he also explored the coast of America to the south in search of a sea passage through the continent. When he returned to Bristol in 1509 his sponsor Henry VII was dead. Sebastian Cabot did not write up an account of his discoveries and many years later he was claiming that the discoveries made by his father were in fact made by himself. His dishonesty on this point makes him a very unreliable source of information. John Cabot was unfortunate, where Columbus had a son who recognized his father's achievements and wrote a valuable biography, Cabot had a son who did nothing to make his father's discoveries better known and who even tried to pass them off as his own.

In the 1490s Columbus landed in South America and also in Central America but at the time of John Cabot's voyage the North American continent was unknown to him. The English claim is complicated by the fact that the American mainland had already been discovered by the Vikings at the end of the tenth century although they had not been able to establish permanent trade or a settlement at that time. Cabot's voyage did not attempt to make a settlement in the new land but it opened up Newfoundland as a regular fishing ground and a place of trade for the Bristol ships. Throughout the sixteenth century voyages across the Atlantic were made every year to bring back the Newfoundland cod.

FERDIMAN. MAGALA.

FERDINAND MAGELLAN
AND THE FIRST
CIRCUMNAVIGATION
OF THE WORLD

THE EXPLORER SAILS AROUND
THE SOUTHERN TIP OF AMERICA

1519 – 1522

'We were three months and twenty days without getting any kind of fresh food. We ate biscuit which was no longer biscuit but its powder; swarming with worms, for they had eaten what was good. It stank strongly of rat's urine. We drank yellow water already putrid for many days… Rats were sold for half a ducat apiece… The gums of both the lower and upper teeth of some of our men swelled, so that they could not eat under any circumstances and therefore died.'

ANTONIO PIGAFETTA, 1525

As a youth of nineteen Ferdinand Magellan witnessed the triumphant return of Vasco Da Gama after his amazing voyage to India when the trade route from Portugal to the East began to open up. These events made a great impression on the young Magellan, and from a youthful age his ambition was to follow in the wake of the great Portuguese explorers and to make new discoveries of his own.

The village of Sabrosa in Portugal's wine district claims to be Magellan's birthplace. He was born in about 1480 to minor gentry and at the age of ten or eleven, after his father died, he was taken to Lisbon to become a page in the household of Queen Leonor. She was consort to Prince John II of Portugal, who was known in his time as the 'perfect prince'.

Magellan was not living in Lisbon at the time when Bartholomew Dias returned from the Cape of Good Hope, but he was old enough to remember the arrival of Christopher Columbus from his first Atlantic voyage.

The last decade of the fifteenth century and the first decades of the following century saw new discoveries and new trade routes opening up almost every year. In 1500 the east coast of Brazil was accidentally discovered by Pedro Alvarez Cabral and the credit for this discovery must go to the Portuguese. The east coast of the American continent, both north and south, was rapidly being explored and filled in on the world map. In 1507 the German mapmaker Martin Waldseemuller published a map in which the American continent was given a name for the first time. He chose to call it after the Florentine banker, Amerigo Vespucci, because he was one of the first people to suggest that north and south were the same landmass and that America was a continent running from the far north to the deep south. Vespucci was very fortunate to have the new continent named after him as he was not an explorer or a navigator and his influence extended only to the south of the new continent and not the north. After Waldseemuller's map was published, the New World across the Atlantic Ocean became known as 'America'. Columbus and other explorers were not honoured as highly as Amerigo Vespucci.

In 1513 the explorer Vasco de Balboa crossed the Isthmus of Panama. He waded out into the Pacific Ocean in full armour waving a sword in one hand and the banner of Castile in the other. He claimed the ocean for Spain. It was becoming more and more evident that there was a whole continent between Europe and Asia and no way through it or round it had been discovered. The continent seemed to stretch from the North to the South Pole. The two great oceans came so close to each other at the Isthmus of Panama that it seemed certain that somewhere there must be a strait or a sea passage joining them together. This theory was an illusion – there was no viable sea passage from the Atlantic into the Pacific in the central and northern parts of America .

New Discoveries By 1517 Magellan was approaching middle age and after voyaging to India, the East Indies and fighting in Morocco he still yearned to make new discoveries. After many years of loyal service to the country of his birth he was spurned by the Portuguese when they refused to offer him the promotion he badly wanted. Portugal had made remarkable progress in developing trade with the East. It was obvious that Columbus had been wrong to assume that the West Indies were near the coast of India, but Magellan was still convinced that there was a western sea passage to reach the spice islands of the Far East. He wanted to lead an expedition to discover the passage but his own country was much too busy developing the route to the east around the Cape of Good Hope. They refused to give him the support he needed.

In the winter of 1518 Magellan approached Charles I of Spain with a proposal to search for a passage around the south of America into the Pacific Ocean. This time his application was accepted. He was given the financial support he needed by the Spanish king and a fleet of five ships. What the king would not do, however, was to pay for good seamen to man the ships and in order to make his voyage Magellan had to recruit his men from the dregs of the Mediterranean Spanish sea ports. This did not deter him from his objectives, he recruited a nucleus of loyal followers to command his five ships and in September 1519 his expedition set sail on the first leg of the great journey. The five ships were the *Trinidad* (110 tons), the *San Antonio* (120 tons), the *Conception* (90 tons), the *Victoria* (85 tons) and the *Santiago* (about 80 tons).

Patagonian Giants Magellan sailed first to the Cape Verde Islands and from there he crossed the Atlantic on the direct route to Brazil. He explored the bay at Rio de Janeiro but soon discovered that there was no passage through to the west. He ventured further south and explored the River Plate but again the result was negative, there was no sea passage. He sailed south again but his crew was already very unhappy about sailing so far into unknown waters. They encountered the Patagonians, men so tall that he described them as giants. Antonio Pigafetta, an Italian who sailed as the official recorder, described how Magellen tricked the Patagonians.

PATAGONIA

Patagonia was the name given by Magellan to the extreme south of America. It is now part of Argentina to the east and Chile to the west. For centuries the inhabitants were thought to be giants, sometimes claims were made that they were nine feet tall.

The manner in which he retained them was that he gave them many knives, forks, mirrors, bells and glass, and they held all these things in their hands. Then the captain had some irons brought, such as are put on the feet of malefactors; these giants took pleasure in seeing the irons, but they did not know where to put them, and it grieved them that they could not take them with their hands, because they were hindered by the other things which they held... (Magellan had the shackles put on their feet...) they began to be enraged and to foam like bulls, crying out very loud 'Setebos' that is to say, the great devil, that he should help them.

As the voyage continued further south it was soon apparent that all was not well. Basically the seamen were afraid of sailing any further into the unknown. On Easter morning 1520 Magellan was greeted by a petition from the captains of the three ships *Conception*, *San Antonio* and *Victoria*.

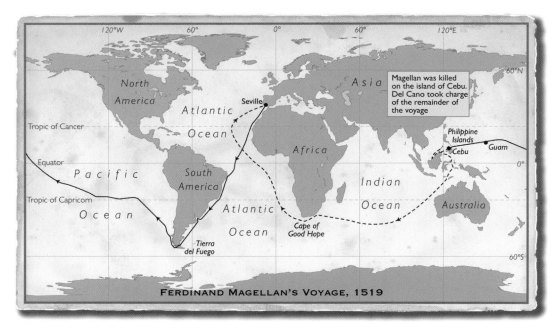

FERDINAND MAGELLAN'S VOYAGE, 1519

They objected to the autocratic policy of their commander and they said that they wished to be consulted about which course their ships were to take. They were unwilling to sail any further along a hostile coast in what they saw as a vain and fruitless search for a passage through the American continent.

The situation was very nearly a mutiny. But Ferdinand Magellan proved equal to the situation. With three of his five ships against him, he was outnumbered and outgunned, but he rejected the petition and sent the captains responsible back to their ships. Then when darkness fell he sent armed men in boats to overpower the *San Antonio* and simultaneously he sent loyal men to take control of the *Victoria*. The *San Antonio* tried to escape by cutting her anchor cable but Magellan had his cannon at the ready and he stopped the ship with a rapid burst of fire. When the *Conception* saw the situation, she too surrendered, and before dawn Magellan's prompt actions had put him back in command of his expedition. He was well aware, however, that nothing but the most ruthless discipline would allow him to keep control of his men. He knew the need for strong discipline and, to show that he meant business, he had the captain of the *Conception* beheaded by one of his own servants. He also hanged one of the ringleaders, Luis de Mendoza, from the yardarm of his own ship, leaving his body dangling from the rope for all to see.

He also hanged one of the ringleaders, Luis de Mendoza, from the yardarm of his own ship, leaving his body dangling from the rope for all to see.

The next problem to arise concerned the *Santiago*. She was reconnoitring to the south when she struck a hidden reef. The seas were so heavy that the ship could not haul off and after hours of punishment from the stormy seas she became a wreck. The weather conditions were so bad that it took four months for the news of the loss of the *Santiago* to reach Magellan and it took even longer for him to find and rescue the crew. By this time it was winter and snow had fallen, the ships were sailing in a cold harsh sea that seemed excruciatingly cold and raw to those brought up in the warm Mediterranean climate. When the mutinous crew of the *San Antonio* realized the situation they had had enough, they overpowered their captain, turned their ship, and sailed for home before Magellan could do anything to stop them. Ferdinand Magellan was down to three ships and he knew that many of his crew were still on the brink of mutiny.

The Land of Fires The voyage struggled on with the three remaining ships. At last Magellan found another passage to the west. His ships entered a strait with choppy waters guarded by sharp rocks on both sides. They sailed past the rocks and battled onwards again. At night they could see fires which they realized were

FERNAND, MAGELLAN,

made by the local inhabitants. Magellan called the land 'Tierra del Fuego' or 'The land of the fires'. They made contact with the Fuegeans but found them a very primitive and poor people. For thirty-eight days and over three hundred miles Magellan's ships battled day and night through the straits. At last, at the end of August, they came to the final headland. The Straits of Magellan opened out to reveal a beautiful great placid sea. Magellan was so taken with the smooth and calm sea that he named it the Pacific Ocean. Little did he know that he had been very fortunate with the weather and at other times he could have been greeted by a sea as high and dangerous as anywhere on earth. Neither was he aware at the time that he was the first to enter into the greatest ocean on the face of the earth by the stormy southern gateway.

Magellan sailed northwards keeping to the coast for a thousand miles. Then he discovered a north west current and he decided to strike out across the ocean on a course which took him with it. It was a rash decision because he had no idea how big the Pacific was or how few and scattered its islands were. He was already short of supplies when he left the land behind, but he made no attempt to find provisions before leaving the coast. He had no charts. He was not to know the scale of the vast watery emptiness into which he rashly led his ships.

Day after day they sailed across the great ocean. Week after week they scanned the horizon for signs of land. Month after month they were

Engraving of Ferdinand Magellan.

Magellan stares thoughtfully into the distance; he holds a scrolled map and a pair of dividers. He was the first to discover the Straits of Magellan and to enter the Pacific from the east. He did not live to complete the circumnavigation of the world.

THE STRAITS OF MAGELLAN

The Straits of Magellan are 350 miles long.

The Atlantic entrance is between Cape Virgenes and Cape Espiritu Santa.

The exit to the Pacific is at Cape Pillar on Desolation Island.

It took Magellan 38 days to navigate the straits.

Magellan discovered the galactic clusters called the Magellenic Clouds, 150 to 200 thousand light years away and only visible in the deep south.

disappointed. Magellan was very unlucky, he had little option but to sail with wind and current but he set a course that did not take him through any of the island groups. If they had discovered the Marquesas, Tahiti or the Fiji Islands then they could have had plenty of fresh food and supplies to replenish their stocks. Somehow they retained sufficient water to stay alive but food was the pressing problem. It was not surprising that the dreaded scurvy set in. It was not possible to cut back on the salted food and there was no supply of fresh fruit or vegetables. Gums became red and sore and swelled to a horrific size. They bled painfully and teeth became loose. The sailors were reduced to chewing the leather on the yardarms to hold the hunger at bay. Men started to die from scurvy and starvation.

They came upon a group of islands, but their hopes were soon dashed as the islands were seen to be barren with no human life and no food. It was a terrible disappointment and Magellan called them the Desaventuradas – the Unfortunate Islands. They had crossed the Equator into the northern hemisphere and they still continued their course to the north and west.

At last, just in time to prevent the *Trinidad* from becoming a morbid coffin ship, an island was sighted on the horizon. It was the isle of Guam in the Philippines where Magellan thankfully made a landing and stocked up his food supplies. On 7 April the ships arrived at the island of Cebu where he struck up a friendship with the local chieftain. What should have been a useful alliance for Magellan proved to be his biggest mistake for the island was at war with its neighbouring isle of Mactan. The chief persuaded Magellan to fight alongside him in the war. Magellan agreed, he was keen to show his friendship and co-operation and he thought himself invincible in his steel armour. He was wrong about his armour, the flashing steel plates only made him an easier target for the enemy. The consequence was that the man who discovered the gateway to the Pacific Ocean was killed in a minor island skirmish and Ferdinand Magellan never completed the circumnavigation of the Earth.

Sebastian del Cano With their leader dead there remained a long and dangerous voyage for the survivors. At least the long crossing of the Pacific was behind them. The three remaining ships sailed on without Magellan and the second-in-command, Sebastian del Cano, took over the leadership of the expedition.

One of the major problems they now faced was that although the deceased commander was Portuguese the expedition sailed under the Spanish flag. The three ships were Spanish vessels in what the Portuguese considered to be their own waters. Magellan's countrymen would show the expedition no mercy when they discovered the ships, and they were therefore obliged to sail well to the south of the main trade routes, so that they did not encounter Portuguese ships on their way from the spice islands to the Cape of

Gums became red and sore and swelled to a horrific size. They bled painfully and teeth became loose. The sailors were reduced to chewing the leather on the yardarms to hold the hunger at bay. Men started to die from scurvy and starvation.

Good Hope. There were so few men left to work the ships that the *Conception* was burnt and her crew was split between the *Trinidad* and the *Victoria*.

The *Victoria*, under the command of Sebastian del Cano, took on a cargo of cloves in the East Indies and set off back to Spain. The *Trinidad* was not so fortunate – the ship was in such a poor condition that it was feared she would not survive the seas at the Cape of Good Hope. It was decided instead to try and get the ship back across the Pacific to Panama. The *Trinidad* never made it to Panama as she was captured by the Portuguese and her crew were thrown into prison. It was not until three years later that they were allowed their freedom and they finally limped home across the Indian Ocean.

The *Victoria* arrived at Seville in September 1522. The cargo of cloves and spices was worth more, ounce per ounce, than a cargo of gold. In spite of all the losses the spices had returned a profit for the sponsors of the expedition. Only thirty-one men completed the first circumnavigation of the world, plus another four when the *Trinidad* finally arrived home in Spain several years later. The thirty-five men who completed the first circumnavigation of the world were the survivors from a total of 280.

It cannot be denied that Magellan's circumnavigation was a voyage that changed the world. The engraving on page 69 is an allegorical glorification of his achievement. He had found a way around the south of America into the Pacific Ocean and he had proved what Columbus had tried in vain to demonstrate, that the Orient could be reached by sailing to the west. He also showed what geographers were beginning to suspect, that the Earth was much larger than they had supposed, that the westward journey was much further than the optimists had imagined and that the Earth was surrounded by water. It was not possible to get around the world by land, the Earth could only be circumnavigated by sea.

The VICTORIA *arrived at Seville in September 1522. The cargo of cloves and spices was worth more, ounce per ounce, than a cargo of gold. In spite of all the losses the spices had returned a profit for the sponsors of the expedition.*

THE FRENCH CLAIM TO CANADA IS SECURED BY JACQUES CARTIER

THE FIRST EUROPEAN TO NAVIGATE THE ST LAWRENCE RIVER

1534 – 1541

'There are people on this coast (Newfoundland) whose bodies are fairly well formed but they are wild and savage folk. They wear their hair tied up at the top of their heads like a handful of twisted hay, with a nail or something of the sort passed through the middle and into it they weave a few birds' feathers. They clothe themselves with the fur of animals, both men and women, but the women are wrapped up more closely and snuggly in their furs; they have a belt about their waists. They all paint themselves with certain tan colours.'

Giovanni da Verrazzano was a Florentine navigator and explorer who was in the employment of Francis I of France. In 1523 he sailed across the Atlantic to explore the American coast and to try and discover a westerly passage to Asia.

At the beginning of March 1524 his ship *La Dauphine* reached Cape Fear on the Florida Peninsula. From there Verrazzano sailed northward, exploring the eastern coast of North America. He made several discoveries on the voyage, the most significant being the site of present-day New York Harbour where he encountered American Indians on Long Island and in the River Hudson. He went on to discover Block Island and Narragansett Bay. Verrazzano wrote interesting but sometimes inaccurate accounts of the lands and inhabitants that he encountered. The most important thing to come out of his voyage was that he became the first to piece together the discoveries north and south of the Equator and thus he completed nearly all the mapping of the east coast of America. Both North and South America were continents and they were joined together by a narrow strip of land. After Verrazzano's survey, the only possible way to find a northern route to the Orient was not through Central America, but through the unexplored cold seas to the north of America.

Verrazzano returned to France on 8 July 1524 and this gave Francis I some claim to the New World north of the Gulf of Mexico. Verrazzano undertook two more voyages to the Americas but he came to a grisly end in the Lesser Antilles. He anchored his ship on one of the islands, apparently Guadaloupe, and when he went ashore he was captured, killed, and eaten by cannibals.

A Forbidding Land Jacques Cartier was the natural successor to Verrazzano. He was born in 1491 near St Malo in Brittany and studied navigation in Dieppe. In 1534, when Francis I of France wanted to send an expedition to explore the northern lands of America, he was forty-three years old. Francis I hoped to discover gold, spices, and, of course, the elusive passage to Asia. Cartier was an experienced navigator by this time and he received the commission. He sailed from St Malo on 20 April 1534, with two ships and sixty-one men. He explored the Gulf of St

Narragansett Bay

Cape Cod

site of New York

Long Island

Block Island

North

40°N

America

Delaware Bay

Atlantic

Chesapeake Bay

Delmarva Peninsula

Ocean

Cape Hatteras

VERRAZZANO'S CIRCUIT IN AMERICA

Cape Fear

70°W

Lawrence as far as Anticosti Island. He did not discover the St Lawrence estuary on this first voyage but he described the land around the Gulf of St Lawrence and he discovered the strong flow of water that implied there was a navigable passage to the east. He found the land and the people on the Labrador coast very forbidding:

If the soil was as good as the harbours, it would be a blessing; but the land should not be called the new land, being composed of stones and horrible rugged rocks; for along the whole of the north shore I did not see one cart load of earth and yet I landed in many places. Except at Blanc Sablon there is nothing but moss and short, stunted shrub. In fine I am rather inclined to believe that this is the land God gave to Cain. There are people on this coast whose bodies are fairly well formed but they are wild and savage folk. They wear their hair tied up on the top of their heads like a handful of twisted hay, with a nail or something of the sort passed through the middle, and into it they weave a few birds' feathers.

NEW YORK
New York has always had a multinational identity. The first person to discover the site was the Italian Giovanni da Verrazzano in 1524, he was the forerunner of the Frenchman Jacques Cartier. In 1609 the site was rediscovered and recognized as an excellent place for a settlement by the Englishman Henry Hudson when he was searching for the North West Passage on behalf of the Dutch. The site was first settled by the Dutch and it became New Amsterdam. The English gained control in 1664 and from that time onwards it became known as New York.

One of Cartier's weaknesses was that he did not communicate well with the Native Americans whom he described as 'wild and savage', but, as he explored to the south, he discovered Prince Edward Island – a place which he found much more to his liking. The coast was low-lying with beautiful trees and meadows, but he could find no sheltered harbour. The shore was very flat with shallow water and dangerous sandbanks. He took the longboat to land ashore at several places. The trees were very fragrant and he was able to identify cedars, yews, pines, elm and ash. They all seemed to be without fruit. There was rich soil in the areas without trees and he discovered wild gooseberries, strawberries and raspberries. At one place he found wild oats growing like rye and they seemed to have been sown there and tilled. He described the heat as 'considerable'. He then went on to describe how he opened up a very successful trading session with the Native Americans. They were a Stone Age people and the metal objects brought for trade therefore held a great value and fascination for them, they would go to any extreme to procure them:

The Savages showed a marvellously great pleasure in possessing and obtaining these iron wares and other commodities, dancing and going through many ceremonies, and throwing salt water over their heads with their hands. They bartered all they had to such an extent that all went back naked without anything on them; and they made signs to us that they would return on the morrow with more furs.

Cartier seized two Native Americans at Gaspé intending to take them back to France in his ship. His motive was to teach them the French language so that they could become useful interpreters to him on his next visit. He returned to France with his findings.

Spices, Copper, Silver and Gold

When Cartier got back to France his report sufficiently excited the curiosity of Francis I for the king to send Cartier back again the following year with his ship, the *Grande Hermione*, plus two other ships with a total complement of 110 men. Cartier's instructions were to explore further inland and, after he had crossed the Atlantic again, he followed his orders implicitly. Guided by the two Native Americans interpreters from his first voyage he sailed up the St Lawrence as far as Quebec and established a base near an Iroquois village. In September he proceeded with a small party as far as the island of Montreal, where he found that navigation up the river was barred by rapids. He was welcomed by the resident Iroquois, but he spent only a few hours among them before returning to spend the winter at his base. He learnt from the Native Americans that there were two rivers leading further west to the interior where he was assured that spices, copper, silver and gold abounded. Cartier wanted to explore further but it was too late in the season and the winter was coming on. The French knew that Quebec lay at a lower latitude than Paris and they therefore expected to find a more moderate winter. They were badly mistaken and the severity of the Canadian winter came as a terrible shock to the French, in fact no Europeans since the Vikings had wintered so far north on the American mainland.

The lack of fresh food through the winter caused an outbreak of scurvy amongst the French. The Native Americans concocted a brew made from hemlock which cured the scurvy but for twenty-five of Cartier's men it was too late and they died from the disease. In May, as soon as the river was free of ice, Cartier was eager to get back again to Paris. He showed his worst side and he treacherously seized some of the Iroquois chiefs, forced them onto his ship and sailed for France. Cartier came home to report that great riches lay farther in the interior and that a great river, said to be two thousand miles long, ran all the way through America as far as the continent of Asia. He had achieved a great deal, but he had not made the most of his opportunities. Through his lack of diplomacy he had destroyed the trust that was badly needed between the explorers and the Native Americans.

Cartier gazes at the New World from the prow of his ship.

Jacques Cartier explored the St Lawrence River as far as Montreal and he became the first to find a route to the interior of the North American Continent. His discoveries gave France a claim to much of Canada.

*Francis I, on the other hand,
maintained that there was a
freedom for all nations to 'navigate
upon the common sea', and he held
up the principle that effective
occupation of territory is the only
criterion for possession.*

The king listened with interest to Cartier's story. He also listened to the fabulous tales told by him by the Native American chief Donnacona, one of the nine Iroquois whom Cartier had captured and brought back to France. King Francis I was still anxious to establish a colony in America and to explore the many possibilities raised by the tales he had heard and by the few pellets of gold brought back to France. The king was well pleased with Cartier's efforts and he rewarded him by giving him the *Grande Hermione*, the ship in which he had sailed. He commissioned Cartier as a captain and master pilot to make more discoveries in what he called the open countries of 'Canada and Ochelaga right into the domain of the Saguenay… comprising an end of Asia'. But the promises were hollow, in spite of his interest in exploration and colonization the king of France did not have the money to finance Jacques Cartier any further.

A French Conquistador At this point a French nobleman called Jean-François de la Roque, le Seigneur de Roberval, offered to raise the funds and to lead a colonizing enterprise. De Roberval was an able and adventurous soldier, he knew something about mining and he fancied himself as a French conquistador. On 15 January 1535, King Francis gave him a commission as lieutenant general of the new country. When Charles V of Spain heard of the plans he lost no time in complaining to the Pope that Francis had violated the papal bull of Alexander VI, the Treaty of Tordesillas. By this time it was a generation since the treaty had been made and Pope Paul III chose simply to ignore the matter. It was the first time the treaty had ever been seriously contested, and the French king asked the Spanish ambassador why the French had been left out when the world was divided between Spain and Portugal? It was a question that several rulers in Europe wanted to ask. Had father Adam, he said sarcastically, left a last will or testament designating Spain and Portugal as his sole heirs? But the Spanish only stiffened their determination to maintain by force their exclusive right to discoveries in America. Francis I, on the other hand, maintained that there was a freedom for all nations to 'navigate upon the common sea', and he held up the principle that effective occupation of territory is the only criterion for possession. He continued to give his support for French colonization on the St Lawrence.

THE ST LAWRENCE

Cartier had no idea of the significance of his discoveries in North America. The St Lawrence flowed from Lake Ontario which in turn was fed from Lake Erie through the Niagara Falls. The great lakes formed the largest freshwater system in the world. It was not the passage to Cathay, but it opened up much of the interior of America. There was far more to be gained by exploring the St Lawrence than the icy waters around Hudson Bay.

The wars in Europe prevented Francis from sending another expedition to the New World until 1541. On this occasion, in order to secure French title against the claims of Spain, he commissioned Jean-François le Seigneur de Roberval, to cross the Atlantic and to found a colony in the lands discovered by Cartier. The latter was appointed as de Roberval's subaltern. Cartier sailed to America first, he arrived at Quebec on 23 August but de

Roberval was delayed until the following year. Cartier made another expedition to Montreal, but, as with his earlier visit, he remained only a few hours and he made no attempt to go even the few miles necessary to get beyond the rapids on the St Lawrence River. Had he done so he might well have discovered Lake Ontario. The maps, based on the knowledge he provided, failed to indicate that he had reached as far as the island at the confluence of the

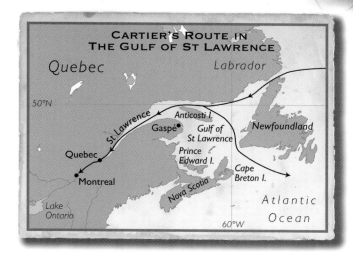

CARTIER'S ROUTE IN THE GULF OF ST LAWRENCE

Ottawa and St Lawrence Rivers. The winter at his new base above Quebec proved just as severe as the earlier one. Cartier was a poor leader, he seems to have been unable to maintain discipline among his men, he had poor relations with the Indians and his actions again aroused the hostility of the local Iroquois tribes.

By the river's edge the French found leaves of gold as thick as a man's fingernail and they also found rocks containing what they thought were diamonds. They gathered ten barrels of the yellow metal and they took home with them half a ton of the diamond stones. In the spring, without waiting for de Roberval to arrive with the main body of colonists, Cartier abandoned his base and decided to sail back to France. He stopped at Newfoundland en route where he encountered de Roberval, and his superior ordered him to go back to Quebec. Cartier disobeyed the order, he stole away during the night and continued his journey back to France. When he arrived in Paris it was found that his gold was iron pyrites and his diamonds were crystals of quartz.

A Tarnished Reputation De Roberval enjoyed no better success than Cartier in Canada. After one winter he abandoned the plan to found a colony and he, too, returned to France. There was huge disappointment at these inadequate attempts and it was another half a century before France again showed any interest in Canada. Cartier received no new commissions from the Crown. He spent his remaining years attending to his business affairs at his estate near St Malo. He had explored the St Lawrence River to the limits of navigation but his failure to proceed any further when he had the time and resources to do so, tarnished his reputation. He was also guilty of disobeying orders and leaving de Roberval to fend for himself in Canada. In defence of Cartier it must be said that he laid the foundations of the French claim to Canada. He gave Canada its name, but this was an accident, he took the Iroquois word 'Kanata' to be the name of the country, when in fact it was the word for 'village'. Without his expeditions, the French language would probably not have been spoken in modern Canada.

Spanish treasure ships scour the Pacific

The Conquistadors exploit the riches of the New World

1519 – 1600

'We arrived at a broad causeway and continued our march… and when we saw so many cities and villages built in the water and other great towns on dry land and that straight and level causeway going towards Mexico, we were amazed and said that it was like the enchantments they tell of…'

Bernal Díaz del Castillo

It was mainly due to the voyage of Christopher Columbus and to the Treaty of Tordesillas that Spain was able to make rapid progress in the development of the New World. The Spanish discovered remarkable civilizations in Mexico and Peru.

Both the Aztecs and the Incas had developed complex societies, rich in art and architecture and with a thorough knowledge of astronomy. The Spanish believed that it was their duty to convert the peoples of the New World to Christianity and when Cortes arrived in 1519 with 500 soldiers he was able to conquer the whole of Mexico in two years and to make the Aztec people subservient to the Spanish. A similar situation arose with the Mayan and the Inca civilizations. After the Spanish had discovered the Incas in Peru it was only a few years before Francisco Pizarro was able to conquer the whole country. This was the sixteenth century and although the Renaissance was flowering in Europe the attitudes of the Conquistadors were only a little removed from the barbaric customs of the Middle Ages. Both the Aztec and Inca civilizations, with their art, their ancient rituals and customs, were brutally and effectively destroyed within a decade. It has to be said that the Spanish introduced a few improvements. Both the Incas and the Aztecs practised live human sacrifice in their rituals and young men and women in the prime of life were sacrificed to their gods. The Spanish must be given the credit for putting a stop to this horrific custom.

Precious Metals Spanish settlements became well established in Central and South America. They were immensely profitable and financed by the gold in Mexico and the silver mines of Peru. The native populations were reduced to virtual slavery, forced to work in the mines whilst the silver and gold they produced was shipped back to Spain in regular convoys of galleons from the New World to the old – all the time steadily increasing the great wealth of Spain. The trade in precious metals was greatly envied by other nations such as the English, the French and the Dutch.

Spain created two viceroyalties in the New World of America. The first, in Central America was New Spain and the second, in South America, was Peru. The voyage of Magellan and the discovery of a sea passage to the south of America motivated the Spanish to do some exploring themselves. An expedition left Spain in 1525 under the command of Garcia de Loaysa and with del Cano (who had been second-in-command to Magellan) as pilot. The mission was to explore the Pacific Ocean from the Straits

THE TORDESILLAS ANTEMERIDIAN

The meridian of the Treaty of the Tordesillas was respected by both Spain and Portugal. The problem arose on the far side of the world where the antemeridian lay at 134° east. Spain claimed that the Philippines were east of this ante-meridian, Portugal claimed that the Spice Islands were west of it. Both the island groups were at much the same longitude so somebody had to be wrong. In fact it was the Portuguese who were right but, by the time it was possible to measure the longitude more exactly the Treaty of the Tordesillas was no longer of any importance.

The historic meeting between Cortes and the Aztec emperor Montzeuma on 8 November 1519.

The wealth and splendour of the Aztecs is well depicted. Little did the Aztecs know that their civilization would soon be plundered and destroyed by Cortes and his followers.

of Magellan and to cross from there to the Spice Islands. They had bad luck with seven ships in the convoy, three did not make the passage through the Straits of Magellan and the rest became separated when they reached the Pacific. Only the *Victoria* completed the mission and sailed as far as the spice island of Tidore.

The Spanish had discovered the Philippines and they were determined to stake their claim to them, but it was several decades before they were able to establish a regular trade route across the North Pacific. The Pacific voyage of Miguel Lopez de Legazpi from New Spain to the Philippines was not achieved until 1564. The return crossing from west to east was first achieved in the following year by Andres de Urdaneta who sailed north to a latitude of 30°. In the same year Alonso de Arellano achieved a faster passage by taking his ship still further to the north. The Spanish were slowly gaining some understanding of the winds and currents of the Pacific.

In the middle of the sixteenth century there had been some exploration in the North Pacific but far less in the ocean south of the Equator. It was obvious that there existed a very large unexplored area to the south and it was generally believed that a great southern continent must exist and was waiting to be discovered. The continent was given a name, the *Terra Australis Incognito* meaning the 'Unknown Southern Continent'.

The Great Southern Continent It was from Callao in Peru that the Spanish sponsored the first expedition to try and find the great southern continent and to establish a colony there. The expedition sailed in 1567 under the command of Alvaro de Mendana. He was given two ships and he took Hernan Gallego with him as his pilot. He also had four Franciscan friars whose job was to convert the heathens of the south seas to Christianity.

The westerly route into the Pacific took the expedition between the Marquesas Islands and the Tuamotu Archipelago. The ships missed both these island groups and consequently they did not sight land until they had been sailing west for sixty-two days. The exception was one small unidentified island in mid Pacific but the wind and current took them away before they could plan a landing. The convoy continued sailing to the west and on 7 February 1568 they reached an island they named Santa Isabel in an archipelago which became known as the Solomons. The reason for the Old Testament name was because they optimistically expected to find gold there and to recreate the riches of Solomon. The name of the group survived but it did not live up to its name and no gold was discovered.

The Solomons were mountainous islands and this convinced Mendana that he had landed near the great southern continent *Terra Australis Incognito*. He explored three neighbouring islands which he named Guadalcanal, Malaita and San

THE SPANISH IN CALIFORNIA

The Spanish explored the coast of California where they made many small settlements. There is a claim that Juan de Fuca explored as far north as Vancouver Island where the Strait of Juan Fuca bears his name but no documentary evidence has been found to support this. In the 1540s Francisco de Coronado explored the upper reaches of the Rio Grande. The area was only thinly populated but in 1598 the province of New Mexico was founded there.

Cristobal. His search did not reveal the mainland of the continent however, and when he realized that he had discovered no more than an island group, he decided to sail to the north across the Equator to where he could take advantage of the prevailing winds to sail back to America. His course took him through the Marshall Islands and close to Wake Island. It was December before he sighted the coast of California. He made his American landfall at Colima Harbour with his long-suffering crew weak and blinded from the terrible ravages of scurvy.

Mendana was not seen as a great commander, his expedition had not discovered the unknown continent and it was deemed to be a failure. But he did not give up hope of finding the southern continent and for many years he planned to make a second expedition. He experienced a lot of opposition. Francis Drake's foray into the Pacific, followed by a similar voyage of the English buccaneer, Thomas Cavendish, a few years later made the Spanish reluctant to sponsor any settlement that the piratical English could easily plunder and destroy. Eventually, nearly thirty years later in 1595, Mendana was at last given command of a second expedition to the Solomons. This time he was given four ships with Pedros Fernandez de Quiros as his second-in-command. The ships carried 378 stalwart men and women who were prepared to make a new settlement many miles from civilization.

Early on this second voyage Mendana discovered the Marquesas where he and his crew were greatly impressed by the grace and beauty of the inhabitants. The visit started well with brisk trade and friendly relations but the islanders had no notion of private property and they helped themselves to anything they fancied on the deck of the ships. The

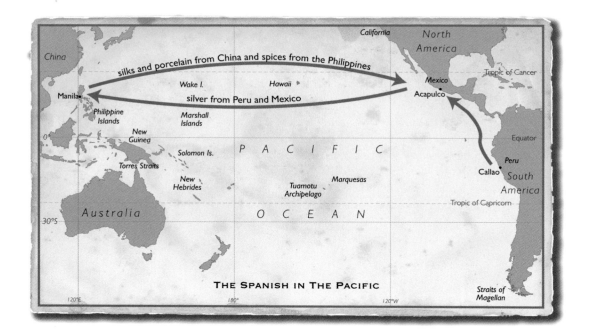

China

California

North America

silks and porcelain from China and spices from the Philippines

Tropic of Cancer

Mexico

Wake I.

Hawaii

Acapulco

Manila

silver from Peru and Mexico

Philippine Islands

Marshall Islands

New Guinea

0°

Solomon Is.

P   A   C   I   F   C

Equator

Torres Straits

Peru

Callao

South America

New Hebrides

Tuamotu Archipelago

Marquesas

Tropic of Capricorn

Australia

30°S

O   C   E   A   N

THE SPANISH IN THE PACIFIC

Straits of Magellan

120°E

180°

120°W

pilfering led to firearms being used and Mendana resorted to a bloody foray in which as many as 200 islanders were killed. It was an ominous start to the expedition when Mendana showed that mass murder was his only solution to the pilfering problem.

As the expedition sailed westwards the explorers encountered the island of Santa Cruz. Mendana knew that he had not reached the Solomons but he decided that the island was just as good a place to make his settlement, and he went ashore followed by the hopeful settlers. The settlement was actually initiated but it was so badly managed that it lasted only two months. Mendana and many others died. The first of Mendana's galleons was lost but the second sailed on to reach the Solomons. It fared even worse than its consorts and was wrecked at San Cristobal with loss of all the crew. By this time the expedition had turned into a total disaster and with Mendana dead, Quiros was able to take over the command. He was a far more capable leader and he eventually managed to get the ships back to Manila with a hundred famished survivors out of the 378 men and women who left Peru.

Converting the Heathen The disastrous voyages of Mendana left the Spanish thinking that the colonization of the Pacific and the search for the great southern continent was a totally unprofitable exercise. But Mendana's fixation was transferred to Quiros and he, in turn, was fired with the will to sail back again. Just like Mendana, after his return to Peru, Quiros tried for years to get sponsorship for another voyage. Quiros campaigned in Spain and he even went as far as Rome to obtain the approval of the Pope. It took him nearly a decade but, by December 1605, he had achieved his ambition and he left Peru in command of three ships with Luis Vaez de Torres as second-in-command. He also carried six Franciscan friars to convert the heathen.

Quiros made an early discovery when the islands of the Tuamotu Archipelago were sighted. He made a landing but did not tarry long. He sailed west for two more months and on 7 April he sighted land again. He discovered an island that he called Australia del Espiritu Santo in the group now known as the New Hebrides. The approach to the island was impressive with high mountain peaks visible on Espiritu Santo and also on the neighbouring islands so that Quiros' spirits were raised by the expectation that he had landed on the elusive southern continent. When the party landed he was able to explore further but it soon became apparent that there was no continent and there was very little in the way of water and other natural resources. The island was not a suitable place to form a colony.

The Straits of Torres When supplies began to run low it was obvious that the ships would not be able to stay so far from civilization for much longer. Quiros set a course to the north, sailing to 38° where he knew he could pick up the westerly winds to take him back to New Spain, but Torres' ship became separated and he took the decision to sail instead for the Spanish base in the Philippines. Torres found his ship had entered the seas near New Guinea. He knew his whereabouts but adverse currents meant that he was unable to clear the east end of the island. The wind and current forced him to sail south of New Guinea. This was how he came accidentally to discover the Straits of Torres lying between Cape York in Australia and the island of New Guinea. He knew very little about Australia but his voyage proved that the great southern continent, if it existed, was separated from New Guinea.

All the Spanish attempts to create new colonies in the Pacific ended up as disasters, but when it came to setting up lucrative new trade routes the Spanish were very successful. The island of Luzon in the Philippines became a centre of trade with the East.

All the Spanish attempts to create new colonies in the Pacific ended up as disasters, but when it came to setting up lucrative new trade routes the Spanish were very successful. The island of Luzon in the Philippines became a centre of trade with the East. The Spanish discovered that the countries of the Orient were very willing to trade in silver and this gave them a more lucrative market for the riches from the Peruvian mines than the market in Europe. The silver was exchanged for Chinese silks and fine porcelain. Thus every year the Acapulco Galleon left the American coast for the Philippines loaded with silver from Mexico and Peru. The crossing from east to west took three months. Later in the year the galleon sailed from Manila in Luzon carrying silks and porcelain. The journey from west to east took about six months. It was an immensely profitable trade and when the English heard of the great treasure ships certain greedy minds began to plan how to intercept them and how to lay their hands on the treasure.

FRANCIS DRAKE AND THE
VOYAGE OF THE *GOLDEN HIND*

THE FIRST ENGLISHMAN TO SAIL AROUND THE GLOBE

1577 – 1580

*'The wind commands me away. Our ship is under sail. God grant we may live so in His fear as the
enemy may have cause to say that God doth fight for her majesty as well abroad as at home, and
give her long and happy life and ever victory against God's enemies and her majesty's.'*

SIR FRANCIS DRAKE, *THE LIFE, VOYAGES AND EXPLOITS OF ADMIRAL SIR FRANCIS DRAKE*

In February 1573 a party of Cimmaron Indians and a small band of Englishmen were exploring the high passes of the Cordilleras mountains on the Isthmus of Panama. After days of climbing they reached a mountain ridge where the Cimmarons pointed to a high tree with a small platform near the top.

Two of the Englishmen, namely Francis Drake and John Oxenham, climbed up to the platform where they were instructed to look in all directions. On the northern horizon was the shimmering Atlantic Ocean from whence they had come; it was an ocean across which they had sailed and which they knew well. Looking to the south they were met with an amazing sight. There in the distance lay another vast ocean which they knew existed but which very few Englishmen had ever seen. The waters that glistened on the misty horizon were those of the Pacific. Drake prayed aloud to God that he might live to sail one day on those distant seas. It became his ambition to captain the first English ship to sail into the Pacific Ocean.

Mule trains carried the silver from the mines of Peru across the narrow passes of the Cordilleras. The mules were well strung out and although soldiers were present it was impossible for the Spanish to protect the full length of the train. As usual, Francis Drake's plan to plunder the Spanish Main was very successful. Drake and his companions were rumoured to have plundered a hundred thousand pesos from the bullion-laden mule trains before they sailed back to England with their booty.

Drake returned as a wealthy man, but money alone was not enough for him to develop his plan to sail to the Pacific. What he needed was royal favour. Queen Elizabeth knew all about his privateering activities in the Caribbean, but it was a matter of opinion whether Drake was a respectable privateer condoned by the queen or simply a pirate who attacked the Spanish galleons purely for his own gain and profit. He was born of the Devonshire minor gentry and he had formed some connections with higher levels of society. Drake was not employed in the service of the queen but he knew that if he continued to lobby in the right places he would get support for his plans. He gained the ear of the queen's favourite, Lord Essex, Sir Francis Walsingham and also of Thomas Doughty, a gentleman adventurer who wanted to accompany him on the mission.

Gentlemen Adventurers By 1577 Drake's scheme to sail into the Pacific had become accepted by the court circle. He was allocated five ships for the voyage and sufficient seamen to man them. His flagship was the *Pelican* of one hundred tons burthen. He was allocated the *Elizabeth* of eighty tons to be captained by John Wynter of Bristol and the *Swan* of fifty tons captained by John Chester. He was also given the *Marigold* of thirty tons captained by John Thomas and finally there was the tiny *Christopher* of only fifteen tons captained by Thomas Moon. In addition to the seamen he carried a Puritanical preacher called Francis Fletcher who

kept a very valuable journal of the voyage. He carried his quota of
gentlemen adventurers which included William Hawkins, a nephew of
the great Elizabethan seaman, John Hawkins, plus the aristocratic
Thomas Doughty, also Gregory Carey who was related to a cousin of the queen and John Chester whose father had been the Lord Mayor of London. In total he commanded 164 men.

*Queen Elizabeth knew all
about his privateering activities
in the Caribbean, but it was a
matter of opinion whether
Drake was a respectable
privateer condoned by the queen
or simply a pirate who attacked
the Spanish galleons purely for
his own gain and profit.*

A detailed description of Drake's ship the *Pelican* (later known as the *Golden Hind*) was written by Nuño da Silva, a Portuguese navigator who first saw the vessel when he was pressed into joining the expedition at the Cape Verde Islands:

*(She) is in a great measure stout and strong. She has two
sheathings, one is as perfectly finished as the other. She is fit for
warfare and is a ship of the French pattern, well fitted out
and finished with very good masts, tackle and double sails. She
is a good sailor and the rudder governs her well. She is not new, nor is she coppered or
ballasted. She has seven armed portholes on each side, and inside she carries eighteen
pieces of artillery, thirteen being of bronze and the rest cast iron... This vessel is
waterfast when she is navigated, with the wind astern and this is not violent, but
when the sea is high she has to labour, she leaks not a little whether sailing before the
wind or with the bowlines hauled out. Taking it all in all, she is a ship which is in a
fit condition to make a couple of voyages from Portugal to Brazil.*

Hatred of the Spanish The voyage to the Pacific was kept a closely-
guarded secret. The sailors had no idea that they had been mustered for a
voyage around the world and they were told that they were bound for
the Mediterranean port of Alexandria. It is hard to believe that the
gentlemen adventurers did not know the true purpose of the expedition and even harder to believe that the crews did not pick up information from the officers and gentlemen as to the nature of the voyage and where they were bound. Drake's history and his hatred of the Spanish were no secret. The convoy was armed to the teeth and it was obvious that they intended to use their gun power if they encountered the Spanish as Drake was determined to do.

THE SPANISH TREASURE SHIPS

Every year the Acapulco Galleon sailed from
Mexico across the Pacific laden with silver from
the mines of Peru. It returned from Manila laden
with silks, gemstones and exotic goods from the
East. The English were very jealous of this
lucrative trade. Francis Drake was the first to
capture a Spanish treasure ship but he was not
the only Englishman to achieve this feat:

1578	Francis Drake
1587	Thomas Cavendish
1710	Woodes Rogers and William Dampier
1743	George Anson

After several delays the little fleet left
Plymouth on 15 November 1577. By the 27th they
were back again where they started. The seas off
Devon and Cornwall were so high that the fleet
was unable to get out of the English Channel.

The second attempt was more successful. The first few weeks of the
voyage were uneventful. It was not until the new year, after he had
cleared the coasts of Spain and Portugal and arrived on the Barbary
Coast of Africa, that Francis Drake resorted to his piratical activities. At
Cape Rhir on 7 January he came across three Spanish fishing vessels.

They stood no chance against the more numerous and well-armed English, Drake bullied them and commandeered their whole catch. He then forced the vessels to accompany him for 900 miles but they were obviously an unwilling liability and later on he decided to set them free again. He rounded Cape Blanc where he found several Portuguese ships at anchor. The Portuguese looked at the new arrivals with fear and suspicion, and rightly so. Drake with his heavy armaments was able to plunder his way through every ship in turn and pilfer anything he found useful for his expedition.

At the Cape Verde Islands he had a stroke of good fortune. He found a Portuguese vessel, the *Maria Santa*, fully provisioned and laden with wine and woollen cloth. He captured the ship, put his own men in charge and renamed it the *Mary*. Aboard the *Mary* was the navigator, Nuña da Silva, who knew the best route to Brazil and also the hazards of sailing the coasts of South America. Drake buttered up da Silva and treated him well. He gave da Silva a place at the captain's table and the best accommodation and thus the navigator was pressed into Drake's service.

The convoy set off to cross the Atlantic and after a spell in the sultry windless seas of the Doldrums they sighted the coast of Brazil. Unlike Magellan, Drake did not waste time exploring the bay at Rio de Janeiro and he did not explore the River Plate. He headed south along the coast towards the latitude where he knew that Magellan had found a passage to the Pacific. By this time frictions had grown up between some of the crew members and in particular between the captain and the gentlemen adventurers; the latter felt that they should be told more about Drake's intentions and where they were going.

The leader of the gentlemen's faction was Thomas Doughty who had been put in charge of the prize ship, the *Mary*. Doughty was an educated man, he was politically astute, he could converse with princes and peers and he did not like having to submit to the authority of a man whom he saw as his social inferior. When he realized that Drake was taking the fleet into unknown and dangerous waters Doughty felt that he and the other gentlemen should have a say in the decisions about where the convoy was going to sail. Drake did not agree. He was the commander of the expedition and he could not possibly do his job if he was obliged to consult Doughty and others on every move.

The frictions increased. Doughty was smooth and compelling. He not only chatted to his fellow passengers but he was also critical about Drake to the navigators and the seamen. Drake knew that to have Doughty behaving in this way was undermining his authority. He called a meeting in an attempt to get support for his plans and he told them what had become obvious when they passed the Straits of Gibraltar – that the ship was not bound for Alexandria. He intended to sail through the Straits of Magellan to the Pacific. The weather became colder and some of the men were suffering from dysentery and fever. Doughty and his followers did not want to sail the dangerous passage to the Pacific. They played on the fears of the seamen and Drake was concerned that he would soon have a mutiny on his hands.

He found a Portuguese vessel, the MARIA SANTA, *fully provisioned and laden with wine and woollen cloth. He captured the ship, put his own men in charge and renamed it the* MARY.

In 1978 a full-scale replica of the GOLDEN HIND *was built to commemorate the four hundredth anniversary of Drake's circumnavigation of the world. Drake's voyage took him into the Pacific and as far north as the site of San Francisco. He returned home with a fortune plundered from a Spanish treasure ship.*

A Death Sentence When Thomas Doughty spoke insolently to Drake, the captain responded by tying him to the mast for two days. The ploy was a failure. Doughty endured the punishment stoically and he cleverly managed to twist the incident round to his own favour. The fleet had arrived at St Julian's Bay, on the coast of what is now Brazil, which was the very place where Magellan's men had mutinied and where one of his ships had deserted him. Drake decided to put Doughty on trial for refusing his authority and trying to subvert the voyage. The jury found Doughty guilty and Drake had the power to decide on the sentence. He decided that the penalty for the crime was death. Doughty claimed that Drake did not have the right to pass a death sentence. Drake claimed that he had a commission from the queen. Doughty asked to see the commission. Drake glibly waved a manuscript around but nobody was allowed to inspect it.

On 2 July Thomas Doughty made his last confession to Francis Fletcher, the ship's chaplain. He and Drake took Holy Communion together and they seemed strangely to have made up their differences. They retired to the cabin where they had dinner and where they conversed cheerfully with each other. Then the whole company assembled on an island in the bay to watch the execution. Doughty spoke his last words to the executioner.

'Strike clean and fair for I have a short neck,'
'Lo, this is the end of traitors' said Drake.

Thomas Doughty was beheaded. Drake called the place 'The Island of True Justice and Judgement'. Others called it 'The Island of Blood'.

Francis Drake had been over-ambitious with the prize ships he had taken. He had not enough seamen to man his six ships through the Straits of Magellan and he therefore decided on some radical changes. The prize ship the *Mary* was broken up as were the *Swan* and the *Christopher,* leaving him with only three ships to tackle the remainder of the voyage. Nobody had ever returned to the Atlantic through the Straits of Magellan so at this point the men already knew that they were committed to a journey around the world.

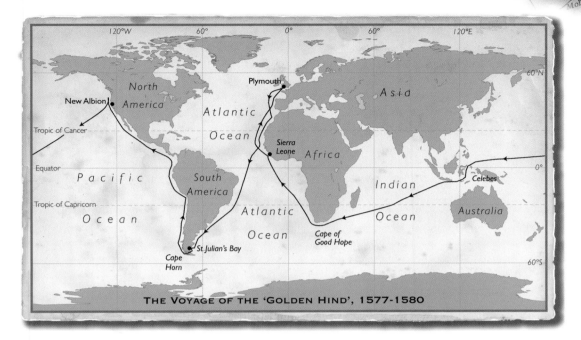

THE VOYAGE OF THE 'GOLDEN HIND', 1577-1580

Drake made a good passage through the straits and at this time he renamed his ship with the name by which she is better known: the *Golden Hind*. He emerged into the Pacific Ocean with his three ships on 6 September 1578 after only seventeen days' sail.

However the Pacific did not live up to its name and it was a very stormy sea which the *Golden Hind* and her two consorts had to face. All three ships were driven to the south by the gale force winds and they discovered by this accident that the land came to an end with open seas to the south. Drake found that there appeared to be another passage around the south of America. He did not have the time to explore further but he had discovered the direct sea route around Cape Horn, an alternative route to the tortuous Straits of Magellan. Drake also found an uninhabited group of islands which he named the Elizabethides after his queen. They were at 57° degrees south, almost at Cape Horn.

They did not catch sight of their consort but they knew she was leaking and that she had suffered much in the passage through the straits. The brave little MARIGOLD *sank and all her crew of twenty-nine went down with her.*

As they were sailing the seas near Cape Horn the smallest ship, the *Marigold*, became separated from the other two. The larger ships searched southwards looking for her. It was all to no avail. The crew thought at one point that they heard cries of distress above the roaring of the winds. They did not catch sight of their consort but they knew she was leaking and that she had suffered much in the passage through the straits. The brave little *Marigold* sank and all her crew of twenty-nine went down with her.

The two surviving ships struggled back to make progress to the north and to find shelter. They became separated in the dark and they were thrown so far apart that they could not see each other's lanterns. Drake spent several days searching for his last surviving consort but the quest was fruitless. The crew of the *Elizabeth* had had enough of executions, storms and the distress calls of their lost comrades. They were not prepared to follow Francis Drake around the world. They deserted and sailed back for home through the Straits of Magellan.

It must have been a time of deep emotions on board the *Golden Hind* when it was realized that Drake's fleet was reduced to a single ship. They had seen a man beheaded. They had heard the distress cries of their own fellow seamen drowning in a strange uncharted sea. Supplies were low and the ship was badly in need of careening. Did the *Golden Hind* on its own have the resources to outwit and outshoot the Spanish in their own territory of the Pacific? Drake was a very experienced privateer and he was confident that he could still beat the Spaniards even with his single ship.

The journey along the coast of Chile was relatively easy after the passage through the Straits of Magellan. There were no settlements to the south but as they sailed further north there appeared signs of civilization. Soon Drake was bargaining with the local inhabitants for food and water. He explored to the north. At the coastal villages he obtained gossip about the movements of the Spanish. The smaller vessels were an easy prey for Drake and with his well-armed ship he could plunder almost at will. What he could not do was to take the ships as prizes for he had not enough crew to man them and to sail them back home again halfway round the world.

A King's Ransom Then he heard the news he was waiting for. A Spanish galleon, the *Nuestre de la Conception* had sailed from Lima and was heading for Panama laden with a king's ransom in silver bars. Drake had little problem in tracking down the treasure ship. He encountered the galleon off Cape San Francisco and he decided to play an old pirate ploy to capture it. Out of the stern he threw wine jars full of sea water tied with ropes to the rear of the ship, then he put on full sail. The drag of the wine jars made the *Golden Hind* sail sluggishly past the treasure ship and the Spaniards concluded that she was a slow, heavy-laden merchantman. Drake had no qualms about flying a Spanish flag to mislead them. Then he cut away the wine jars and as his ship raced forwards she was easily able to catch up with the treasure ship. As she came closer to the *Conception* the guns of the *Golden Hind* were trained on the galleon and when she drew alongside there was a deafening roar of cannon. Drake's gunners did a fine job, the treasure ship lost her mizzen mast on the first salvo and the rear deck was strewn with splintered wood, broken beams and rigging. In the confusion Drake sent a boarding party to the lee side of the Spanish ship. The action was over in a matter of minutes; the unprepared Spaniards did not have time to fire a single shot.

Drake himself then boarded the *Nuestre de la Conception* and he went below decks to examine his booty. He found fourteen chests full of silver and gold coin. He found large quantities of gold and silver plate. He found gemstones and jewellery. But in the hold glistened no less than 1,300 bars of pure silver. The silver weighed about twenty-six tons and the English stared in disbelief as it was transferred from the treasure ship to the *Golden Hind*. The action ranked amongst the most barefaced and outrageous thefts in history.

Drake had achieved one of his prime objectives but he still had to get his treasure back to England. As far as he was aware there were three ways to get home with his haul. The first option was the way he had come – through the Straits of Magellan, but he had good reasons for ruling out this dangerous possibility. A second alternative was to strike out across the Pacific, to navigate the Indian Ocean and to round the Cape of Good Hope. Drake thought there was a third possibility. There was a route that had never been sailed before, it was a passage across the north of America called the Straits of Anian. Expeditions had searched the east coast of America to find a North West Passage to Cathay. The search had not been successful but, with good fortune, Drake could find the western end of the passage and find his way back to the Atlantic by this new and shorter route.

It was necessary to get away from the scene of the crime before news of his haul became known on the Panama coast. The *Golden Hind* followed the American coastline northwards for several days then Drake headed out to sea hoping to pick up the coastline again further to the north. He was successful in finding the coast again but although he continued northwards, perhaps as far as the forty-ninth parallel, he did not find the passage he sought. It would indeed have been a magnificent voyage of discovery if he had found a sea passage to the north of America.

By this time the *Golden Hind* was leaking badly, barnacles covered the hull below the water line and Drake needed to find a safe place to land, to careen her bottom and make repairs to masts and rigging. He found a haven, in a latitude which from its description could have been anywhere between 38°and 48° north. It is hard to believe that, seven years before the attempt at Roanoke to form an English settlement on the east coast of America, there was an English ship exploring the coast of California. Drake's landing was not of course an attempt at forming a colony but even so it gave the San Franciscans a very early claim to be discovered by the English. The place called 'Drake's Bay' to the north of the Golden Gate was, in all probability, the place where Drake landed, where he repaired his ship and where he made friendly contact with the local Native Americans. It seems surprising that Drake did not discover San Francisco Harbour but he recorded that there was fog along the coast and for this reason he did not realize that there was anything to explore. He is not the only captain to have sailed past one of the finest natural harbours in the world. James Cook did exactly the same thing at Sydney Harbour two centuries later. Botany Bay and Drake's Bay have something in common.

> *The silver weighed about twenty-six tons and the English stared in disbelief as it was transferred from the treasure ship to the* GOLDEN HIND. *The action ranked amongst the most barefaced and outrageous thefts in history.*

New Albion Drake called the place where he landed 'New Albion'. He got a good reception from the local Native Americans and there was singing and dancing when the two cultures met as described by Richard Hakluyt in his description of the voyage:

The newes of our being there, being spread through the countrey, the people that inhabited round about came downe, and amongst them the king himselfe, a man of goodly stature, and comely personage, with many other tall, and warlike men.

In the fore front was a man of goodly personage, who bore the sceptre, or mace before the king, whereupon hanged two crownes, a lesse and a bigger, with three chaines of a marvellous length: the crownes were made of knit worke wrought artificially with fethers of divers colours: the chaines were made of a bonie substance, and few be the persons along them that are admitted to weare them.

In coming towards our bulwarks and tents, the sceptre bearer began a song, observing his measures in a dance, and that with a stately countenance, whom the king with his garde, and every degree of persons following, did in like manner sing and daunce, saving onely the women which daunced and kept silent. The General permitted them to enter within our bulwarke, where they continued there song and daunce a reasonable time. When they had satisfied themselves, they made signs to our General to sit downe, to whom the king, and divers others made several orations, or rather supplications, that would take their province and kingdome into his hand, and become their king, making signes that they would resigne unto him their right and title of the whole land, and become his subjects.

Drake now had to accept that the only way to get home again was to strike out across the North Pacific. He left the coast of California, sailing across many leagues of uncharted ocean. He was unlucky not to sight the Hawaiian Archipelago but his course took him to the south and, after an uneventful crossing with the trade winds behind him, he arrived in the Caroline Islands at the end of September 1579 after a Pacific crossing that lasted for sixty-six days.

A Favourable Wind Drake was now faced with the double problem of having to avoid both the Spanish and the Portuguese. But as he threaded his way through the Spice Islands he could not resist calling there where a friendly chieftain allowed him to cram his ship with as many spices as he could carry. It was January 1580, and he was working the *Golden Hind* through the treacherous coral outcrops of the Celebes, when his ship ran onto a reef and stuck fast. In the panic that followed every available part of the cargo was unloaded in the hope of refloating the ship. But Drake refused to unload his silver. Out came the cables and the boats. Men heaved at oars and strained at the windlass in a futile attempt to pull the ship off the reef. The *Golden Hind* would not budge. Every stratagem resulted in failure but Drake was determined not to lose his silver. In desperation he called upon the ship's chaplain Francis Fletcher to pray to God for a favourable wind. Fletcher agreed to his captain's request but first he called upon every member of the ship to repent of his sins. This of course included the captain and the question of the execution of Thomas Doughty was brought to the fore. Soon afterwards there was a sudden change in the wind. The Almighty had heard the request. The breeze carried the ship off the reef and the men were free to continue the voyage.

SIR FRANCES DRAKE

Was Francis Drake the greatest seaman of Elizabethan England or was he no more than a pirate and a buccaneer?

DRAKE THE GREAT SEAMAN:

• Drake's navigation around the world was a piece of superb seamanship.
• Without Drake the English might well have been defeated by the Spanish Armada.
• Drake was knighted and honoured by his queen and his country.
• His ship the *Golden Hind* was held in such high regard that it was preserved at Deptford.

DRAKE THE PIRATE:

• Drake's buccaneering activities in the Caribbean were a major factor in escalating the war between England and Spain.
• Drake did not have the right to execute Thomas Doughty.
• Drake did not have the right to defrock the priest Francis Fletcher.
• Drake promised his men a share of his profits, but his promise was never honoured.

Fletcher received no reward for his work, in fact he received a severe punishment. Drake was furious with Fletcher for bringing up the question of Thomas Doughty and the incident still played hard on his conscience. He called the ship's company together and solemnly excommunicated Francis Fletcher from the Christian Church. Did Drake, as captain of the ship, have the power to defrock a priest? Certainly not, but the decision had to be accepted and poor Fletcher was forced to become an object of ridicule and to carry a placard 'Ye Falsest Knave That Liveth' strung around his neck.

To say that the voyage home from Indonesia was uneventful would not be true. It took another year for the *Golden Hind* to navigate across the Indian Ocean, around the Cape of Good Hope, and northwards along the Atlantic coast of Africa. The ship made a landing at Sierra Leone. Then came the final leg along the Barbary Coast, round the Iberian Peninsula and across the choppy seas of the Bay of Biscay. It was 26 September 1580 when the *Golden Hind* finally docked at Plymouth. 'Is the queen alive and well?' yelled Drake to the men on the dockside.

A Priceless Hoard From that day on, as Drake well knew, it was up to the English people to judge his voyage and his decisions. What he had achieved seemed impossible. To have sailed around the world was in itself a magnificent triumph. To make new discoveries at Cape Horn and off the west coast of America was also a great accomplishment. He had returned with a priceless hoard of silver stolen from under the very noses of the Spanish. Was the treasure the greatest prize of the voyage? His sponsors certainly thought it was, their investment of £5,000 had brought a return of £600,000!

The country was boundless in its admiration. Queen Elizabeth's reaction was to confer a knighthood on Francis Drake (see page 88). The *Golden Hind* was repaired, re-rigged and preserved in a dock at Deptford for all time, a symbol to show that Englishmen would never forget the voyage of Sir Francis Drake.

THE QUEST FOR
A ROUTE TO THE ORIENT

EXPLORERS PERISH IN THEIR SEARCH FOR
THE NORTH EAST AND NORTH WEST PASSAGES

1553 – 1631

*'Being furnished with one tall ship of her Majesties, named The Ayde, of two hundred
tunne, and two other small barks, the one named The Gabriel, the other The Michael,
about thirty tun apiece, being fitly appointed with men, munition, victuals, and all things
necessary for the voyage, the sayd Captain Frobisher with the rest of his company came
aboord his ships riding at Blackwall, intending (with Gods helpe) to take the first winde
and tide serving him, the 25th day of May, in the yere of our Lord God 1577.'*

THE PRINCIPAL NAVIGATIONS VOYAGES, TRAFFIQUES AND DISCOVERIES
OF THE ENGLISH NATION RICHARD HAKLUYT (1598)

'There is one way left to discover, which is to the North', wrote Robert Thorne in 1527. 'For out of Spain they have discovered all the Indies and occidental and out of Portugal all the Indies and the seas oriental.'

Expanding nations such as the English and the Dutch were very keen to become involved with trade from the East. The profits made on spices alone easily warranted the investment required in finding new trade routes, but if the English and the Dutch were excluded from the Spanish and Portuguese waters then the only alternative was to find another passage to Cathay. If another route to the Orient existed from northern Europe then it could only be discovered by sailing west across the north of America or east across the north of Asia.

Historically the North East Passage to the north of Asia seemed at first to hold the better promise. In 1553 Sir Hugh Willoughby in the first expedition funded by the Company of Merchant Adventurers, sailed from England with three ships to search for a passage with Richard Chancellor as his second-in-command. He wintered in Lapland inside the Arctic Circle. When he resumed his voyage in the spring his fleet soon became scattered by storms but Willoughby successfully rounded the northernmost cape of Norway and sailed on until he reached the Novaya Zemlya archipelago. It took him many months of sailing and as the summer was coming to an end he decided to sail back to Lapland where he hoped to winter again and to make another attempt in the following year. He made the terrible mistake of leaving his return until too late and he found his ships hampered by the ice and desperately short of supplies. The outcome was that Sir Hugh Willoughby and all his crew died from the cold and the scurvy. Richard Chancellor however, managed to find a route into the White Sea to Archangel on the northern coast of Russia. From there he travelled overland and made his way to Moscow. The Russians gave him a warm welcome. He was able to establish a trade route from Moscow via the River Volga to Archangel and from there by sea around the north of Norway to England.

Barbaric Customs The next attempt to find the passage was in 1556 with the expedition of Stephen Burrough in the *Searchthrift*. His single ship was a tiny vessel with a crew of only eight. Burrough actually got as far as the Kara Sea, and from there he reached the straits between Novaya Zemlya and the mainland of Asia but he was prevented from sailing any further by the ice. He made contact with the nomadic tribe of the Samoyeds but he was so appalled by their barbaric customs that he made no effort to befriend them and he decided that his only option was to turn for home. He wintered successfully at Archangel on the White Sea, the same spot as used by Chancellor, but he was unable to penetrate further to the east and by the spring he was back in England.

In 1580 came the third attempt. This was the Jackman and Pet expedition with two ships sailing from Harwich on 30 May. By August they had reached as far as the Kara Sea but, like the other explorers before them, they could not get through the ice. The explorers found

Barents did not survive the winter, he died and many of his crew with him. The ship was lifted up and broken by the pressure of the ice and the survivors were forced to get home in an open boat.

themselves surrounded by ice floes and as the season advanced the two ships became separated. The expedition was another miserable failure. Pet was defeated by the ice like the others before him, although he battled his way back through heavy seas and eventually reached home with his crew almost dead from exposure. Jackman's fate was even worse, his ship perished with all hands off the coast of Norway. The disaster was the last straw for the English, too many ships and too many lives had been lost. No more attempts were made to find the passage to the East.

The other nation interested in finding another route to the Orient was the Dutch. Their most significant expedition in the sixteenth century was that of Willem Barents who sailed from the Netherlands in 1596. Barents penetrated further north than anybody before him and he reached the northern limit of the Novaya Zemlya archipelago. As with the English expeditions the sea was frozen and there was no way forward. His ship became trapped in the ice and he was forced to spend the winter on an ice floe with his men as shown in the opening picture on page 98. The crew were fortunate enough to find driftwood with which they were able to build a hut to protect them from the elements. The winter was a terrible ordeal however, with little fuel to keep the men warm and with very limited food supplies. Barents did not survive the winter, he died and many of his crew with him. The ship was lifted up and broken by the

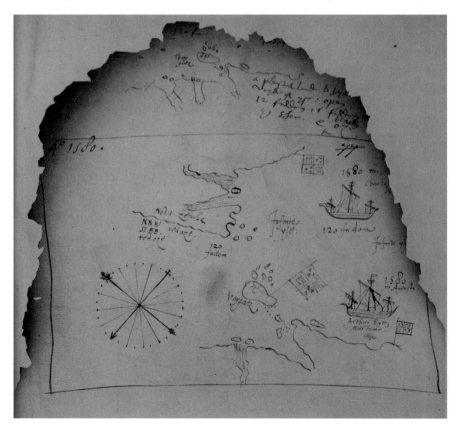

Chart made by Hugh Smyth during an expedition led by Arthur Pet and Charles Jackman on the GEORGE and WILLIAM, which set out in May 1580 to find a northern route to China. The chart shows the two ships, and English standards on the islands of Vaygach and Novaya Zemlya, off the Arctic coast of Russia.

pressure of the ice and the survivors were forced to get home in an open boat. It was a miracle that anybody at all could survive the ordeal they had to go through, but nearly half of Barents' crew eventually managed to return to the Netherlands.

Martin Frobisher Barents's expedition was the last attempt for many years to find a North East Passage. Opinion was moving rapidly towards the north west where it was generally thought that the passage would be much easier. As early as 1509 Sebastian Cabot discovered what turned out to be the entrance to Hudson Bay and it was natural to assume that he had found the eastern end of the passage. It was not until nearly seventy years later, in 1576, that Martin Frobisher commanded an expedition to explore what later became known as Hudson Bay and to look for the fabled Straits of Anian that were assumed to connect the bay to the Pacific Ocean. Money to support the exploration came from a wealthy merchant called Michael Lok who hoped to gain trade and profit from the discoveries of the voyage.

Frobisher had two small vessels, the *Gabriel* and the *Michael*. He lost the *Michael*, a vessel of only twenty tons, when the crew of the ship deserted him early in the voyage. He sailed on into Hudson Bay where he made contact with the Inuit. He searched the borders of the bay and he found what he thought was the entrance to the Straits of Anian but the winter was coming on rapidly and he dared not stay longer to explore further. He returned to England with an Inuit on board and with some samples of black rock streaked with what he thought was gold. What he had found was in fact no more than a small bay within the greater bay of Hudson. He was also mistaken about the gold in the rocks but this was not proved until he had made other expeditions to Hudson Bay to obtain more samples.

> ## THE INUIT
> Many regions around Hudson Bay and along the coasts surveyed by the explorers were inhabited by the Inuit (then known as Eskimos). The local tribes knew how to survive the winter, how to keep warm, how to build igloos from the ice and where to find food even in the depths of winter. The explorers made little use of the Inuit when, if they had studied their way of life, they could have eased much of their own sufferings.

Martin Frobisher managed to get backers for two more voyages. He sailed again to America in 1577 and also 1578, but on these voyages he spent his time looking for what he thought was gold ore rather than seeking the North West Passage. It was left to John Davis, a scholarly man who was more interested in geography than in profits, to take up the search from where Frobisher left off. In 1585 Davis discovered the Cumberland Sound and on his third voyage he entered Baffin Bay and sailed north to a latitude of 73°. Even at this high latitude he did not discover a passage to the Pacific.

The persistence of the Tudor explorers has to be admired when the limitations of their ships and the hardship of their voyages are taken into account. After the expeditions of Frobisher and Davis interest in the North West Passage waned for a time but there were still many advocates of a northern passage to Cathay. In 1610 Henry Hudson explored the perimeter of the bay named after him. He could find only a few icy

The crew mutinied and they put Hudson with his son and five loyal seamen into an open boat to fend for themselves. They were never seen again.

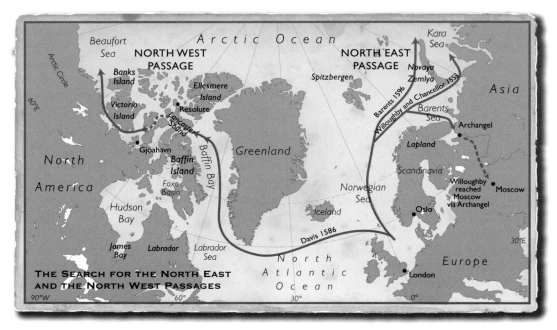

THE SEARCH FOR THE NORTH EAST
AND THE NORTH WEST PASSAGES

inlets but no navigable straits. He discovered James Bay to the south but he knew that he had not found the entrance to the fabled Straits of Anian. Much to the disappointment of his crew Hudson decided to winter in the bay and when the spring came he decided to spend another season exploring. This was too much for his long-suffering seamen. The crew mutinied and they put Hudson with his son and five loyal seamen into an open boat to fend for themselves. They were never seen again.

This should have been the end of the bitter cold hunt for the North West Passage but there were still backers prepared to put money into the search and, in 1631, two rival expeditions sailed from England. Thomas James from Bristol captained one of the expeditions. He was backed by local merchants and his ship was called the *Henrietta Maria* :

THE NORTH WEST PASSAGE

The search for a North West Passage began in the sixteenth c̶e̶n̶t̶u̶r̶y̶ ̶a̶n̶d̶ ̶l̶a̶s̶t̶e̶d̶ almost until the twentieth. Vast sums of money were spent on exploration and many lives were lost. In spite of all the failures there did exist a northern sea passage from Atlantic to Pacific, but it was passable only in exceptionally warm conditions.

One Captain James, a man of great learning, experience in navigation, and well seen in the mathematical science, set sail from Kingrode (in the Bristol Channell), to discover the North-West passage to the East Indies… (the ship) was well furnished with all necessaries, and victualled for 18 months; having but 20 men and 2 boys.

Drifting Ice The second expedition was sponsored by the London merchants and led by Luke Foxe, a hard-bitten Yorkshireman. By the end of June Thomas James was in Hudson Bay navigating the treacherous drifting ice. His ship cleared the ice floes and came to open water, but not for long. The further west she sailed the more numerous became the icebergs. At the same time Luke Foxe was also exploring to the north and west seeking a sea passage. He got as far as the entrance to Lancaster Sound but he found ice barring the way in every direction. Two days later his ship struck against a rock and heeled over. The expedition nearly perished at this point but, in due course, the crew managed to free the ship and they got underway again. On 29 August there came what was an historic encounter. Thomas James with the *Henrietta Maria* met with the London ship captained by Luke Foxe. They were fierce rivals but James showed hospitality to his countrymen:

In the morning Captain Foxe and his friends came aboord of mee, where I entertained them in the best manner I could, and with such fresh meat as I had gotten from the shoare... In the evening, after I had given his men some necessaries, with Tobacco and other things which they wanted, hee departed aboord his ship and, the next morning, stood away South-South-west since which time I never saw him.

'I was well entertained by Captain James', wrote Foxe. 'With varietie of such cheere as his sea provisions could afford, with some Partridges; we dined betwixt decks, for the great cabin was not bigg enough to receive our selves and followers...'

James still had time to return home before the cold weather set in, but he was determined to winter in Hudson Bay. Foxe was invited to stay with him but he had already decided to return to England. James sailed to the south and found an anchorage in the bay that bears his name. He stripped his ship of the sails and rigging and partly submerged her so that she could not be carried away by the drifting ice. The ship had lost her rudder and the crew feared that she might no longer have been seaworthy. The crew had to carry provisions for over a mile across the ice to winter in the primitive huts they had built onshore. Thomas James himself movingly described the scene as his ship was abandoned and left to survive the winter in the ice:

Our men that were ashoare stood looking upon us, almost dead with cold and sorrowes, to see our misery and their owne. We lookt upon them againe, and both upon each other, with woeful hearts.

Our men that were ashoare stood looking upon us, almost dead with cold and sorrowes, to see our misery and their owne. We lookt upon them againe, and both upon each other, with woeful hearts. Darke night drew on, and I bade the Boate to be haled up, and commanded my loving companions to goe all into her, who (in some refusing complements) expressed their faithful affections to mee, as loth to part from me. I told them that my meaning was to goe ashore with them. And thus, lastly, I forsook my ship.

The expedition was short of provisions, particularly fresh fruit and vegetables. Needless to say the dreaded scurvy struck the crew. It was difficult to find firewood. The ground was frozen to a depth of ten feet. Many were sick and four men died in the bitter northern winter. When at last the spring came and the ice began to melt they were greatly relieved to find that the ship was still seaworthy and they managed to recover the rudder from the seabed. James then sailed north to latitude 65° 30′ but he found himself surrounded by ice. He spent the summer months exploring Hudson Bay but finally, to the great relief of his weary men, he gave up the search and decided to return home. Both James' and Foxe's voyages were characterized by courage and hardship, but like their predecessors both were failures in their quest for the elusive passage to Cathay. They were the last of their generation to search for the North West Passage.

A Losing Battle The whole story of the attempts to find the northern route to Cathay is a tale of disaster and privation. Whether it was the passage across Asia or the passage across America the end result was always the same. A tale of bitter cold, of hunger and scurvy. Long winters were spent in the most inhospitable places without fresh food. It is the tale of a losing battle against the elements. The results were heartbreaking with many ships destroyed by storm and ice and with hundreds of lives lost in the most depressing of circumstances. Not a stone was left unturned to find the passage but the result was always a bitter disappointment.

Did these journeys change the world? They certainly would have done had they been successful but in the end all that came out of a huge investment was a hard-won knowledge of the inhospitable northern reaches of the American continent.

THE HISTORIC VOYAGE
OF THE *MAYFLOWER*

THE PILGRIM FATHERS
ESTABLISH NORTH AMERICA'S
FIRST SUCCESSFUL COLONY

1620

'In the name of God, Amen. We, whose names are underwritten… Having undertaken
the Glory of God, and Advancement of Christian Faith, and the Honour of our King
and Country, a Voyage to plant the first colony in the northern Parts of Virginia…'

MAYFLOWER COMPACT, 1620 –1647

Soon after the voyage of Christopher Columbus, crossings of the Atlantic became more and more frequent. By the end of the sixteenth century voyages to the Americas had become commonplace and by the early seventeenth century it was such a regular occurrence that it becomes impossible to record every crossing.

By the year 1600, in spite of several attempts at colonization by the English and the Dutch, and the fact that much of the eastern coastline had been charted and explored, no permanent settlements had been made in the New World. By this time a crossing of the Atlantic was seen as a minor voyage compared to the great expeditions into the Pacific. Even so, the Atlantic voyages could still change the world and one such voyage was that of the *Mayflower* which left Plymouth in 1620 with the avowed intention of creating a self-supporting colony in the New World.

By the later years of the reign of Queen Elizabeth there had been many radical changes in the religious attitudes of northern Europe. The Protestants had made the break with Rome and many new forms of religion became established. In England the Presbyterians and the Puritans wanted to simplify their religion and to do away with altars, crucifixes and religious relics. When Queen Elizabeth died in 1603 the Puritans hoped that James VI of Scotland would support them in their desire to be allowed to worship in their own simple fashion.

Fear of Persecution At the manor house of Scrooby in Nottinghamshire a group of Reformers met every Sunday to hold their services. Their leader was William Brewster who ran the posting inn in the village of Scrooby which was a staging point on the Great North Road. The reformers had two or three priests who supported their ideas and who acted as ministers but their religious meetings were frowned upon by the authorities. The fear of persecution caused them to consider emigrating to Holland where they felt sure that they would receive a warm welcome and where they would be allowed to worship as they wished. In 1608 they arranged for a ship to collect them from a point near Boston in Lincolnshire and to carry them across the North Sea to Holland. Their plans were betrayed. The king's officers were waiting to arrest them when they boarded their ship. Their goods were ransacked and the ringleaders were held in jail for a month.

The pilgrims did not give up their plan to get to Holland and, at a later date, they arranged for another ship's captain to pick them up at a point on the River Humber from where they hoped to sail secretly to Amsterdam. They were to make their own way from Scrooby to the rendezvous. The men were to walk overland but the women and children were to travel by boat along the River Idle to the River Trent and from the Trent to the Humber where they hoped to find their ship and to board her. The boat carrying the women and children reached the Humber at a point near Immingham and although they were very close to the rendezvous unfortunately the boat became stuck on a mudbank as the tide receded. Once again the pilgrims were betrayed. Cavalry and foot soldiers arrived on the scene. Some of the men had managed to board the ship but they could only watch helplessly as their wives and children were seized and dragged away by the soldiers. William Bradford described the incident as seen from the ship:

... the Dutchman (the ship's captain seeing the horse and foot soldiers) swore the sacrament; and having the wind fair, weighed anchor, hoisted sails and away. But the poor men which were got aboard were in great distress for their wives and children, which they saw thus to be taken, and were left destitute of their help; and themselves also, not having a cloth to shift them with more than they had on their backs, and some scarce a penny about them, all they had being aboard the bark. It drew tears from their eye, and anything they had they would have given to be ashore again; but all in vain, there was no remedy, they must thus sadly part.

The women and children were held in prison for a time but they were finally released and eventually they were able to make their way to an emotional reunion with their husbands and fathers who had sailed to Amsterdam. The Reformers stayed in Amsterdam for about twelve months. Then they decided to move to the university town of Leiden where they hoped that they would have better prospects. They worked hard at their jobs and they stayed in Leiden for nearly ten years. John Smyth practised as a physician and William Brewster taught English at the university. They had great respect for the Dutch who did not interfere with their chosen form of religion, but they were still not satisfied with their lives. They wanted their children to be brought up speaking English, and after a few years they talked of moving back again to England.

Freedom of Worship After much discussion about what was the best way forward they came up with a possible solution. The Virginia Company had been granted a large tract of land between the latitudes of 34° and 45° in North America. An arrangement was made with the company that the Reformers should try and make a settlement somewhere in these latitudes on the American coast. The pilgrims had the revolutionary idea that they would be able to support themselves by fishing, farming and trading with the Native Americans. Most important to them was that if they could form a successful self-supporting colony in the new land of America then they would have won the freedom to worship as they pleased.

Sussana, the wife of William White, was carrying a child who was born on the ship and Stephen and Elizabeth Hopkins' child was also born at sea.

They made their plans thoroughly and carefully. At Delftshaven they boarded a ship called the *Speedwell*. They made their farewells to Holland and they sailed from there to the English Channel where they landed at Southampton. Friends in England had decided to join in the venture. They came from all over the country. The company numbered just over a hundred in total counting women and children.

Several of the company were from Scrooby and they had been part of William Brewster's original group of Reformers. William Bradford and

VICTUALS

A typical catering stock for crossing the Atlantic with 200 people in the 1620s:

- 8,000 pounds of salt beef
- 2,800 pounds of salt pork
- A few beef tongues
- 600 pounds of salted cod
- 15,000 brown biscuits
- 5,000 white biscuits
- 30 bushels of oatmeal
- 40 bushels of dried peas
- 1½ bushels of mustard seed
- 1 barrel of salt
- 11 firkins of butter
- 1 hogshead of vinegar
- 10,500 gallons of beer
- 3,500 gallons of water
- 2 hogsheads of cider

his wife Dorothy were from Austerfield, only a few miles from Scrooby but over the county boundary in Yorkshire. John Carver and his wife Katherine were from the Nottingham/Derby area. Edward Winslow and his wife Elizabeth were from Droitwich in Worcestershire. Christopher Martin was from Great Burstead in Essex. William Mullins and his family were from Dorking in Surrey; their daughter Priscilla married John Alden who joined the ship at Southampton. John Howland was from Fenstanton in Huntingdonshire. Edward Fuller was from Norfolk. Myles Standish and his wife Rose came from Lancashire; he was not one of the pilgrims but a professional soldier who came to help with the defence of the settlement. Humility, the one-year-old daughter of Edward Tilley, was the youngest person on board but, by the time they reached America, two babies had been born on the voyage. Sussana, the wife of William White, was carrying a child who was born on the ship and Stephen and Elizabeth Hopkins' child was also born at sea. Isaac and Mary Allerton with their three small children were part of the Leiden group. Their daughter Mary who was four years old, lived until 1699 and became the last survivor of the *Mayflower* voyage. The pilgrims had decided for very sound reasons that the elderly, the weak and infirm, should not make the first journey across the Atlantic and they were left behind in England:

We came to this resolution, that it was best for one part of the Church to go at first, and the other to stay, viz: the youngest and strongest part to go. Secondly, they that went should freely offer themselves. Thirdly, if the major part went, the pastor to go with them; if not, the Elder only. Fourthly, if the Lord should frown upon our proceedings, then those that went to return and the brethren that remained still there to assist and be helpful to them, but if God should be pleased to favour them that went, then they also should endeavour to help over such as were poor and ancient, and willing to come. These things being agreed, the major part stayed and the pastor with them.

'Truly doleful was ye sight of that mournful parting, to see what sighs and sobbs and praires did sound amongst them, what tears did rush from every eye, and pithy speeches pierced each harte', wrote John Robinson who was to stay behind. At Southampton the *Speedwell* was joined by a second ship, called the *Mayflower*, which had also been chartered to take them across the Atlantic Ocean. The little convoy made its way to Plymouth where final preparations were made for the long voyage ahead. They completed their provisioning and set sail again on 5 August. The seas were heavy as they worked their way along the English Channel and the captain of the *Speedwell* reported that his ship was so leaky he dared not sail any further. They were driven back to Dartmouth where they put in to make the necessary repairs. The ships then sailed out from Dartmouth and beat their way again into the stormy seas of the English Channel. They cleared Land's End but then there was another distress call from the *Speedwell*, the captain reported that his ship was leaking and she could not possibly survive long enough to cross the Atlantic. They had to return to port a second time. Would they ever make it across the Atlantic Ocean? The shipwrights discovered that the *Speedwell* carried a main mast that was much too high for her and she also carried too many sails. This put an extra strain on the ship and it forced open the seams of the hull and caused the leakage. When a proper mast had been fitted the ship was seaworthy again but she did not sail to America. The ill-fitting mast was a plot on the part of the master and men of the *Speedwell*; they did not want to go on the journey. They had planned the whole episode so that they could remain in England.

The true pilgrims were transferred from the *Speedwell* to an already overloaded *Mayflower*. On 6 September the ship left England for the third time. A whole month had been wasted by the delays and frustrations. They were way behind their schedule, but at last they were favoured with a fair wind and the ship made good progress. The unseasoned travellers suffered from seasickness as the *Mayflower* pitched and rolled her way out into the Atlantic.

The time has come to give a description of the vessel that carried a hundred hopeful pilgrims to a new life in a new land. There is very little evidence with which to piece together the nature of the ship but we are told by William Bradford that she weighed about 'nine score burden' or 180 tons. This is frequently quoted as being a very small vessel but Drake's *Golden Hind* by comparison weighed in at only a hundred tons. We know that the *Mayflower* had at least two decks because the shallop, a boat that could carry twenty-five people under sail, was described as being stored between the decks. We also

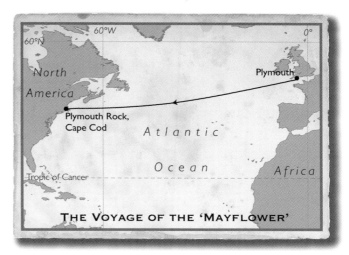

THE VOYAGE OF THE 'MAYFLOWER'

know that she was an old ship; she was described as 'leaky and unwholesome' and one of her beams was 'bowed and cracked'. Searches have been made of the English records for ships with the name 'Mayflower' and there were many with this name, but the majority can be ruled out as being too small or the wrong age to fit the description. The most likely candidate however, is a ship called the *Mayflower* that fought against the Spanish Armada in 1588 – this would make her over thirty years old at the time of her Atlantic voyage. It is very moving to think that the ship which carried the Pilgrim Fathers to America was a veteran of the Spanish Armada.

The construction of seagoing vessels the size of the *Mayflower* is well known. The ship would be about ninety feet long and twenty-five in the beam. She carried three masts with mainsails and topsails on the main mast and the fore mast. There would be a spritsail on the jib at the front of the ship and the mizzenmast probably carried a lateen sail which made the ship more manoeuvrable when tacking into the wind. The main

The MAYFLOWER *in the Atlantic, battling her way to the west. After an engraving by Marshall Johnson.*

There is no Atlantic crossing to compare with that of the MAYFLOWER. *The Pilgrim Fathers were the first to prove that it was possible to create a self-supporting colony in the New World.*

deck was open to the elements with a forecastle to the front where the sail-makers practised their craft. There was a half deck to the rear with a poop deck mounted above at the stern of the boat. Below decks afforded shelter from the elements for the passengers but it was dark and gloomy, a miserable place with the ship rolling and pitching all the time. A canvas was rigged on the main deck to give the passengers a little more living space. The gun deck carried four cannon to both port and starboard. Beneath the gun deck and below the level of the water line was the hold of the ship; this was where all the stores and supplies were kept. Here were the water casks, the beer casks and the food supplies with a galley to heat and prepare the food. Here too lived the ship's rats continually gnawing into the stores.

After making good progress through most of September the *Mayflower* was hit by heavy weather and for many days she tacked in vain making very little progress to the west. The problem of finding the longitude was almost impossible, the dead reckoning of the navigators was the only way to estimate how far they had travelled. With no islands or landmarks on the voyage it was impossible for the pilgrims to know how much longer they had to suffer at sea. The passengers wrote about great storms where their frail vessel was thrown around like a cockle shell. Sails were torn and shredded by the winds and the ropes and timbers groaned and creaked in protest. There was a frightening incident when one of the main beams broke and gave way with a great crack and became dislodged from its position. Luckily the pilgrims were very practical people and they had a large screw on board with which the cracked beam could be jacked back into position. A new timber post was cut to hold up the broken beam in its place.

Few of the passengers dared to go above decks when the storms were raging and they spent most of their time huddled together below in the darkness. But one young man, John Howland by name, felt himself in need of fresh air and he climbed out onto the main deck above. A huge wave broke across the ship and carried him over the side. By the greatest of good fortune he was able to catch hold of a trailing rope and he hung on grimly for dear life. He was taken well below the surface of the sea but he still managed to keep hold of the rope and the crew eventually managed to haul him back on board.

In October Elizabeth Hopkins gave birth to her child. It was a boy and they called him Oceanus.

Land at Last It was 11 November when at last the *Mayflower* sighted land; the passage had taken sixty-six days. The ship was riding the seas off Cape Cod and they found that she was much further north than the crew had expected. They tried to sail to the south but found themselves in danger of hitting a sandbank, so they decided to anchor in the calm waters of the great bay at Cape Cod. Soon, for the first time in over two months, they were able to set foot on land. For several days they explored the region around the bay that measured thirty miles across. The long sea voyage was behind them, but they had to make a home in the wilderness that now greeted them. The many delays meant that the ship had arrived at almost the worst time of the year. The winter was coming on and there was a wind so cold that the clothes froze on their backs. There was nobody to welcome them. There were no houses. There were no crops. There was nowhere to shelter except in the ship they had arrived in. In the woods were wild animals and sometimes the Native Americans would appear. The Native Americans would be another danger that they would soon have to face.

They stepped ashore at a place they chose to call Plymouth Rock. They fell upon their knees. They kissed the ground and they gave thanks to God that he had brought them across the 'vast and furious ocean'.

The settlers found a sheltered harbour that seemed to be a suitable place to build their settlement. They stepped ashore at a place they chose to call Plymouth Rock. They fell upon their knees. They kissed the ground and they gave thanks to God that he had brought them across the 'vast and furious ocean'.

The pilgrims were skilled and resourceful men and women. They built a store house and a fort to house the guns and serve as a place to worship. Christmas was approaching and they began to build their first dwellings. These were wooden houses with thatched roofs made of reeds, they had fireplaces with hearths for cooking and they had chimneys to take the smoke away. There was abundant fish in the bay but their nets were too coarse to catch the smaller fish they saw swimming there. Their food was monotonous but with care and rationing they knew that they should have sufficient to get them through to the next harvest. They were very successful with their hunting expeditions and they discovered a store of corn buried beneath the ground by the local Native Americans.

Things seemed to be improving at last. They knew that the Native Americans were not far away and they were very anxious to make contact with them and to prove that their intentions were friendly. Edward Winslow described an expedition in search of the Native Americans who were very reluctant to come forward:

We marched through boughs and bushes, and under hills and valleys, which tore our very armour in pieces and yet could meet with none of them, nor their houses, nor any fresh water, which we greatly desired and stood in need of… We had brought neither beer nor water with us, and our victuals was only biscuits and Holland cheese, and a little bottle of aquavitae, so as we were sore a-thirst. About ten o'clock, we came into a deep valley full of brush… and long grass, through which we found little paths of tracks, and there we saw a deer, and found springs of fresh water, of which we were

The settlers had wild turkey with berries to give flavour. There was pumpkin pie to eat and the Native Americans brought venison with them to the feast. According to Edward Winslow there were ninety Native Americans at the thanksgiving and they stayed for three days.

heartily glad, and sat us down and drunk our first New England water with as much delight as ever we drunk drink in all our lives.

The winter was cold and wet. Then, after all they had suffered and all their hard work, there came a great sickness so terrible that many of the new settlers died in that first hungry winter of 1621. Only one of the pilgrims died on the voyage but fifty-one died in that miserable winter. After all they had suffered to reach their new world this was the bitterest blow of all.

First Harvest Supper In March the survivors sowed the seeds of their first harvest. They planted thirty acres of corn and six acres of barley and peas. In April they said their goodbyes to the *Mayflower* when she left the harbour to return to England. At last the weather grew warmer, they were able to enjoy the summer and to gather in their first harvest. On 4 November 1621, nearly a year after they had arrived on American soil, they were able to hold their first thanksgiving service. By this time the pilgrims had made contact with the local Native Americans, relations were good and they too were invited to partake in the first harvest supper. The settlers had wild turkey with berries to give flavour. There was pumpkin pie to eat and the Native Americans brought venison with them to the feast. According to Edward Winslow there were ninety Native Americans at the thanksgiving and they stayed for three days. It was a lot of mouths to feed for the small colony but the hospitality was worthwhile to cement friendly relations between them.

In the next decade other ships followed the Pilgrims to the New World. The Puritans of East Anglia were very interested in the settlement at Plymouth. They too wanted to create a colony in the New World so that they could worship as they chose without interference from others. John Winthrop of Groton in Suffolk was given permission by the English crown to form a colony in America to be known as the Massachusetts Bay Colony or the Massachusetts Bay Company.

Thus in 1630 a fleet of eleven vessels was assembled to create what was effectively the first mass settlement in America. Puritans from all over England flocked to join Winthrop's venture and when the fleet sailed in 1630 there were 700 prospective settlers and eleven ships in the fleet. In its time it was the largest fleet ever assembled for the colonization of a new continent. The flagship was the *Arbella*, named after Arbella Clinton, daughter of the fifth Earl of Lincoln. It was on the *Arbella* that Winthrop preached his sermon of the 'City on the Hill' in the Puritan tradition – ' For we must consider that we shall be a city on a hill. The eyes of all people are upon us.'

RECORDS OF THE PLYMOUTH COLONY

The number who sailed from Plymouth	100
The number who died in the first year	51
Executed for murder	1
The number still alive in 1679	12
The number still alive in 1690	3

The last survivor was Mary Cushman (née Allerton) who died in 1699 (she was aged four on the *Mayflower* voyage in 1620)

New Settlers The *Arbella* was accompanied by the *Ambrose*, the *Jewel*, the *Talbot*, the *Whale,* the *Success* and the *Mayflower*. (The latter was not the same vessel as that used by the Plymouth colony.) Another four ships carried the freight and livestock for the new settlement. The fleet left England in April 1630 and it arrived at Massachusetts in July. The passage must have been sheer hell for the death rate on the Atlantic crossing was no less than two hundred. Another hundred of the passengers had had enough of the primitive conditions and they returned to England as soon as they could find a ship to take them home, leaving about 400 new settlers.

The place chosen for the new colony was called Salem, but it was not an ideal site and many therefore moved on to create settlements at Boston and Watertown. Boston became the largest settlement and the main centre of the new colony. In spite of the short distance from Boston to Plymouth the new colony had little contact with the Plymouth separatists and the colonies grew independently of each other. The history of the Boston settlement is well documented, it grew rapidly and it became the state capital of Massachusetts.

Winthrop's fleet was one of many to follow in the wake of the Pilgrim Fathers. Little did the first pilgrims know when they held their thanksgiving, that they were setting a precedent to be followed by millions of families long after them. Little did they know how many people would follow them to the New World of America. Little did they know how many descendants would be proud to claim them as their ancestors in the centuries yet to come. Little did they know how much the voyage of the *Mayflower* would change the world.

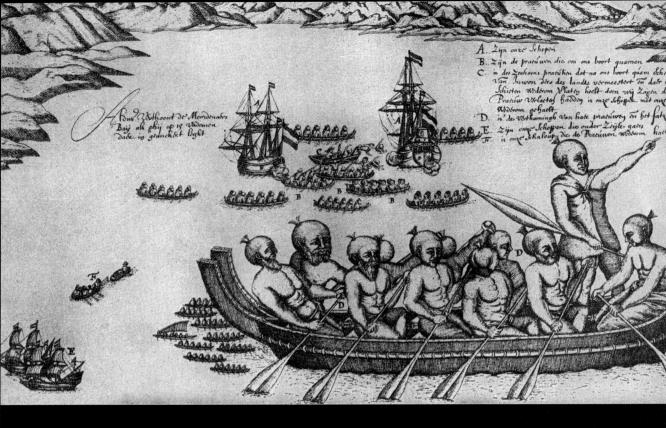

A. Zijn onze Schepen
B. Zijn de praeuwen die om ons boort quamen
C. n des Zeehaens praeuken dat na ons boort quam uht
   van Inwon des des landes vermeestert en dat
   Schieten wederom platten doen wij Zigen de
   Praeuw veelactej hadden is onze Schip met onse
   weder geh aelt
D. in de Vethoeningh van hate praeuwen en het sat...
E. Zijn onze Schepen die onder Ziijle gaen
F. n onse Shaloupe die de Praeuwen weder...

A Kuo Zuthoont der Moordenaes
Baij alz schip op 15 vademen
dale is gedruckt light

ABEL TASMAN
DISCOVERS TASMANIA

THE DUTCH EXPLORATION
OF THE SOUTH PACIFIC

1642 – 1643

'The pilot mayor and the under-mate of the Zeehaen reported as follows: That they had rowed fully a mile round said point where (they) had found high and level land with greenstuff (unplanted, being forthcoming from God and nature), fruit-bearing timber in abundance, and a

In spite of the failure to find the North East and North West Passages the Dutch and the English were still very keen to become directly involved in the spice trade. They both concluded that the best way forward was to form a company with its own ships to sail to and trade with the Far East; they knew that the route around the Cape of Good Hope was the better one.

In 1602 the Dutch formed the Vereenigde Oostindische Compagnie, abbreviated to VOC. The English rival, the East India Company, was floated in London the previous year, but the Dutch raised £540,000 in capital which was more than eight times the money raised by the English.

The Dutch successfully negotiated with the sultan of Bantam for a base which they called Batavia on the island of Jakarta. The name was the ancient Roman name for the Netherlands. By the 1620s the Dutch were well established in Indonesia. At this time there had been several sightings of a land to the south, which became known by the name of New Holland because the Dutch were the first to make the sighting. In 1606 Willem Jansz took his ship the *Duyfken* ('Little Dove') along the south coast of New Guinea and south to the west side of the Cape York peninsula. Jansz therefore has a claim to be the first European discoverer of Australia but he remained totally unaware of his achievement. In 1616 Dirk Hartog in the *Eendracht* charted some of the west coast of New Holland and, in 1627, Pieter Nuyts in his ship the *Gulden Zeepard* charted the south coast at a latitude of 35° for a distance of nearly a thousand miles. It was known from these sightings that there was a great land to the south but the coast was barren and uncompromising. The Dutch made no formal claim to the land and they made no attempt to colonize it.

In 1642, when Anthony Van Dieman was the governor general of Batavia, it was decided to send out an expedition to explore the South Seas. The aims were twofold. One was to try and make new discoveries in the south and the other aim was to try and find a faster passage from Batavia to Cape Horn and thence to Europe by sailing in the deep southern latitudes. Abel Tasman was the man chosen as leader of the expedition. He was given two ships, the *Heemskerck* and the *Zeehaen* with Franchoys Visscher, the noted pilot and surveyor, as his second-in-command and with a complement of 110 men.

The early part of the voyage was through well-charted waters, and he sailed west as far as Mauritius in the Indian Ocean. Then Tasman crossed the Tropic of Capricorn and continued south until he had reached a latitude of more than 40°. His instructions were to continue south to between 52° and 54° but it was so long since he and his crew had seen land that he was reluctant to go any further in that direction. He was in unknown waters but there was no sign of any land. What he did discover however was the roaring forties and with the help of these favourable winds he made very good progress sailing to the east. He saw nothing of New Holland for he was well south of the Australian mainland. Then, after many months without a sight of land, he came across the southern

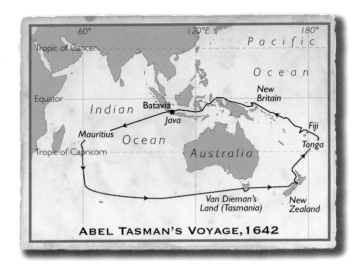

ABEL TASMAN'S VOYAGE, 1642

coast of a land he called Van Dieman's Land. Tasman generously named his discovery after his superior in Batavia but posterity determined that it should be called Tasmania after the man who had discovered it.

Abel Tasman searched for a place to land. He sent the ship's carpenter, a strong swimmer, to swim through the rough surf and set up a pole with an inscription to take possession of the land for Holland. He was wary of the local inhabitants who he pictured in his own drawing in an open boat – see page 114. He was able to get fuel and fresh water but little in the way of food. He stayed only ten days but in that time he managed to chart a fragment of the coastline.

After leaving Tasmania he continued sailing to the east at the same latitude. On 13 December he sighted what became his greatest discovery. Another land appeared on his horizon, with great mountains and an iron-bound rocky coast which looked so dangerous that he was not prepared to risk his ship by going in any closer. There was no doubt in his mind that he had discovered the coast of the great southern continent. He sailed along the inhospitable cliffs but he could find nowhere to land. Eventually he arrived at a bay where he was able to anchor his ships and to make a landing.

Warlike Maori Tasman had not reckoned with the warlike attitudes of the local population. The Maoris were frightened and confused to see such a large strange craft appear on their coast carrying strangely clad men who rowed their boats ashore facing in the wrong direction. The Maoris ran out to the shore shouting their war cries and with weapons raised to defend their territory. There was a hostile skirmish on the beach and four of Tasman's men were killed. Tasman called the place Murderer's Bay. It was this most unfortunate and depressing incident which prevented him from exploring the new land further, and it was also one of the reasons why Tasman did not discover that New Zealand consisted of two islands. What he thought was a very deep bay was actually a strait between two islands. After leaving the bay he followed the coastline all the way to the furthest cape. He charted the north coast of the North Island but he did not attempt to land again. Beyond the northernmost cape there were three islands that he named 'Three Kings Islands' for it was Twelfth Night and he thought the name was appropriate.

He did not have the time or the instructions to

TASMANIA
When Abel Tasman discovered Tasmania he called it Van Dieman's Land after his superior, Anthony Van Dieman. It is only fair that it became known to posterity as Tasmania. At the time Tasman thought he had discovered part of the continent of New Holland – it was nearly two centuries later that Tasmania was found to be an island.

travel so far to prove his theory but he had proved what was required of him. He had discovered the roaring forties and an alternative route to Chile, South America and Cape Horn.

Tasman called New Zealand 'Staten Land' meaning 'Land of the (Dutch) State General'. He was convinced that it stretched all the way to Cape Horn and that it joined up with another 'Staten Land' discovered twenty-seven years earlier by his countrymen Jacob le Maire and Willem Schouten. In 1616 Le Maire and Schouten had discovered a strait, now known as the Strait Le Maire, that gave them a passage to Cape Horn. It was Le Maire who gave it the name Cape Hoorn after his birthplace in Holland but it was the English spelling 'Cape Horn' that prevailed, partly because of the horn-shaped terrain around the cape. They called the land to the east of the strait 'Staten Land' and like Tasman they thought it was part of the great southern continent.

Dangerous Breakers On leaving New Zealand Tasman turned his ships to the north where he made two more discoveries. The first was a landing at Tongatapu, one of the southernmost islands of the Tonga Group. The islanders were amazed to see him. They gave him a very friendly reception and they provided his ships with food and fresh water. It was an idyllic ten days for the seamen who had endured so much and who had been so long at sea. Tasman then sailed on to discover Fiji where he encountered one of the greatest dangers of the Pacific islands, a coral reef with sharp rocks and dangerous breakers. He got his ships off the reef with difficulty and he managed to make a landing. On the return leg of his journey he was still making new discoveries, including the islands which came to be New Britain and New Ireland followed by a landing on New Guinea before returning to his starting point at Batavia.

Tasman circumnavigated Australia without seeing anything at all of the coastline. It was an amazing voyage, but he did have the great advantage over other European explorers in that he started and ended his voyage at Batavia. It took him only ten months of sailing to complete his circuit. He lost only ten men on his expedition. The Dutch followed up the 1642/43 voyage with another expedition in 1644. This second exploration was much shorter than the first but Tasman added the coastline of the Gulf of Carpentaria to the map and two thousand miles of the coast of northern Australia. He also sailed as far as the Straits of Torres but he did not confirm the existence of the strait, he thought he had reached a shallow bay.

At this point in time the Dutch seemed to have Australia and New Zealand well within their sights, but for some reason they did not choose to follow up the discoveries made by Tasman. Their base at Batavia was a staging point for nearly all the voyages across the Pacific Ocean and they were therefore better placed than any other European country to explore and colonize the islands and land masses in the Pacific. The history of the world would have been very different if the Dutch had followed up their discoveries. It was well over a century later that James Cook completed his surveys of Australia and New Zealand and demonstrated the true nature and extent of the main land masses in the southern hemisphere.

SCHOUTEN AND LE MAIRE

A Dutch expedition led by Willem Schouten and Jacob Le Maire rounded Cape Horn in 1616 and they were responsible for giving the cape its name. They discovered a strait now known as the Strait Le Maire between Tierra del Fuego and an island they called Staten Land. They believed the land to be part of the great southern continent. When Abel Tasman landed on the coast of New Zealand he called it Staten Land, in the belief that it was part of the land discovered by Le Maire. The incident illustrates well the optimistic belief in the great southern continent.

THE ORIGINAL ROBINSON CRUSOE AND THE BUCCANEERS OF ENGLAND

THE EXPLOITS OF WILLIAM DAMPIER, WOODES ROGERS AND ALEXANDER SELKIRK

1680 – 1709

'The inhabitants of this country are the miserablest people in the world.
The Hotmadods (Hottentots, the Nama people of Namibia) of Monomatapa,
though a nasty people, yet for wealth are gentlemen to these...'

WILLIAM DAMPIER, *A NEW VOYAGE AROUND THE WORLD*

It would be a gross over-simplification to say that after the discoveries of Abel Tasman there were no more significant sea voyages made in the seventeenth century, but by this time the early fever for exploration had cooled down. The Spanish and the Portuguese were interested only in the lucrative spice trade and the consolidation of their position in the Pacific.

The Dutch too were anxious to increase their quota of the spice trade and they were eager to expand their base at Batavia. The English turned their interests towards developing the American colonies where the early settlements were growing very rapidly and the French likewise wanted to develop their colonial investments in Canada and Louisiana. There was a great deal of inland exploration going on, particularly at the western frontier of the developments in North America but exploration by sea had slowed down.

In the 1680s the English buccaneer William Dampier made an appearance in the Pacific Ocean. Dampier was a very extrovert and complex character but he did more than any other explorer of his generation to add to our knowledge of the countries on the far side of the world. He was born in 1652 to a farming family at East Coker near Yeovil in Somerset. He was an educated man, but he yearned for adventure and when he was orphaned at the age of sixteen he went to sea as an apprentice to a Weymouth ship owner. He started life in the merchant service but later in his life he became a naval officer. He married above his station to Judith, a relative of the Duchess of Grafton, but she passed quickly out of his life and there is no evidence that he ever spent any time with his wife.

Pirates and Buccaneers After a decade of service in the navy Dampier left so that he could follow his own career. He became a lumberjack at Campeche on the Gulf of Mexico where he rose to become a plantation manager. It was at Campeche that he saw his opportunity to make a fortune by joining a party of buccaneers who operated their illegal activities along the Spanish Main in Central America. He spent several years of his life with the pirates, plundering settlements, capturing ships and running illegal cargoes. This episode of his life covered most of the 1670s.

Dampier was a very gifted man who had no obvious need to tarnish his reputation by buccaneering and piracy but he was always quick to take advantage of any opportunity open to him. He began to keep a journal in which he recorded every place he visited, he wrote about the people and their customs and also the wildlife and the geography of each country. He had a great natural talent for describing the natural history and the way of life in the places he visited. His journal was his most valued possession and it was also the most precious thing that he left to posterity. He describes how he took great care of it:

Portrait of William Dampier by Thomas Murray.

In many ways Dampier proved himself to be a brilliant man. He sailed round the world three times and he wrote a bestselling account of his travels. He was very interested in studying nature and he kept a journal of the islands and the wildlife he discovered. In the portrait he is holding his precious journal in his hand.

Foreseeing a necessity of wading through rivers frequently in land marsh, I took care before I left the ship to provide myself a large joint of bamboo which I stopt at both ends closing it with wax, so as to keep out of any water. In this I preserved my journal and other writings from being wet, that I was then forced often to swim.

Considering the size and length to which Dampier's journal grew it must indeed have been a large joint of bamboo to hold the many thick parchments. Later on in his career he kept the journal wrapped in an oilskin cloth and whenever he thought his ship was in danger of floundering the first thing he would do was rush down to his cabin to take care of it.

In the 1680s he was chosen by the British admiralty as the leader of an expedition to map and explore some of the lesser known regions of the world. He knew the importance of wind and weather patterns in navigation and he took an interest in the winds, storms, seasons, tides and currents of the 'Torrid Zone', by which he meant the tropics. His knowledge was remarkable and his approach was very scientific, he produced maps and sailing instructions to help navigators to make the most of the winds and currents in the tropics. On his visit to the Galapagos Islands, like a famous scientist from a later century, he was fascinated by the giant tortoises and he made observations of their courting habits:

It is reported of these creatures that they are nine days engendering, and in the water, the male on the female's back. It is observable that the males, while engendering, do not easily forsake their female. For I have gone and taken hold of the male, when engendering, and a very bad striker may strike them then, for the male is not shy at all. But the female, seeing a boat when they rise to blow, would make her escape, but that the male grasps her with his two fore fins and holds her fast.

Another of his accounts concerns the giant spiders found in the Caribbean islands, which looked as though they could bite off a man's finger. He describes some of the revolting seventeenth-century uses of the spiders:

Here are also a sort of spiders of a prodigious size, some near as big as a man's fist, with long small legs like the spiders in England: they have two teeth, or rather horns an inch and a half or two inches long, and of a proportional bigness, which are black as jett, smooth as glass, and have their small end sharp as a thorn; they are not strait but bending. These teeth we often preserve. Some wear them in their tobacco-pouches to pick their pipes. Some preserve them for toothpickers, especially such as were troubled with the tooth-ache; for by report they will expel that pain, though I cannot justify it of my own knowledge. The backs of these spiders are covered with a dark yellowish down, as soft as velvet. Some say these spiders are venomous, others not; whether it is true I cannot determine.

In 1688 Dampier's wanderings took him to the coast of Australia or New Holland as it was known at that time. Parts of the north and west coast had already been discovered earlier in the same century by the Dutch voyages from Batavia. Discoveries had been made by Jansz (1606), Hartog (1616), Nuyts (1627) and Tasman (1644) but Dampier found himself on an unknown part of the coastline. His ship, the *Cygnet*, reached a point near Melville Island and he decided to explore to the west. The land he found was barren and totally unsuitable for a settlement. Had he found a green and fertile land, as Cook did in the next century on the east coast, then Dampier could have recommended the land for settlement and thereby taken more of the credit for the discovery of Australia.

When he returned with his findings, the English appreciated that Dampier may have discovered something of value and, after an interval of eleven years, the Admiralty offered him a commission and a ship called the *Roebuck* to explore further. Thus, in 1699 we find Dampier on the west coast of Australia for a second time, on this occasion near the point where Dirk Hartog landed in 1616. Dampier made a landfall at a place he called Shark Bay near the island named after Hartog. He navigated along several hundred miles of coastline in the hope of reaching the location where he had landed with the *Cygnet* in the previous decade. The *Roebuck* however, was not man enough for the job

AUSTRALIA

There were many visits to Australia before Cook:

1606	Willem Jansz reached the Cape York peninsula.
1616	Dirk Hartog touched on the west coast.
1627	Pieter Nuyts explored a thousand miles of the south coast.
1642	Abel Tasman reached Tasmania.
1644	Tasman explored much of the north coast.
1688	Dampier at Melville Island.
1699	Dampier on the west coast.

Dampier made two visits to Australia and he had the opportunity to survey the coastline and pre-empt Cook as the discoverer. One reason for not following up his discovery was that the coast was barren and unsuitable for settlement.

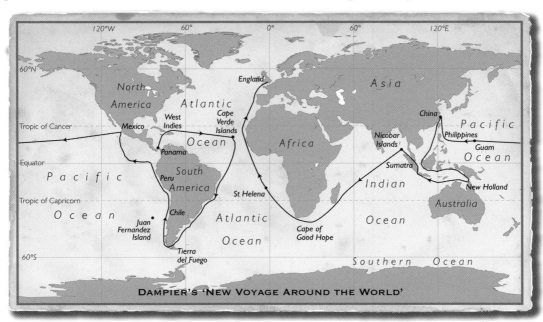

DAMPIER'S 'NEW VOYAGE AROUND THE WORLD'

and Dampier was forced to abandon his search as the state of his ship deteriorated. In spite of his leaky ship he sailed to the northern coast of New Guinea and he proved the existence of a strait between New Guinea and New Britain.

In between his two visits to Australia, William Dampier published an account of his earlier voyages; the title alone tells how much of the world he had seen by the time he was in his forties. His book was well written and it was very well received. It went through four editions in two years. The title page gives a good indication of the extent of his voyages:

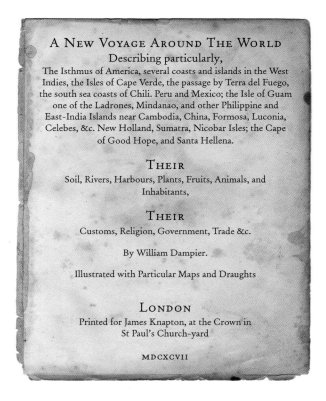

A NEW VOYAGE AROUND THE WORLD
Describing particularly,
The Isthmus of America, several coasts and islands in the West Indies, the Isles of Cape Verde, the passage by Terra del Fuego, the south sea coasts of Chili. Peru and Mexico; the Isle of Guam one of the Ladrones, Mindanao, and other Philippine and East-India Islands near Cambodia, China, Formosa, Luconia, Celebes, &c. New Holland, Sumatra, Nicobar Isles; the Cape of Good Hope, and Santa Hellena.

THEIR
Soil, Rivers, Harbours, Plants, Fruits, Animals, and Inhabitants,

THEIR
Customs, Religion, Government, Trade &c.

By William Dampier.

Illustrated with Particular Maps and Draughts

LONDON
Printed for James Knapton, at the Crown in St Paul's Church-yard

MDCXCVII

The Torrid Zone After his return from Australia Dampier went on to publish a second book of voyages and discoveries. It contained a supplement to his voyage around the world, also his voyage to 'Tonquin' in Asia, his 'Campeachy' voyages from much earlier in his career, and his discourse on winds, tides and currents in the 'Torrid Zone'. By the time his book was published he had sailed twice around the world but although he was middle-aged he was by no means at the end of his adventures. In 1704 he rounded Cape Horn to enter the Pacific Ocean and it was there that he left the Scotsman, Alexander Selkirk, marooned on the Pacific island of Juan Fernandez, 400 miles off the coast of Chile. (The opening picture shows Selkirk making his cats and kids dance before some distinguished visitors.) This was at the request of Selkirk himself; he hated

ROBINSON CRUSOE
It is typical of our obsession with fiction that everybody has heard of Robinson Crusoe but few have heard of Alexander Selkirk. For four years Selkirk was stranded in isolation on the Pacific island of Juan Fernandez. When Daniel Defoe heard the story he used it as the basis of his novel *Robinson Crusoe* but the true story of Alexander Selkirk is even more amazing.

Dampier so much that he was not prepared to sail another league further in the same ship. Other versions say that Selkirk left the ship because it was unseaworthy and in a very bad state of repair. If this is true then it seems he made a good decision for one of the ships subsequently floundered on a reef and became a total loss. William Dampier, as usual, survived.

Woodes Rogers A few years later another expedition left Bristol for the South Seas under the command of Captain Woodes Rogers. This was a blatant buccaneering voyage, sponsored by Bristol merchants who hoped to get a large profit out of Rogers' enterprise. Rogers had two ships, the *Duke* of 320 tons and the *Duchess* weighing in at 260 tons. He carried William Dampier with him as pilot, the ideal man for a voyage set on piracy and plunder. Captain Rogers must be credited with some degree of gallantry; he described in his log the events of 14 February, St Valentine's day, when the ship was heading for the island of Guam:

We had a bull dog which we sent with several of our nimblest runners to help him in catching goats; but he distanced and tired both the dog and the men, catched the goats, and brought 'em to us on his back...

In commemoration of the ancient custom, of chusing valentines, (Rogers) drew up a list of the fair ladies in Bristol, that were in any way related to, or concerned in the ships, and sent for his officers into the cabin, where every one drew and drank a ladies health in a cup of punch, and to a happy sight of 'em all, which I did to put 'em in mind of home.

Woodes Rogers' ship successfully rounded Cape Horn and in 1709 his ships arrived at the island of Juan Fernandez in the South Pacific. Alexander Selkirk was still alive. He had survived for five long and lonely years of isolation on the remote Pacific island. Woodes Rogers described Selkirk with amazement:

At first he never ate anything till hunger constrained him, partly for grief and partly for want of bread and salt... he made fire by rubbing two sticks of piemento together upon his knee, a wood which served him both for firing and for candle, and refreshed him with its fragrant smell. He soon wore out all his shoes and clothes by running through the woods; and at last was forced to shift without them...when his powder failed, he took them (the goats) by speed of foot; for his way of living and his continual exercise of walking and running, cleared him of all gross humours, so that he ran with wonderful swiftness through the woods and up the rocks and hills, as we perceived when we asked him to catch goats for us. We had a bull dog which we sent with several of our nimblest runners to help him in catching goats; but he distanced and tired both the dog and the men, catched the goats, and brought 'em to us on his back...

When Selkirk heard that Dampier was on the rescue ship however, he was still not sure that he wanted to return to civilization but, in the end, he chose rescue as the lesser of two evils. Alexander Selkirk kept an account of his experiences on the island and this was published on his return home. The book became very well known but it became badly distorted. It was studied by Daniel Defoe who used it as the basis of his popular fictional work *Robinson Crusoe.*

Silks and Gemstones Let us return to the voyage of Woodes Rogers. After picking up Alexander Selkirk the convoy sailed northwards into the North Pacific where the Acapulco Galleon, the *Nuestra Senora de la Incarnation,* was successfully captured. The booty was a cargo of silks and gemstones which were taken to India where they were sold for a very good price. Woodes Rogers managed to avoid the Spanish men-of-war and with the help of a Dutch convoy he got his ships safely back home again. The Bristol merchants got a very handsome return from their investment.

Dampier was a brilliant man who made remarkable discoveries and who recorded his exploits in a clear and lucid style, yet he does not rank amongst the great captains and explorers of the world. In spite of his brilliance we cannot admire Dampier. The reason is not just because of his buccaneering activities which some have tried to excuse on the grounds that it was an acceptable way to make a living in his times. Too many people, such as Alexander Selkirk, hated Dampier and did not want to sail on the same ship as him. When he returned from his second voyage to Australia complaints were made against him by his officers, he was court-martialled and found guilty of cruelty. This was in an age where seamen were tied to the gratings and lashed for minor offences, even keel-hauling was condoned and the horrors of the African slave trade had been witnessed by many captains. What Dampier did to his own men to be convicted of cruelty must have been horrific indeed!

ROGGEVEEN DISCOVERS EASTER ISLAND AND ANSON'S FLEET STRIKES GOLD

THE SEARCH FOR NEW ISLANDS IN THE GREAT SOUTH SEAS

1721 – 1769

'But the principal failing occurred in the sailing,
And the Bellman, perplexed and distressed,
Said he had hoped at least, when the wind blew due East,
That the ship would not travel due West!'

LEWIS CARROLL 1832–1892

In the first decades of the eighteenth century the high seas were still littered with pirates and buccaneers, all following in the wake of men like Drake and Dampier and sometimes trying to claim some respectability for their activities. The Spice Islands and the Spanish trade routes in the Northern Pacific were well known but the true nature of the Pacific was far from understood, particularly in the south.

Many small islands still remained undiscovered but there also persisted a belief that there was a great mass of land left to find, namely the great southern continent. Australia and New Zealand had both been discovered but only as isolated landings, and before 1760 the maps of both these countries were in a very fragmentary form. Nobody had sailed as far south as Antarctica since temperatures below zero and icebound seas made this impossible within the limitations of the sailing ships of the time. It was known that scurvy could be avoided if regular supplies of fresh food could be found but the causes of the disease were not properly understood. It was impossible for any captain to look after the health of his crew for more than a few weeks away from land. Latitudes could be measured with reasonable accuracy but longitudes were little more than guesswork based on the dead reckoning system of navigation which was the only one available at the time. Observations of the satellites of Jupiter, and of events such as solar and lunar eclipses occasionally provided reliable longitudes for sites on land but the accurate observations required for these techniques were virtually impossible to make on the swaying deck of a sailing ship.

Solid Stone Statues One significant voyage to the Pacific in the early eighteenth century was that of the Dutchman Jacob Roggeveen. He was sponsored by the Dutch West India Company (WIC), the great rival of the Dutch East India Company, known as the VOC who held sway in Indonesia. The WIC was not legally allowed to trade in the Pacific but they decided that provided they entered the ocean from the east around Cape Horn and not the west they were safe from molestation by their rivals. One of Roggeveen's aims was to discover the great southern continent. He entered the Pacific in 1721 via the Cape Horn route. He had three ships under his command and when he had entered Pacific waters he soon made a fascinating discovery. On Easter Sunday 1721 he became the first explorer to discover and land on an inhabited island off the coast of Peru to which he gave the name of Easter Island. In spite of its isolation the island was inhabited, but what struck the Europeans more than anything were the wonderful great stone statues arranged in

EASTER ISLAND

How were the great stone statues on Easter Island created?

Roggeveen thought they had been made from cement, mixed on the site and therefore there was no problem in transporting them. He was wrong, and it was confirmed that the statues were made of solid stone but how were they carved and moved to the beach? For many years extraterrestrial beings were suggested, but the quarries for the stone were discovered. The great statues had been carved at the quarries and they were transported to the beach using levers and wooden rollers. Easter Island was so isolated that it seemed impossible for the Polynesian canoes to reach it from any other inhabited island. The language and the culture was very close to that of Tahiti, and it became apparent that the Polynesians had been able to cross the thousands of miles of ocean to settle on the island.

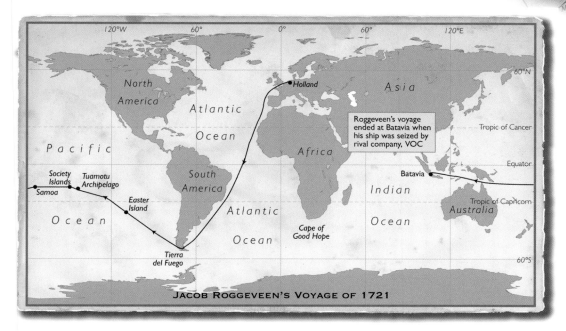

JACOB ROGGEVEEN'S VOYAGE OF 1721

Roggeveen's voyage ended at Batavia when his ship was seized by rival company, VOC

long lines on the beach with their backs to the sea. The statues were huge, two or three times the height of a man and they were so ancient that they belonged to an era many generations before the current inhabitants of the island. The local people had no idea how the statues came to be there, they had existed long before living memory. The Easter Island statues were solid stone monoliths hewed out of solid rock. Roggeveen did not believe they were monoliths however, and he explained their presence by saying they were made *in situ* out of mud and plaster. He traded with the islanders for food and water but he was unable to cope with the inevitable pilfering which took place when the natives swarmed inquisitively all over his ships. The first contact between the two cultures ended in tragedy. In a disastrous attempt to stop the pillaging Roggeveen's men opened fire and killed about twelve of the Easter Islanders.

Roggeveen then sailed westwards from Easter Island losing one of his ships, the *African Galley*, on an atoll in the Tuamotu Archipelago. He continued to the west and sailed through the Society Islands and the Samoas but although he saw many undiscovered islands on his horizons his experiences at Easter Island prevented him from stopping to investigate any of his sightings. He did not sail south to search for the southern continent but he persisted on a westward course. At last he reached the Dutch outpost of Batavia but, even though he was amongst his own countrymen, he was not able to enjoy the fruits of his voyage. His ships were seized by his rival company, the VOC. Thus Easter Island was the only notable discovery of the voyage, but considering that it was his first command at the age of sixty-two and that he was a lawyer by profession Roggeveen made a creditable contribution to global knowledge.

Whilst the countries of Western Europe continued to make minor discoveries to the south the Russians were very active in the North Pacific. This was in the time of Peter the Great, whose reign was from

1689 to 1725. He was the most progressive of the Russian tsars. In the last years of the seventeenth century, from 1697 to 1699, the Kamchatka Peninsula was discovered and charted by Vladimir Atlasov. The extent of Siberia into the western shores of the Pacific was still unknown but in 1728 the navigator Vitus Bering was given directions to explore the Pacific Ocean to the north of the Kamchatka Peninsula. Bering followed his instructions implicitly and sailed northwards into the arctic circle to a latitude of 67.5°. He was halted by a wall of ice in the Arctic Sea. He had passed through the straits between the continents of Asia and America, the straits that came to bear his name.

Several years later, in 1741, Vitus Bering was given two ships and instructions to sail across the North Pacific at the latitude of the Aleutian Archipelago, with Aleksey Chirikov as his second-in-command. The two Russians lost contact with each other but they both reached the American coast. Bering landed and made observations of the coastline but Chirikov sailed back to Russia by the cautious method of following the Aleutian Islands without making a landing on any of them. It was another generation before the findings came to be published but they added more knowledge about the coastlines in the far north of the Pacific Ocean.

THE BERING STRAITS

- – – – Bering, 1728
- ·········· Bering, 1741
- – · – · Chirikov, 1741
- ——— Cook, 1778

It was at much the same time, in the 1740s, that the British introduced a new-style navy. The war of the Austrian succession was being waged in Europe and the British found themselves fighting against both the Spanish and the French. The government decided to make a double strike against the Spanish. A large fleet was despatched to the Caribbean under the command of Admiral Edward Vernon and a smaller fleet under the forty-three-year-old George Anson, was sent into the Pacific by way of Cape Horn with instructions to try and capture the Manila Galleon. Anson was ordered to 'annoy and distress' the Spanish settlements. If possible he was to take Manila and leave it garrisoned with British troops. Anson was a very strict captain, he was hard on discipline with no quarter given to any who opposed him.

Anson's fleet was in very poor shape and it should never have been sent off for a voyage around Cape Horn. His flagship, the *Centurion,* was of recent construction as were the fourth-rate *Gloucester* and the little sloop *Tryall*. His three other ships, namely the *Pearl*, the *Severn* and the *Wager* were all old, leaky or rebuilt vessels. He took with him two supply ships, the *Anna* and the *Industry* making a total of eight ships in all. He commanded a total of 1223 sailors but half of these were recruited against their will from the Portsmouth dockside by the strong-arm tactics of the press gang. He also carried 529 untrained soldiers including a number of elderly Chelsea Pensioners who had been forced out of a comfortable retirement to serve on the high seas.

The fleet set sail on 20 September but progress was painfully slow because Anson's fleet was obliged to escort a merchant fleet across the Bay of Biscay. It took five weeks to get to Madeira. At last the ships set out for the open Atlantic. They were well provisioned but heavily overloaded, in fact they were so low in the water that the lower hatches had to be kept closed. When the ships reached the Doldrums the overcrowded space below decks was a hell on earth. It was an airless, dark, swaying dungeon full of filth and disease. Fever and dysentery took their toll and men began to die. Burials at sea became a daily occurrence.

The survivors reached Brazil on 21 December. They were able to get fresh food and the sick were taken on shore to recover, but they could not stay long for the Spanish knew about the expedition and they were only a few hundred miles away on the same coast. Anson sailed on to the Straits of Magellan. The *Severn* and the *Pearl* gave up the battle, they turned tail and deserted back to England. The *Wager* survived the ordeal of reaching the Pacific but she was driven onto the rocky coast of Chile by the gales. Her crew of 140 were marooned far from civilization. They managed to salvage the ship's boats and to sail the 3000 miles to a Spanish settlement in Peru where they were taken as prisoners. The escape from Peru is a story in its own right; one of the survivors was the midshipman, John Byron, who became a circumnavigator many years later.

Juan Fernandez Anson made for the island of Juan Fernandez with his remaining ships and men. The *Gloucester* also made it to the island but with two out of every three of her crew dead and with the remaining survivors so weak, they needed help to bring them into port. The store ship *Tryall* made it to Juan Fernandez and so did the *Anna* but the latter was so rotten that she had to be emptied of all provisions and burnt. The condition of the *Tryall* was little better, she was not fit enough to sail any further. The armada of ships that left England was sadly depleted. When Anson's crew had rested and recovered they quickly gained their strength and the commander was able to sail north to the isthmus of Panama where he had a rendezvous with Admiral Vernon. The plan was that the British army would conquer and control the Caribbean, so Anson should have been greeted in Panama by friendly British faces. Things did not go according to plan.

When the ships reached the Doldrums the overcrowded space below decks was a hell on earth. It was an airless, dark, swaying dungeon full of filth and disease. Fever and dysentery took their toll and men began to die. Burials at sea became a daily occurrence.

WAS RUSSIA CONNECTED TO AMERICA?

Peter the Great is the best remembered of the Russian tsars. He wanted to know more about his country so he sent the explorer Vitus Bering to Siberia to chart the most remote part of his empire. It took Bering three years just to cross Russia from Moscow to the east coast. Bering mapped the Kamchatka Peninsula. He discovered two chains of islands, the Kurils connecting with Japan and the Aleutians linking Russia with America. He followed the Russian coastline hoping to reach America but he found his ship turning back again to the west. He had sailed through what later came to be known as the Bering Straits.

Panama was infested by mosquitoes and Vernon's army had no defence against them. The soldiers contracted malaria and many of them died in Panama leaving the army as badly depleted as George Anson's ships.

There was still one card in Anson's favour. The folklore memory of Francis Drake was still alive nearly two centuries later and the Spanish settlements in Chile and Peru surrendered to him without a fight. Anson was able to lay his hands on three prize ships and he put into effect his plan to lie in wait for the Manila Galleon. He waited in vain. The Spanish had been warned about his presence and the galleon took refuge in Acapulco. George Anson could probably have taken the galleon if the Spaniards had not been forewarned but he had other problems to contend with. The foremast of the *Gloucester* was so rotten that it snapped clean off. The hull was leaking and there was nine feet of water in the hold. The pumps were manned day and night but the sailors were losing the battle against the leaks. There was no alternative but to abandon the *Gloucester* and set her on fire. Then the *Tryall* was scuttled in favour of the three Spanish prizes which were in far better condition. There was nothing left to plunder on the coast of New Spain but somehow Anson had to get his men home again. His next problem was to get his ships into shape for the voyage across the Pacific. On 6 May 1742 he set sail to the west.

It should have taken about fifty days to cross the northern Pacific but Anson's fleet took 114 days – he did not know the wind patterns and his lack of knowledge more than doubled the time of his crossing. But his ships arrived eventually at the Chinese port of Macao on the Canton River where George Anson bullied the Chinese into refitting his ship. He knew that the next Manila Galleon, the *Nuestra Senora de Cobadonga*,

Commodore George Anson on the island of Juan Fernandez.

An engraving from the authentic journal of Anson's expedition. There is a hive of activity: trees are being felled, the sick are being carried ashore, food is under preparation.

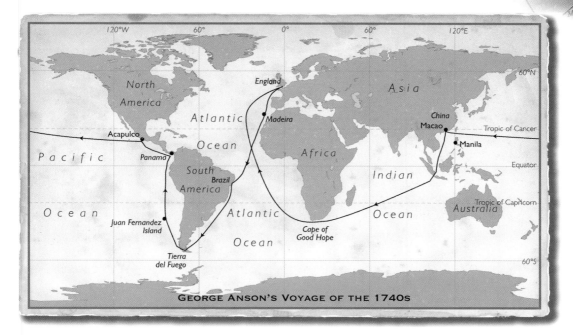

GEORGE ANSON'S VOYAGE OF THE 1740S

would be sailing soon and this time he planned to capture it. The *Cobadonga* had 530 men and 60 guns, the *Centurion* mustered only 237 men and fewer guns. The odds were very much against the British and the Spanish captain, when he saw a ragged ship coming towards him, was not unduly concerned. But manning the *Centurion* were hardened desperate men who had seen many of their colleagues die and had been through hell and high water to get to the Pacific. The treasure ship was their last desperate hope of making anything out of all their sufferings. If they did not take the Manila Galleon then they could not face the public if they ever managed to get their ship back home again.

Anson's men fought like demons to take the *Cobadonga*. Grapeshot from the *Centurion* tore the Spanish sails to shreds and a steady fusillade from the small arms quickly demoralized the Spaniards. The *Nuestra Senora de Cobadonga* surrendered. The British found that she really was a treasure ship. There were concealed caches of gold and silver to be found all over the ship, there was jewellery and there were gemstones, but best of all the galleon carried a chest of silver estimated to be worth £55,000 – it was a king's ransom and a truly magnificent haul.

The *Centurion* eventually returned to England with her treasure. The ship received a rapturous welcome and Anson was seen as a successor to Sir Francis Drake. His exploits were judged by his backers to be a great success but they did not take into account the loss of seven ships and 1500 men out of the original 2000. Most of the deaths were due to shipwreck and scurvy. How is it possible to value the lives of so many seamen when less than a quarter returned home? It was the last of the great buccaneering voyages.

Adventures in South America John Byron was a midshipman on board the *Wager* in 1741 during George Anson's voyage round the world. He was the second son of the fourth Baron Byron and grandfather of the poet

Lord Byron. John Byron was one of the lucky men to return alive from Anson's voyage to the Pacific, but he did not sail round the world with his commander. After entering the Pacific the *Wager* became separated from the rest of the fleet and she was wrecked off the coast of Chile. The survivors set off by land to the north and after three years of hardship Byron and his colleagues reached one of the Spanish settlements in Peru where they were held as prisoners of war. In 1745 Byron was at last repatriated and he was able to pick up his naval career again. He proved himself to be a very capable officer and for the next two decades he worked himself up through the rankings. In 1764 he was appointed to the command of two ships, the *Dolphin* and the *Tamar* with Captain Mouat as his second-in-command. He was sent by the British government to make new discoveries in the North Pacific. His instructions were to retrace the steps of Drake as far as New Albion in California and then to search for the fabled Straits of Anian that were still believed to exist at the Pacific end of the North West Passage.

The *Dolphin*, allocated to Byron, was a very smart ship fitted with new copper plating on the hull. The copper was an experimental protection against the ravages of the teredo worm. The experiment proved to be very successful and it was also found that the drag of the ship was diminished by the smooth hull and she therefore moved faster through the water. The two ships made good progress to the South Atlantic and they anchored at Port Desire in Patagonia. Charles Clerk, who was one of the officers on the *Dolphin*, wrote to his friend Dr Macy at the Royal Society in London concerning the Patagonian giants. His letter was published in the *Philosophical Transactions of the Royal Society*:

He set what was a world record in his times by completing a valueless circumnavigation of the globe in only twenty-two months.

…(they) are certainly nine feet if they don't exceed it… (they are) prodigious stout, and as well and proportionately made as ever I saw people in my life… there was hardly a man there less than eight feet; most of them considerable more; the women, I believe, run from 7½ to 8.

It is hard to believe that a man as careful as Charles Clerk could declare that he had seen men who were nine feet tall. It is possible that he only viewed the Patagonians from a distance and that he was fooled by the perspective into seeing them as much larger than they were. It is also possible that he was enjoying a joke at the expense of the Royal Society.

Byron's ships made a good passage through the Straits of Magellan into the Pacific but it was at this point that Byron chose to diverge from his instructions. His mission was to sail to the west coast of America as far as California and this would mean running the gauntlet of the Spanish presence all along the coast. It would therefore be necessary to keep well away from the coastal settlements if the ships were not to be molested. Byron argued that he could not take the risk of being so long at sea when some of his crew were already showing symptoms of scurvy. He abandoned the idea of sailing to California as being far too risky. He sailed westwards for several months but he made no attempt to look for uncharted land. In fact he saw little in the way of land until he came to a chain of islands in the neighbourhood of the Solomons that he called the 'Islands of Disappointment'. He reasoned that if he followed the chain of islands he would discover the fabled southern continent, but he made no attempt to follow up his theory, claiming the sickness of his crew as his excuse. He set what was a world record in his times by completing a valueless circumnavigation of the globe in only twenty-two months.

The *Dolphin* had no sooner berthed in England than it was decided to send her round the world a second time. In spite of the fact that very little evidence had been found there was a growing conviction that a great southern continent was waiting to be discovered. Samuel Wallis had been chosen to find this *Terra Australis Incognito*.

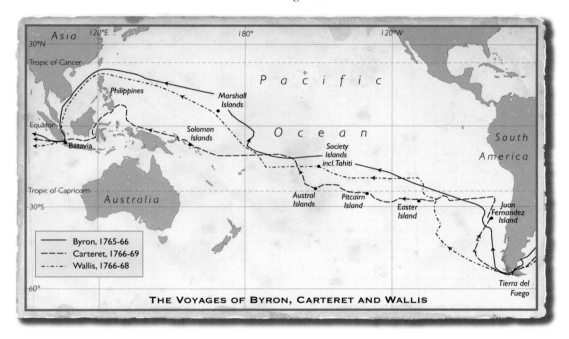

THE VOYAGES OF BYRON, CARTERET AND WALLIS

Samuel Wallis had Philip Carteret as his second-in-command and the latter was provided with the smaller vessel called the *Swallow*. Carteret accepted the *Swallow* but she was a very slow ship and she could not keep up with the gleaming copper-bottomed *Dolphin*. He expected to be provided with a much better ship later in the voyage but when his new ship simply did not materialise he realized that he was doomed to sail round the world in the small, frail and sluggish vessel. It was a miracle that the *Swallow* managed to survive the Straits of Magellan. Wallis waited patiently at first for his consort to catch up with him, but the two ships parted company in the rough seas to the west of Cape Horn. Again the voyage was fated. Wallis suffered badly from sea sickness and he was not well enough to attempt to explore any of the uncharted ocean. Two expensive British voyages of exploration were both failures. The only consolation was that Wallis did in fact make a major discovery in the South Pacific. He found the island of Tahiti, the jewel of the South Seas.

Advanced Civilization At Tahiti the *Dolphin* was at first welcomed by a shower of stones, but soon the Tahitians realized that the ship wanted to trade with them for food and supplies and relationships improved very quickly. The British were able to study the Tahitian lifestyle at first hand. It was obvious that there was an advanced civilization on Tahiti compared to other islands in the Pacific. There were stone products and manufactured items, there was farming and cloth, some kind of social hierarchy existed. There were priests. There was a religion and a respect for the dead. The island seemed to have been created with a ready food supply, even the bread seemed to grow on the breadfruit tree. There was no writing and therefore no legal system, which was confusing to the Europeans because it meant that they could not understand the Tahitian idea of ownership. The Tahitians simply helped themselves to anything they fancied from the ship. They had no iron, and this was the reason why the iron nails became a valuable item of barter. The nails could be worked into knives and simple agricultural instruments and this was of value on Tahiti. The concept of morals was very different from Europe. Tahitian girls gave themselves freely to the European men, and it was hardly surprising that a ship's nail came to be the price of their favours. Wallis soon found that nails were being extracted from the ship's timbers and if he allowed the situation to continue the ship was in danger of falling apart.

The chief of the island was a buxom woman called Purea or Oborea. She seemed to belong to the leading family of Tahiti and the others all deferred to her authority. The political situation was very volatile however, civil wars were frequent and when Cook arrived in Tahiti in 1769 Purea had been deposed and she was only found with great difficulty, living in much reduced circumstances and comparative poverty.

Tahiti was the only discovery of any significance in Wallis' circumnavigation. He did not overstay his welcome and because of his illness he wanted to sail again for home as soon as possible. Trailing behind Wallis with his sluggish ship came Philip Carteret. The two ships followed a similar course across the Pacific but Carteret did not have the luck to sight Tahiti. He did make a few minor discoveries. He stumbled upon Pitcairn Island and later in the voyage he became the first European to sail through the straits between New Ireland and New Britain, showing for the first time that they were separate islands. This discovery, considering the bad state and unseaworthiness of the *Swallow*, was a fine achievement. Carteret must still be given credit as one of the greatest of circumnavigators. To get his sluggish vessel through the Straits of Magellan, across the Pacific Ocean, and back again to England was a marvellous triumph. It was not until 20 May 1769 that the *Swallow* at last docked in England, exactly a year later than the *Dolphin*.

No further discoveries of any significance were made, but the voyages did pave the way for the greatest navigator of them all. James Cook arrived in Tahiti two years later than Wallis with his ship the *Endeavour* when he came to observe the Transit of Venus. Before describing Cook's voyages however, there is one more explorer who deserves his place in history. He is the Frenchman Louis-Antoine de Bougainville who visited Tahiti in 1768, the year between the visits of Wallis and Cook.

Louis-Antoine de Bougainville explores the Pacific's flora and fauna

The Frenchman enjoys an idyll on Tahiti and encounters the Great Barrier Reef

1766 – 1769

'I concur that it is difficult to conceive of such a large number of low-lying islands and land almost submerged, without supposing that there must be a continent nearby. But Geography is a science of facts.'

Louis-Antoine de Bougainville, *Voyage autour du monde*

Louis-Antoine de Bougainville was born in Paris in 1729. He entered the army at the age of twenty-four and he served as aide-de-camp to General Louis-Joseph de Montcalm.

He distinguished himself against the British in Canada during the Seven Years War. In 1763 he left the army to join the navy. In the following year he successfully established a French colony in the Falkland Islands but for political reasons the colony was ceded to Spain only four years later.

After only two years in the navy Bougainville was selected as leader of a French expedition to explore the South Pacific. His two ships left France late in 1766 and they returned in 1769. The voyage turned out to be the first French circumnavigation of the world but it was also a scientific voyage to study the flora and fauna of the Pacific islands and it has a claim to be the first voyage to carry professional scientists. Bougainville took the naturalist, Philibert Commerçon, with him to study the flora and fauna of the southern hemisphere and he also took the astronomer, Pierre Antoine Veron, the man who became the first person to measure the longitude of the Philippines with any degree of accuracy. Charles Routier de Romainville came as a draughtsman to draw charts of the voyage and Prince Nassau-Siegen, a French nobleman, came as a passenger and gentleman adventurer.

Bougainville was allotted two ships for his expedition. The larger was the *Boudeuse*, a 550-ton frigate, forty metres in length, with a complement of eleven officers and a crew of 203. She was a new ship, launched only a few months before the expedition left France, but she had not been properly overhauled and unknown to Bougainville, who was still a relatively inexperienced sailor, she was already in a poor state of repair. The second ship, the *Etoile*, was a 480-ton storeship, thirty-four metres long, with a complement of eight officers and 108 men. Nicolas-Pierre Duclos-Guyot was the second-in-command. Bougainville, again because of his relatively short naval career, relied heavily on Duclos-Guyot for decisions concerning the safety of the ships. The command of the smaller vessel was given to François Chenard de la Giraudais and he had Jean-Louis Caro l'Aine as his second-in-command.

Carved on the tree trunks they found inscriptions and other signs of recent European visitors. They had landed at the place that had been used by the British expedition of Wallis and Carteret the year before.

Port Galant The convoy made a good Atlantic crossing and the ships stopped briefly in Montevideo for supplies and provisions. At the end of the year 1767 the two ships arrived near the southern tip of America. The passage through the Straits of Magellan was chosen in preference to the Cape Horn route. This may have been the wrong decision for the seas were very high and the ships were forced to find a sheltered bay and wait for the weather to improve before they could make any further progress. The *Boudeuse* and the *Etoile* anchored at a place in Patagonia they called Port Galant where they found a number of recently felled trees. Carved on the tree trunks they found inscriptions and other signs of recent European visitors. They had landed at the place that had been used by the British expedition of Wallis and Carteret the year before. New Year's Day, 1768, was quite fine and Bougainville therefore decided to send out two of his longboats to do some exploring. One was sent along the shoreline to investigate a bay to the west, the other was sent into the middle of the straits to examine some islands he called the Isles Royales. He then despatched a third boat to explore the southern shore of the strait where he hoped to find the entrance to a sea passage called the Canal Barbara. On 4 January some of his men climbed the mountain behind Port Galant, which on a clear day afforded a good panorama of the strait.

The weather deteriorated rapidly and the ships were confined to harbour – for the next two weeks Bougainville and his crew were trapped in Port Galant experiencing gale-force winds, torrential rain, temperatures below freezing and heavy snow in spite of the fact that it was high summer. Some of the indigenous population turned up to visit the ships and to nose around out of curiosity. There was much discussion about whether or not the visitors were the fabled Patagonian Giants but the French soon discovered that the giant tradition was in error. Some of the Patagonians had large feet and many had very large heads of hair but, statistically speaking, they were not significantly taller than any other race.

Eventually, on 16 January, the ships were able to leave the little harbour and to sail at last to the west. They headed for a channel on the north east side of an island they called Isle Louis-le-Grande. The *Etoile* was able to reach the island but the weather and tidal conditions prevented the *Boudeuse* from making any progress out of Port Galant. Another nine miserable days were lost before Bougainville managed to get his ship underway again on 25 January. Suddenly the conditions improved rapidly and the ships sailed quickly up Paso Ingles, past Isla Carlos III and the entrances to Rivière Batchelor and Baie St Jerome. Later that day they rounded Cap Quad to enter Long Reach and they found themselves in the final stretch of the Straits of Magellan. Conditions remained good the following day and the two ships rounded Cap des

Portrait of Louis-Antoine de Bougainville who commanded the first French ship to sail around the world.

His book VOYAGE AUTOUR DU MONDE *made a great impression on French society in the decade before the French Revolution. He very nearly reached the East Coast of Australia before Cook, but he was forced to keep his distance by the breaking waters of the Great Barrier Reef.*

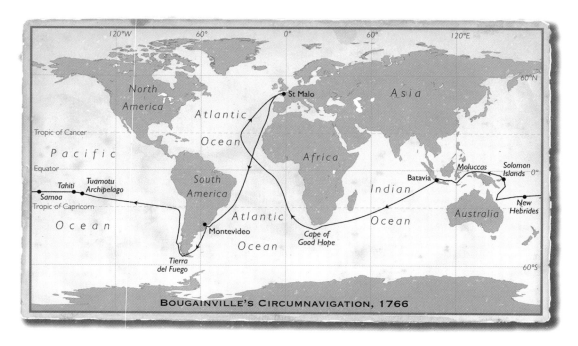

BOUGAINVILLE'S CIRCUMNAVIGATION, 1766

Pilier and the Twelve Apostles rocks to enter the Pacific Ocean at last. The final stretch from Port Galant to the Pacific had been negotiated without any stoppages.

Tropical Peaks Bougainville took his ships northwards along the coast of Chile and sailed almost as far as the tropics before he headed west into the Pacific. He passed through the Tuamotu Archipelago and he charted a few islands but made no landing. After two months of uneventful sailing the peaks of a high tropical island appeared on his horizon. The island was Tahiti.

Bougainville was very taken with Tahiti and its inhabitants. He had every right to think that he was the first European to discover this beautiful island. He deduced from the reactions of the Tahitians that his was not the first European ship to anchor there, but the language problem meant that he was unable to work out who had preceded him.

The French called the group of islands the Archipel de Bourbon. Bougainville found an anchorage at a place called Haitaa on Tahiti-Nui. The French received the same attentions as the British had experienced on their visit to Tahiti. Vegetables, fruit, island pigs and fish were readily exchanged as the Tahitians swarmed around the ship in their canoes. The attentions of the brown-skinned and dark-haired Tahitian girls with their garlands of scented flowers, and their readiness to bestow their favours on the white men for the shirt off their back or a ship's nail, made them irresistible.

LOUIS-ANTOINE DE BOUGAINVILLE

Bougainville, who commanded the first French ship to circumnavigate the Earth, was very unfortunate not to be the discoverer of Tahiti; he was preceded less than a year before by the Englishman Samuel Wallis in the *Dolphin*. The French called the island 'Cythera' and Bougainville took a Cytherian back to France with him to mix in Parisian society. After his return to France he became secretary to Louis XV and because of his naval experience he served as *chef d'escadre* (commodore) in operations of the French fleet off North America (1779 – 82) in support of the American Revolution. In 1782, after a French defeat off Martinique he carried the blame and was court-martialled. He survived the worst of the French Revolution and lived out his retirement in Normandy.

In his book *Voyage Autour du Monde* Bougainville described an incident where 'In spite of all our precautions, one young woman came aboard into the poop, and stood by one of the hatches above the capstan... the young girl negligently allowed her loincloth to fall to the ground, and appeared to all such eyes as Venus showed herself to the Phrygian shepherd. She had the Goddess's celestial form.' This was an exceptional case and did not seem to have been premeditated. There was no way that Bougainville could prevent his sailors from taking advantage of the island girls but he was at pains to explain that the respectable married women did not solicit their favours:

Married women are faithful to their husbands, they would pay with their lives for any unfaithfulness, but we are offered all the young girls. Our white skin delighted them. They express their admiration in this regard in the most expressive manner. Furthermore the race is attractive, with men five feet ten inches tall, many reaching six foot, a few exceeding this. Their features are very handsome. They have a fine head of hair which they wear in various ways. Several also have a long beard which they rub as they do their hair with coconut oil. The women are pretty and, something that is due to the climate their food and water, men and women and even old men have the finest teeth in the world. These people breathe only rest and sensual pleasures. Venus is the goddess they worship.

Bougainville met Ereti, the chief of the district, and he received permission to set up a camp on shore. A Tahitian building situated close to a freshwater stream was allocated to the French. It was a place where they could take their sick ashore to recover their health and they were given permission to draw water from the stream. The few sailors who were suffering from scurvy were quickly restored to good health by the fresh food. New timbers were needed to repair the ships and Ereti took the visitors around and indicated which trees could be felled

Music and Fireworks Relations between French and Tahitians were generally good, but the biggest problem in the south sea paradise was the light fingers of the Tahitians, and the continual thieving which Bougainville could control no better than Wallis before him, or Cook and others after him. He set a guard on the camp to keep the thieves away. Pilfering apart, the two cultures got along extremely well with each other. The French entertained the Tahitians with music and a fireworks display. The Tahitians reciprocated with their own forms of song and music and their traditional wrestling displays.

On 12 April strong winds sprang up and created problems for the anchored ships. Haitaa was on a sheltered part of the coast but it was a poor harbour. The cables and hawsers used to anchor the ships were frayed by the sharp coral and over the next few days several anchors were lost. Fortunately for the French, the wind did not drive their untethered ships onto

'In spite of all our precautions, one young woman came aboard into the poop, and stood by one of the hatches above the capstan ... the young girl negligently allowed her loincloth to fall to the ground, and appeared to all such eyes as Venus showed herself to the Phrygian shepherd. She had the Goddess's celestial form.'

the surrounding coral. Bougainville's nautical inexperience showed
again. He had made an unfortunate choice of anchorage and he should
have been better advised about the problem of sharp coral rocks below.
The motion of the ship scraped the anchor ropes against the coral and
Bougainville lost no less than six anchors as a result.

A problem of a different sort arose when the petty thieving became
intolerable. Guns were fired and three Tahitians were wounded.
Bougainville prevented the incident from escalating further by putting
four soldiers in irons and giving peace offerings to the Tahitians. Frictions
were beginning to show, the time had come to leave and the French
started to load their ships.

*Today the Indians asked us to fire a few shots in their presence. We complied to their
request and caused a great deal of fear, all the animals shot at having been killed
stone dead. They brought more refreshments than ever and after that the scoundrels
had a great time. Apart from thefts, these are the best people in the world. All the
women are weeping over our departure and the people are very eager for us to return.
We sowed in the presence of the cacique and to the great satisfaction of the people:
wheat, maize, beans, peas, lentils and the seeds of various vegetables.*

When he sailed from Tahiti Bougainville took a Tahitian called Ahutoru
with him. Ahutoru was a young man keen for adventure and he was
very quick at picking up a strange language. It was not until the ships
had left Tahiti that Bougainville decided to investigate a curious incident
that involved Ahutoru and which had happened whilst they were there.

The Botanist's Assistant The botanist Philibert Commerçon was in his
element as he roamed the island examining and collecting new
specimens. He found several plants that he thought would make good
anti-scorbutics. He had a valet called Jean Baret who accompanied him
on his expeditions. The Tahitians were very interested in the botanist's
assistant for they quickly deduced that she was actually Jeanne Baret – a
woman! She had travelled all the way from France and managed to pass
herself off as a young boy. The French had had their suspicions about the
botanist's assistant early in the voyage but they had accepted the
explanation that she was a young boy and they were taken in by her
disguise. The Tahitian Ahutoru, who knew nothing of
French male or female fashion, saw straight away that
Jeanne Baret was a girl. Ahutoru's interest brought the
matter to a head and the captain explained the dilemma in
his journal:

*I have taken steps to ensure
that she suffers no
unpleasantness. The court
will, I think, forgive her
for this infraction of the
ordinances. Her example
will hardly be contagious.
She is neither ugly nor
pretty and is not yet 25.*

*Yesterday I checked a rather peculiar event on board the Etoile. For
some time, a rumour had been circulating on the two ships that Mr
de Commerçon's servant, named Baret, was a woman. His build, his
caution in never changing his clothes, or carrying out any natural
function in the presence of anyone else, the sound of his voice, his
beardless chin, and several other indications had given rise to this
suspicion and reinforced it. It seemed to have been changed into a*

certainty but a scene that took place on the island of Cythera. Mr de Commerçon had gone ashore with Baret who followed him in all his botanising, (and) carried weapons, food, plant notebooks with courage and a strength which had earned for him from our botanist the title of his beast of burden. Hardly had the servant landed than the Cytherans surrounded him, shouting that it is a woman and offered to pay her the honours of the island. The officer in charge had to come and free her. I was therefore obliged, in accordance with the king's ordinances, to verify whether the suspicion was correct. Baret, with tears in her eyes admitted that she was a girl, that she had misled her master by appearing before him in men's clothing at Rochefort at the time of boarding, that she had already worked for a Genevan as a valet, that born in Burgandy and orphaned, the loss of a lawsuit had reduced her to penury and that she had decided to disguise her sex, that moreover, she knew when she came on board that it was a question of circumnavigating the world and this voyage had excited her curiosity. She will be the only one of her sex (to have done this) and I admire her determination all the more because she has always behaved with the most scrupulous correctness. I have taken steps to ensure that she suffers no unpleasantness. The court will, I think, forgive her for this infraction of the ordinances. Her example will hardly be contagious. She is neither ugly nor pretty and is not yet 25.

There was a happy ending to the affair. The French accepted that they had a woman on board and she was treated with respect by the crew for the remainder of the voyage. As Bougainville foretold, Jeanne Baret became the first woman to circumnavigate the earth.

The ships sailed west from Tahiti and they passed through the Samoan Islands and the New Hebrides. Bougainville recognized that the people in this part of the Pacific were a different race from those in Tahiti; they were Melanesian as opposed to Polynesian, they were darker skinned and their facial features were different. He continued sailing west until he entered into waters not previously navigated by any European ship. At this point on his voyage Bougainville was heading directly for the east coast of Australia at a latitude of about 15° south. Then, in the evening of 4 June, the crew on the *Boudeuse* heard the sound of breakers and they fired cannon to warn the *Etoile*, which was following behind, of the danger ahead. The next morning a low sandy island could be seen on which Bougainville bestowed the name, Le Bature de Diane (Diane Bank). They proceeded cautiously and on the next day the ships arrived at a coral reef. The danger from the white surf breaking on the reef was very obvious, it was the cause of great concern to the French and Bougainville wisely decided to turn his ships and to set a course for the north east to take them away from what could have been a terrible disaster.

Bougainville Reef The reef, later called Bougainville Reef, was an outlier of the Great Barrier Reef off the eastern coast of Australia and the sailors' trepidation was therefore well-founded. Some of the crew believed that they had been able to see land from the masthead away to the south west. At this point of his voyage Bougainville was set to make history and to discover the east coast of Australia for France. It was not to be. The seas were far too dangerous to cross and he wisely kept his ships

WOMEN SAILORS

Jeanne Baret was the first woman to sail round the world. In England Joseph Banks tried to emulate Philibert Commerçon's feat and he arranged to pick up a lady botanist, disguised as a man called Mr Burnett at Madeira. Banks withdrew from the expedition and consequently Ms Burnett did not sail with Captain Cook.

There are many examples of women at sea, who usually disguised themselves as men and frequently lived a life of piracy:

• Alwilda. A legendary figure from the ninth century, she was a pirate but married Alf, King of Denmark.

• Grace O'Malley (1530 – 1603). The 'Pirate Queen of Cannaught', there is a story that she once met Elizabeth I.

• Mary Read and Anne Bonny (1698 – 1720). Both were transvestite pirates. They were caught and sentenced to death but 'pleaded their bellies' – that is they declared their sex and showed that they were pregnant.

• Ching Shih (fl. 1805). The leader of the infamous 'Red Flag Fleet' with 1500 ships. She terrorized all the shipping from the Chinese coast to Malaysia.

well off the white breaking water. Bougainville knew about the discoveries made by Dampier in 1688 and 1699 and he correctly deduced that he was on the opposite side of the land discovered by Dampier when the latter was exploring the west coast. Bougainville was badly in need of fresh water and supplies but he knew that the land found by Dampier was very bleak and inhospitable. He therefore assumed that the east coast would be no more hospitable than the west and he decided against trying to land there:

Such extensive breakers announce a low coast and when I see that Dampierre, in this same latitude of 15° 35' abandoned the western coast of this barren land, where there is not even any drinking water and whose approaches bristle with shoals and reefs, I conclude that the eastern coast is no better and I am inclined to think, like him, that all this land is nothing more than a mass of islands and banks. Moreover these pieces of wood, these fruits, this seaweed which we are finding, the quietness of the sea, the currents, everything, tells us that we have had land to the SE for several days and I am led to believe that it tends SE and NW, as do the reefs that defend it.

The expedition arrived at the northern end of the Solomon Islands. At first Bougainville did not recognize them as the Spanish discoveries from two hundred years ago. The ships sailed on but the winds dropped and they were becalmed. Islands could be seen in all directions and only then did Bougainville begin to suspect that he had reached the islands described by Quiros two centuries before him. He did not realize however, that a large island to the west of an isle he called Aoba was in fact Quiros' Espiritu Santo. Had he sailed further to the north he might have deduced that it was the same island for he could have identified the distinctive bay of St Phillip and St James and the estuary of the River Jordan. The *Boudeuse* and the *Etoile* veered to the south and they passed through the strait between Espiritu Santo and Malekula. Several smaller islands were seen off the south coast of Espiritu Santo. Bougainville despatched his small boats to search for good anchorages but he did not intend to stay for long.

By this time his supplies were low, his men were suffering from scurvy and the ships were badly in need of refitting. The last goat and dog were killed to be eaten as by now several members of the crew were reduced to making meals out of the ship's rats.

He sailed on towards New Britain. By this time his supplies were low, his men were suffering from scurvy and the ships were badly in need of refitting. The last goat and dog were killed to be eaten as by now several members of the crew were reduced to making meals out of the ship's rats. He knew that by sailing west he could reach the Moluccas and from there he could sail to the Dutch base of Batavia where he would be able to get fresh provisions and repairs to his ships.

It was September 1768 when he stopped firstly at Buru in the Moluccas and soon afterwards on the north coast of Java where he made his way to Batavia. There, for the first time since leaving France, he was able to get up to date news of what was happening in Europe. He discovered that a British ship had left Batavia only twelve days before his arrival. The ship was the little *Swallow* that had gallantly crossed the Pacific under Philip Carteret. When he had refurbished his ship and taken on fresh supplies Bougainville sailed west again. He crossed the Indian Ocean and he rounded the Cape of Good Hope. It was on 26 February 1769 that he caught up with the *Swallow* in mid Atlantic. 'His ship was very small', noted Bougainville of Carteret, '[it] went very badly and when we took leave of her, she remained as it were at anchor. How he must have suffered in so bad a vessel may well be conceived'. At the end of March Bougainville landed at St Malo in Brittany having lost only seven men on his voyage, a statistic which compares very favourably with other circumnavigators of his time.

On his return to France Bougainville wrote a very scholarly account of his journey entitled *Voyage Autour du Monde*. It was very well received throughout Europe. He had a lot of sympathy with the people of the Pacific and he helped to create the popular belief in the noble savage and the moral worth of man in his natural state. His often quoted opinion of the Pacific was that, 'it is difficult to conceive such a number of low islands and almost drowned lands without a continent near them'. At the same time he had not found a continent in the South Seas and he maintained that, 'if any considerable land existed hereabouts we could not fail meeting with it'.

Brilliant Career Louis de Bougainville never made another voyage of exploration but after his voyage around the world he had a brilliant career. In 1772 he became secretary to Louis XV and from 1779 to 1782 he served as a *chef d'escadre* (commodore) in operations of the French fleet off North America. This was during the French support for the American Revolution but after a French defeat off Martinique on 12 April 1782, he was court-martialled. He lived long enough to experience the French Revolution but he escaped the Massacres of Paris and after the worst excesses of the revolution were over he settled on his estate in Normandy. When Napoleon came to power Bougainville was made a senator, a count, and a member of the Legion of Honour. The largest of the Solomon Islands is named after him and also a strait in the New Hebrides group. Perhaps his best known memorial is the plant genus Bougainvillea that he brought to Europe from Brazil which became very popular amongst the gardening community.

Captain Cook's epic voyage on board the *Endeavour*

The charting of New Zealand and the east coast of Australia

1768 – 1771

'Was it not for the pleasure which Naturly results to a man from his being the first discoverer even
was it nothing more than Sand or Shoals this kind of service would be unsupportable especially in
far distant parts like this, Short of Provisions & almost every other necessary. People will hardly
admit of an excuse for a man leaving a coast unexplored he has once discov'd, if dangers are his
excuse he is then charged with Timerousness & want of Perseverance, & at once pronounced the most
unfit man in the world to be employ'd as a discoverer, if on the other hand he boldly encounters all
the dangers and Obstacles he meets with & is unfortunate enough not to succed he is charged with
Temerity & Perhaps want of Conduct.'

FROM COOK'S JOURNAL

It was the third day of June in the year 1769. On the Pacific island of Tahiti the astronomer Charles Green was using his telescope to project the image of the sun onto a screen.

As his clock ticked away the seconds he watched carefully until he could see a small black disc making contact with the bright image of the sun.

The passage of the planet Venus across the face of the Sun was such a rare event that well over a century could elapse between transits. The astronomers had calculated that if two observations of the Transit of Venus were made from two widely separated points on the Earth's surface, then it was possible to estimate the distance from the Earth to the Sun, which was known as an astronomical unit. This was why the British government, with the support of the Royal Society, had sent a ship to the southern hemisphere to observe the transit. If the results were successful then the scale of the whole solar system could be determined and eventually it would be possible to use the results to measure the distance to the nearest stars.

The leader of the expedition was a man of forty-one. His name was James Cook and his ship was called the *Endeavour*. Cook was born in the village of Marton in Cleveland in the North Riding of Yorkshire. His father was a farm labourer. At the age of seventeen James Cook left his first job as a grocer's assistant on the quayside at Staithes to go to sea as an able-bodied seaman. He worked in the North Sea coal trade for John Walker of Whitby and he proved himself to be an exceptional sailor. He worked his way up through the ranks until, at the age of twenty-six, he was offered the command of his own vessel. At this point in his career Cook decided to leave the merchant service and he signed up for the Royal Navy. He rose to become a ship's master, but he also showed great skill at map making and navigation. His qualities were well known to the British navy. He was a very fine seaman and an excellent commander. James Cook was without doubt the best man to lead the expedition to the southern hemisphere.

Scientists and Greyhounds The *Endeavour* carried the usual quota of seamen and marines but there were also several scientists on the voyage. Charles Green was the official astronomer. Joseph Banks, a gentleman of great fortune and an avid collector of flora and fauna of all kinds, arrived with his retinue to be included on the voyage. His friend Doctor Solander was a botanist, a pupil of the great Carl Linnaeus who instigated the

THE TRANSITS OF VENUS

1639	First observation of a transit of Venus by Jeremiah Horrocks.
167 0s	Edmund Halley demonstrates how to find the Sun's distance from the Transit of Venus.
1761	Transit of Venus observed in Europe, the Atlantic and Indian Oceans.
1769	Transit of Venus observed from Tahiti.
1874 and 1882	Transits of Venus.
2004 and 2012	Transits of Venus.

classification system of that name for all living things. Joseph Banks brought two artists with him: Sydney Parkinson to sketch his specimens and Alexander Buchan to draw the landscapes. He also had a skilled draughtsman called Herman Sporing and four servants to attend to his needs, two black and two white and, lest we forget, two greyhounds accompanied him to help with all the hunting and shooting he planned for the voyage. If the *Endeavour* was unfortunate enough to encounter hostile Spanish or French ships in the Pacific then Joseph Banks would have no problem about convincing them that the expedition was a peaceful voyage to further the interests of science.

Soon after the observations of the Transit of Venus were completed James Cook opened his secret instructions from the Admiralty. It was a badly kept secret, for everybody on board knew that the other main purpose of the voyage was to make new discoveries in the South Seas. Cook's instructions were to sail south from Tahiti down to a latitude of 40° degrees. It was hoped that somewhere in that vicinity the expedition would discover the great southern continent, the *Terra Australis Incognita*, which many geographers still thought to exist in the southern hemisphere. The *Endeavour* carried out her instructions implicitly but south of Tahiti she discovered nothing but high seas, wind and storms. After reaching 40° south the instructions were to head to the west along the line of latitude. If the account given in Abel Tasman's journal was correct then this course was guaranteed to find a landfall, but it was well over a century since Tasman's voyage and nobody had ever attempted to rediscover his findings.

Land Ahoy The *Endeavour* was still sailing to the west when on 6 October there was a shrill and excited call from the masthead. Nicholas Young, the youngest sailor on the ship, was perched high on the mast pointing excitedly ahead and shouting 'land'. It was evening and there were differences of opinion about whether or not Young Nick's eyes deceived him. When morning came however, there could be no doubt. A wonderful land had appeared on the horizon, with green forests and river valleys, hills and mountain ranges towering above them. Joseph Banks made an entry in his Journal:

In the evening a pleasant breeze. At sunset all hands at the mast head; land still distant 7 or 8 leagues, appears to be larger than ever, in many part 3, 4 and 5 ranges of hills are seen one over the other and a chain of mountains overall, some of which appear enormously high. Much difference of opinion and many conjectures about Islands, rivers &c, but all hands seem to agree that this is certainly the Continent we are in search of.

The land was, of course, New Zealand. The next day Cook made the first landing. It was a great tragedy that the first contact with the Maoris ended in a shooting incident when one of the Maoris was killed. The landfall seemed obviously to be the country discovered by Tasman. Cook sailed firstly to the south, then he changed his mind and decided to turn back to follow the coast to the north. Soon he reached the easternmost cape of New Zealand and he sailed into what he called the Bay of Plenty. Here he got a much better reception from the Maoris, with excellent trade

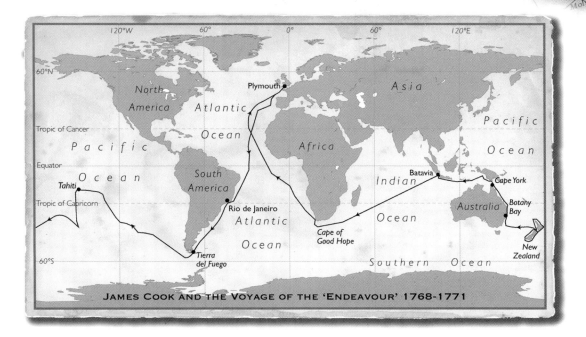

JAMES COOK AND THE VOYAGE OF THE 'ENDEAVOUR' 1768-1771

and re-provisioning. Charting the coast of the new land was a formidable task. The *Endeavour* tacked and re-tacked for several weeks as Cook battled against the elements to reach the northernmost cape. By Christmas Day he had rounded the cape and he rediscovered the Three Kings Islands first found by Tasman on Twelfth Night 1643. The charting of the west coast of the island proved to be just as difficult as charting the east coast and at one point the *Endeavour* was driven back so far that it took her two days just to regain her former position. At last a high mountain was sighted which Cook named after Lord Egmont, the First Lord of the Admiralty. Then he entered into calmer waters in what he took to be a large bay. He discovered a group of small islands in sheltered waters where he chose to anchor his ship. He did not know it at the time but he had crossed the straits destined to be named after him. He had landed on the South Island.

The *Endeavour* explored the bay. The crew discovered that it was not a bay but rather a sea passage between the North Island they had been charting and another landmass to the south. The *Endeavour* sailed through the straits. It was soon recognized that there were two islands and when they came out of the straits Cook first turned to the north to complete the circuit of the North Island. Then the ship turned to retrace her steps to survey and chart the South Island. It was probably Banks who insisted on calling the channel between the islands the Cook Straits, and it was probably Cook who insisted that a large island they passed later be called Banks' Island. It was a little unfortunate that it was not an island at all but was firmly joined to the land by a low hidden isthmus. The explorers were still confident that they were sailing along the coast of

On 5 May, as they weighed anchor, the sailors made a large catch of sting-ray in their nets. Cook thought to call the place Sting-Ray Harbour but he looked at his ecstatic botanists drying, pressing and arranging their specimens and he decided to call it Botany Bay.

the great southern continent. Then, as they encountered Stewart Island and discussed whether or not it joined the mainland, it was evident from the swell of the sea that there was no more land beyond. Sure enough, the coast ran to the west then turned sharply towards the north east. By March the *Endeavour* was sailing along the treacherous rocky western coast of the South Island, keeping a respectful distance away. By the end of March the ship was back again at the anchorage they called Queen Charlotte Sound. On 1 April the ship left New Zealand and the last sight of land was christened Cape Farewell.

Australia The discovery and the charting of New Zealand, together with the observation of the Transit of Venus, made the voyage into a great success. But more was to come. Cook knew that Abel Tasman had made another landing some distance to the west at a place he called Van Dieman's Land. Cook set his sails for the west in the hope of making more discoveries. The wind and the currents took him further north than he had intended, but as luck would have it the northerly course caused him to discover another new coastline. When dawn broke on 19 April the first lieutenant, Zachary Hicks, was at the lookout. He could see land to the north and he gave a great shout. Again, the land was not a small Pacific island; it soon became obvious that they had discovered a great landmass. They knew of the country called New Holland many miles to the west, but it was a barren country, nothing like the promising green landscape that now greeted them. Cook brought his ship in closer and he decided to follow the coastline to the east. Soon the lie of the land turned to the north as the *Endeavour* followed the coast. Cook was very keen to make a landing, but the bays were full of high surf and the rocks looked treacherous. He continued to the north and it was the end of April before he discovered a sheltered bay where the ship could anchor.

The captain rushed up through the hatch and onto the deck in his nightshirt. All around lay broken timbers of the ship. There was a great jagged hole in the side. The Pacific Ocean was pouring into the hold. The ship was sinking.

The water supply was poor but adequate. Some contact was made with the aboriginals but they were very shy and ran off as soon as Cook's men approached them. The botanists were delighted with the landing and with the new country. There were new specimens to be found everywhere they searched and although they saw very little wildlife some large mammals had left evidence of their existence behind them. Cook stayed for eight days. He would have liked to have stayed longer but he had an inkling that there was still a great deal of country to be explored to the north. On 5 May, as they weighed anchor, the sailors made a large catch of sting-ray in their nets. Cook thought to call the place Sting-Ray Harbour but he looked at his ecstatic botanists drying, pressing and arranging their specimens and he decided to call it Botany Bay. As they sailed from Botany Bay they noticed inlets that might lead to other sheltered harbours, Cook called one of the places Port Jackson but he did not stop to explore. As they departed the sun appeared from behind a rain cloud and Sydney Parkinson recorded 'Two of the most beautiful rainbows my eyes ever beheld. The colours were strong, clear and lively.' The inner rainbow was so bright that its reflection could be seen in the water.

Hidden Reefs The voyage to the north had everything the explorers and the scientists could wish for. There were new headlands and coastlines for the surveyors to plot. New animals and plants were found at every landing and the natural history collection continued to expand. But Cook knew the risk he was taking by keeping his ship too close to the shore. The broken water showed the existence of hidden reefs below the surface and he had to keep a lookout on the mast for every yard of the way; sometimes he had one of the ship's boats go in front of the *Endeavour* to look for danger. They crossed the Tropic of Capricorn and continued to the north. Cook retired for the night. It was 11 June, there was a full moon and the captain decided to sail on through the night. He retired to his bunk with instructions to call him in an emergency. The night progressed and all seemed well until there was a loud splintering crash and suddenly the ship was jolted to a halt. The *Endeavour* had struck a reef and the swell was causing the ship to rock up and down on the sharp coral, scraping the boards and planking. The captain rushed up through the hatch and onto the deck in his nightshirt. All around lay broken timbers of the ship. There was a great jagged hole in the side. The Pacific Ocean was pouring into the hold. The ship was sinking.

As he crossed the Indian Ocean he began to lose men daily. By the time he anchored at Cape Town he had lost over thirty of his crew. It was a terrible loss to the man who in more than two years at sea had not lost a single man to scurvy.

The guns, the ballast and all unwanted stores were unloaded. The boats were put out and as many hands as possible heaved at the oars. The ship refused to move. The pumps were manned and water was pumped out of the hold as every man on the ship, including the aristocratic Joseph Banks, took his turn at the handle. It made little difference and the ship stayed firmly on the reef. They waited for the tide to rise hoping that the higher water level would float the stricken ship. She still stubbornly refused to move. All hopes were put on the night tide, which some claimed was higher than the daytime tide. The capstan was manned and a rope taken to a fixed rock. Weary hands worked the pumps. Strong arms heaved on the oars. As many hands as could fit around the capstan heaved their weight. Joseph Banks conveys the fear of all on board:

The dreadful time now approachd and the anziety in every bodys countenance was visible enough: the capstan and Windlace were mannd and they began to heave: fear of death now stard us in the face; hopes we had none but of being able to keep the ship afloat till we could run her ashore on some part where out of her materials we might build a vessel large enough to carry us to the East Indies.

The *Endeavour* deigned to move a fraction. The slightest motion was enough to spur the men into a greater effort. At last the ship was coaxed off the sharp coral and into the open water. The relief was seen in every face as the ship was floating again.

Rest and Repairs The problems were not yet over. A sail was wrapped around the hull of the ship and used to fother the hole where the coral had done its worst. The *Endeavour* hobbled into a river estuary where she was heeled over for repairs. It gave the men a well-earned rest. The botanists were able to collect their specimens again. Banks' greyhound chased a kangaroo but lost the race in the bushy undergrowth. Cook now had a taste of how dangerous it was to sail so close to the Great Barrier Reef. The rest of the journey was strewn with dangerous reefs. At one point the ship was caught in a dead calm with a tidal rush carrying her rapidly towards certain death where the sea poured like a waterfall over the coral. At the last second came a breath of wind, described as a mere 'cat's paw' of air, which filled the sails for a few seconds and enabled the ship to get clear of the danger.

The *Endeavour* reached the northernmost point of Australia at Cape York. James Cook landed and took possession of the land in the name of King George III and called it New South Wales. He did not explain why North Wales had been ignored. After three more months of sailing the ship reached Batavia where at last she could be repaired – the shipwrights discovered that her keel was worn down to a thickness of a quarter inch in one place. The outpost of the Dutch Empire was planned as a Dutch city with canals and grand houses. In the heat of the tropics the stagnant water of the canals made an ideal breeding ground for the mosquito and Batavia was well known as a cesspool of malaria and tropical diseases. For the first time on the voyage Cook began to lose his seamen. He left Batavia at the earliest opportunity and he stopped at Princes Island to take on fresh provisions. He also took dysentery on board. As he crossed the Indian Ocean he began to lose men daily. By the time he anchored at Cape Town he had lost over thirty of his crew. It was a terrible loss to the man who in more than two years at sea had not lost a single man to scurvy.

It is an amazing fact that both New Zealand and Australia were discovered and charted in the same voyage. If the *Endeavour* voyage had been the only one made by James Cook then his place in history would be secure. But Cook went on to make two more, each of them almost as great as his first. In his second voyage he became the first explorer to take his ship into the Antarctic Circle. Over the course of three years he made three visits to the Antarctic seas and he effectively circumnavigated Antarctica at the very limits of the ice shelf. He disproved once and for all the existence of a habitable continent to the south of Australia. He penetrated at one point to an astonishing 71° south before he was forced to turn his ship in the bitter cold with her sails as hard as boards and the ropes frozen in the blocks. Much of Cook's second voyage was spent searching for lost islands in the Pacific such as Espiritu Santo discovered by the Spanish in the sixteenth century. He visited Easter Island, the Marquesas, the New Hebrides, New Caledonia and the Tonga Isles. Cook was able to find these specks of land in the Pacific, to map and chart them, and to measure with certainty their latitudes and longitudes.

After the return from his second voyage Cook was given an admiralty pension and a place at the Greenwich Hospital as a reward for his efforts. But he insisted on coming out of retirement to lead a third great voyage to the Pacific. This time the main object was to find the western end of the North West Passage. He sailed to the North Pacific and he charted the west coast of America. He took his ships around the icy seas of Alaska and through the Bering Straits. There he was met with a solid and impenetrable wall of ice making it impossible for his ships to enter the North West Passage. The voyage was not a failure for Cook made an important discovery in the North Pacific when he stumbled on the Hawaiian Archipelago. It is surprising that the Spanish had never discovered Hawaii; their treasure ships crossed regularly from the Philippines to Panama but for centuries they kept rigorously to their sailing instructions and their regular route.

There are good reasons for naming Cook as the greatest of all the maritime explorers. He was the first captain to know his position on the surface of the globe to within a few nautical miles. He completely solved the problem of scurvy. His maps and charts were exemplary and many were still in use hundreds of years after his death. He was an excellent disciplinarian and he always commanded respect from his men. He knew exactly when to take calculated risks. Perhaps most important of all, he had a great respect for the people of the islands he visited and he always knew how to get their co-operation. It was a great irony that on his final voyage, in one of the few mistakes he made, he was killed by the natives of Kealakekua Bay in Hawaii.

Minimal Losses In some respects, such as the finding of the longitude, he was very fortunate for both the theoretical and the practical methods came to fruition at the same time. On his first voyage he carried the nautical almanac and a professional astronomer to enable him to calculate his longitude from the observations of the Moon. On his second and third voyages he carried one of the earliest ship's chronometers, which told him the time at Greenwich wherever he was on the surface of the world. A simple measure of Cook's success as an explorer is the number of men he lost on his voyages. Apart from the crossing of the Indian Ocean on his first voyage his losses were

Portrait of Captain Cook by William Holl II, after the painting by Nathaniel Dance.

Cook was fortunate to be the first explorer to carry a chronometer on his ship, and hence he was able to provide accurate estimates of longitude for the first time. He mapped and charted a greater length of coastline in the Pacific Ocean than anyone before or since.

A simple measure of Cook's success as an explorer is the number of men he lost on his voyages. Apart from the crossing of the Indian Ocean on his first voyage his losses were minimal. No seaman ever died of the scurvy on Cook's voyages.

minimal. No seaman ever died of the scurvy on Cook's voyages. This was partly due to new knowledge about the cause of the disease and to his use of sauerkraut as a method of obtaining the necessary vitamin C. He also realized that to keep scurvy at bay fresh food was necessary and he planned his route to supply his ship with as much fresh fruit and vegetables as he could obtain, wherever he happened to be on the surface of the earth.

James Cook was a close and silent man, his one fault was that he would seldom if ever discuss problems with his officers. There were times when he was the only person on board who knew where the ship was sailing to next. He had a few close friends and he got on extremely well with Joseph Banks on his first voyage, which was a great credit to both men considering their widely different social backgrounds. He had a very loyal and long-suffering wife who three times waited three long years for him to return home from his voyages and who usually became pregnant soon after his return. On the third voyage he did not return. Elizabeth Cook bore him six children and she lived as a widow until her death fifty years later.

THE TRANSATLANTIC VOYAGES
OF GREED AND DESPAIR

THE SLAVE TRADE AND ITS ABOLITION

'The stoppage of all further importations from Africa… is the very shortest and safest path by
which the Slaves can travel to the enjoyment of their true liberty.'

WILLIAM WILBERFORCE, *A LETTER ON THE ABOLITION OF THE SLAVE TRADE*

Edward Colston was one of Bristol's greatest benefactors. He had endowed almshouses, schools and charities, not only in Bristol but in places as far afield as London, Surrey, Devonshire and Lancashire. 'This great and pious benefactor was known to have done many other excellent charities', reads his memorial.

'And what he did in secret is believed to be not inferior to what he did in public.' Are we allowed to ask what Edward Colston did in secret? Are we allowed to ask how he made his great wealth and how he came to be a great benefactor? In Colston's time it was no secret, but in later centuries very few asked the question. He owned sugar plantations in the West Indies and his vast fortune was built on the transatlantic slave trade. Edward Colston did more than any other man of his time to bring the slave trade to Bristol.

In Liverpool there is a memorial to Foster Cunliffe who was three times mayor of the thriving eighteenth-century seaport. He is described on his memorial as 'a merchant whose sagacity, honesty and diligence procured wealth and credit to himself and his country, a magistrate who administered justice with discernment, candour and impartiality. A Christian devout and exemplary.' Are we allowed to ask how Foster Cunliffe came to be so wealthy? Like Colston he believed himself to be engaged in a very respectable trade: the transportation of Africans torn forcibly from their homes to be transported in chains under appalling conditions to the other side of the Atlantic where they lived the rest of their lives as slaves.

In the seventeenth century London held a monopoly on the African slave trade and ports such as Bristol and Liverpool looked on with envy when they were not allowed to partake in the profits. In 1698 the embargo was lifted and several provincial ports immediately began trading to the African coast. Bristol was the best placed port to take advantage of the new laws and it took only two decades for Bristol to overtake London's dominant position in the trade, a place which she held for about three more decades until the middle of the eighteenth century. In the 1750s it was Liverpool that took the lead and which handled the bulk of the trade until abolition in 1807.

THE PLANTATION OWNERS

The plantation owners were amongst the wealthiest merchants in England and they socialized with the highest levels of society. They endowed schools and almshouses and many were devout Christians. They kept black servants whom they treated well. The source of their wealth was in a distant country and very few people witnessed the human sufferings from which they made their profits.

Triangular Voyage The transatlantic slave trade involved a triangular voyage. The first stage was from the home port with a cargo of manufactured goods. There were pots and pans, clothing and metal objects that would fetch a good price on the African market. The pots and pans were not new, they were mostly secondhand, collected from the market stalls. There are records of the dealers looking for holes in the pans and testing to see if they held water.

When they reached the African coast the slavers sold their wares and loaded up the ship with their human cargo. Press gangs were employed by the local slave dealers to roam the interior and to capture as many people as possible. Sometimes the gangs were able to take advantage of local feuds to capture Africans from neighbouring tribes. The slavers loaded their human cargo for the next leg of the voyage:

> *Deep freighted now with human merchandise,*
> *The vessel quits the shore; prepar'd to meet*
> *The storms, and dangers, of th' Atlantik main;*
> *Her motion scarce observ'd, save when the flood*
> *In frequent murmurs beats against her prow.*
>
> *Whilst groans and loud laments, and scalding tears,*
> *Mark'd the keen pangs of others. – Female shrieks,*
> *At intervals, in dreadful concert heard,*
> *To wild distraction manly sorrow turn'd;*
> *And ineffectual, o'er their heedless limbs,*
> *Was wav'd the wiry whip, that dropp'd with blood.*
>
> William Roscoe

Alexander Falconbridge, who was employed as one of the ship's surgeons, described the conditions between the decks as the slavers left Africa to take their live cargo to America:

...having occasioned the port-holes to be shut, and the grating to be covered, fluxes and fevers among the negroes ensued. While they were in this situation, my profession requiring it, I frequently went down among them, till at length their apartments became so extremely hot as to be only sufferable for a very short time. But the excessive heat was not the only thing that rendered their situation intolerable. The deck, that is the floor of their rooms, was so covered with blood and mucous which had proceeded from them in consequence of the flux, that it resembled a slaughter-house. It is not in the power of the human imagination to picture to itself a situation more dreadful or disgusting. Numbers of the slaves having fainted, they were carried up on deck, where several of them died and the rest were, with great difficulty, restored. It had nearly proved fatal to me...

Tobacco and Cotton The death rate amongst the Africans was very high. When at last they reached the sugar plantations in the West Indies, or in later years the tobacco and cotton plantations of the southern

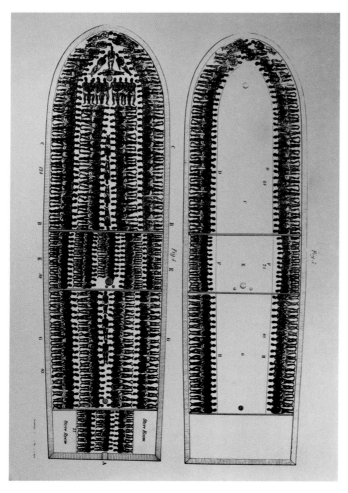

United States, the slaves were sold off to spend the rest of their lives working on the plantations. There are records of slaves bought for £3 or £4 in Africa and sold for £30 each on the plantations. The size of the ships varied greatly. Sometimes a merchantman would carry a few slaves for a small profit, but usually the whole ship was dedicated to slave transport. In the later years the largest slavers could carry as many as four hundred Africans in terrible conditions. Both the first legs of the voyage were very profitable but there was still more profit to be made. On the final leg across the Atlantic to Europe the ships carried sugar, rum and timber from the Caribbean. Tobacco was shipped from Virginia and in the later decades of the eighteenth century raw cotton was carried to Liverpool to feed the rapidly expanding mills of Lancashire.

A few slaves were carried on the third leg of the voyage. It became very fashionable for wealthy households to include at least one black servant in their retinue. In most cases they were very well treated. The general public was kept in ignorance of the appalling conditions in Africa and America. It did not last for ever; the sailors and the ships' surgeons were the only people who witnessed the horrors of the middle passage at first hand but soon the English middle classes were becoming more conscious of the dreadful sufferings of the blacks. Hannah More was born at Fishponds near Bristol. She received a good education and she was a great favourite of Samuel Johnson and his circle. It was Johnson who coined the phrase, 'how is it that we hear the loudest yelps for liberty amongst the driver of Negroes?' Soon men such as Thomas Clarkson and William Wilberforce became involved and a society was created for the abolition of slavery. Hannah More's poetry helped to bring attention to the problem:

When the slaving ships came to cross the Atlantic on the middle passage they were packed with as many bodies as the ship could carry. A large ship could carry as many as four hundred in dreadful conditions of squalor. The hold shown on page 153 was only 3 ft 3 inches in height. People in Europe did not see this leg of the voyage, neither did they see the conditions on the sugar and tobacco plantations.

> *When the fierce sun darts vertical his beams,*
> *And thirst and hunger mix their wild extremes;*
> *When the sharp iron wounds his inmost soul,*
> *And his strained eyes in burning anguish roll;*
> *Will the parch'd negro own, ere he expire,*
> *No pain in hunger, and no heat in fire?*

The Wrongs of Africa It was a long and protracted battle. Wilberforce brought forward bills for abolition in 1787 and again in 1791 – both were defeated in the Commons. In Liverpool William Roscoe spent thirty years fighting for abolition. In 1806 he was elected to represent Liverpool as a Member of Parliament and he had the satisfaction of voting in favour of the Abolition Bill. His two-part epic poem on 'The Wrongs of Africa' was written and published in the 1780s.

> *Ah! Why, ye sons of wealth, with ceaseless toil,*
> *Add gold to gold, and swell the shining pile?*
> *Your general course to happiness ye bend,*
> *Why then to gain the means neglect the end?*

THE MIDDLE PASSAGE

The middle passage involved the transportation of human cargo across the Atlantic in the most appalling conditions of squalor. Apart from the slaves themselves, the only people to witness the horrors of the voyage were the sailors and the ships' surgeons. We are indebted to men like Alexander Falconbridge, a surgeon, and John Newton, a slaving captain, for their descriptions of terrible middle passages. John Newton was completely reformed and became a vicar. He wrote some of our best loved hymns such as 'Amazing Grace' and 'How sweet the name of Jesus sounds'.

The abolition of transportation of slaves was not the end of slavery. John Gladstone, whose son William Gladstone became a greatly respected prime minister, owned extensive sugar plantations in Demerara. Gladstone claimed that his estate was 'proverbial for humanity'. It was impossible to find a plantation owner who did not echo the same sentiments. They all knew of other plantations where the slaves were badly treated but it was always somebody else who was guilty. The plantation owners had no problems in aligning their occupation with their religion; they were frequently devout churchgoers, respectable members of society, and from the tens of thousands of pounds they made by tearing Africans from their homes and putting them into slavery they gave a few hundred to the church. Their correspondence frequently refers to captives 'shipped by the grace of God' and phrases such as, 'God sent the ship to her desired port in safety'. They boasted that they paid for medical services to help the negroes, but the services were only provided when it was profitable for them to get a sick slave back to work again. John Pinney, a Bristol plantation owner, explained:

Avoid as much as possible the calling in of a Doctor to the Negroes; they are so exorbitant in their charges, it is impossible for an estate to support it. Simples, good nursing and kitchen physic are the only requisites to recover sick negroes; I was very successful in my practice, and have no doubt that you will be equally so.

Smallpox Epidemic Medical practice was very primitive, and still relied on eighteenth-century folklore rather than sound scientific knowledge, but when an epidemic of smallpox broke out on Pinney's plantation the isolation techniques were well known and slaves were innoculated against the disease. The incident serves as a good illustration of the hypocrisy of the slave dealers. The blacks responded to the vaccine in exactly the same way as the whites, yet the slavers frequently tried to justify their business with the pathetic excuse that the negroes were a different species from the whites. John Pinney does actually refer to them as 'human' flesh but he still tries to appease his conscience in a way that was typical of

WILLIAM WILBERFORCE AND THOMAS CLARKSON

The two most prominent abolitionists were William Wilberforce and Thomas Clarkson who both campaigned tirelessly to make the slave trade illegal. Wilberforce had connections in high places and he was a great friend of William Pitt the Younger. Clarkson went to great lengths to get information on the trade and he frequented the dockside pubs in Bristol and Liverpool to get information from the common sailors.

all the merchants in the trade. 'But surely God ordained them for ye use and benefit of us', wrote Pinney. 'Other[wi]se his Divine Will, would have been manifest by some particular Sign or Token.' The obvious signs of distress and suicide amongst the slaves were conveniently not seen as 'God's Sign or Token'.

The most active group against slavery were undoubtedly the Quakers. They included William Champion who withdrew from the sugar trade and sold off his lucrative plantations in the West Indies. The Quaker-controlled banks changed their policy and refused credit to companies directly involved in the slave trade. Thomas Clarkson was himself a Quaker and when the abolitionist movement gained ground Dr Long Fox and James Harford were just two of many Quakers who opposed slavery on the very just principle that it represented a gross violation of human rights.

A Million Slaves In 1790 Eli Witney invented the cotton gin, which was a simple device that could extract the seed from the lint by mechanical means. It meant that a plantation slave could produce fifty pounds of cotton per day instead of the one pound produced before the invention. Witney's cotton gin was widely plagiarized and he made nothing from it whereas the cotton magnates made a fortune from it. With this invention the manufacture of cotton became highly profitable and generated the Lancashire cotton industry which helped to fuel the industrial revolution. By 1810 the transportation of slaves was illegal but there were still a million slaves on the cotton plantations. The plantation owners could easily breed their own slaves to replace the old and infirm and, by the time of the American Civil War, there were four million slaves working on the plantations.

The transatlantic slave trade comprised many voyages. None of these journeys can be singled out as a great one. But if we are trying to identify voyages that changed the world then it has to be admitted that not all of them changed the world for the better. The story would be incomplete if we ignored them.

> Whene're to Afric's shores I turn my eyes,
> Horrors of deepest, deadliest guilt arise;
> I see, by more than Fancy's mirror shown,
> The burning village and the blazing town:
> I see dire victims torn from social life,
> The shrieking babe, the agonising wife;
> She, wretch forlorn! is dragg'd by hostile hands,
> To distant tyrants sold, in distant lands!
>
> Hannah More

John Harrison and the
search for Longitude

The dedicated watchmaker wins the £20,000 prize

1741 – 1773

'Two lunar months are past, and more,
Since of these heavens half a score
Set out to try their strength and skill,
And fairly start for Flamsteed Hill…
But take care Rev. Maskelyn,
Thou scientific harlequin,
Nor think, by jockeying to win…
For the great donor of the prize
Is just as Jove who rules the skies.'

'The Astronomical Racers' or 'Greenwich Ho' by CP

The problem of scurvy had plagued every long sea voyage since seafarers first gathered enough courage to leave the land behind them. It was well known in ancient times that the condition was a problem of diet.

The lack of vitamin C was not identified specifically until many years later, but the fact that scurvy was caused by a deficiency of fresh food was obvious. Sufferers recovered quickly when they came to land and when they were able to eat fresh fruit and vegetables. In the middle of the eighteenth century the problem was studied more methodically. Dr James Lind, an Edinburgh doctor, made a serious study of the disease and in 1754 he published his paper 'A Treaty on the Scurvy'. He chose to dedicate the book to George Anson who had lost so many men to the disease on his circumnavigation of the world a few years earlier.

James Lind knew that by giving the sailors citrus fruits, lemon juice and fresh vegetables in their diet it was possible to prevent the onset of scurvy. The problem was that the fruits did not keep long enough for a prolonged voyage and the disease reasserted itself when the fresh food ran out. Attempts were made to preserve the fruit by bottling. Unfortunately the idea did not work because Lind and others did not realize that vitamin C was destroyed by the boiling process used in the bottling. Lind's work had opened up other areas of research, however, and other foods emerged that contained the required vitamins and which could preserve them over the period of a long voyage.

Pickled Cabbage In 1768 when James Cook sailed from Plymouth in the *Endeavour* he carried 7860 pounds of a concoction called sauerkraut, a disgusting German dish of pickled cabbage which was strongly recommended in Dr Macbride's *Historical account of the New method of Treating the Scurvy at Sea*. Macbride thought he had solved the problem and Cook was eager to know if the sauerkraut really did keep the scurvy at bay. Getting the sailors to eat the pickled cabbage was another matter but Cook solved it by means of modern psychology:

The Sour Krout the men at first would not eat until I put in practice a method I never once knew to fail with seamen, and this was to have some of it dress'd every Day for the cabin Table, and permitted all the Officers without exception to make use of it and left it to the option of the Men either to take as much as they pleased or none at all; but this practice was not continued above a week before I found it necessary to put everyone on board to an Allowance, for such are the tempers and disposissions of Seamen in general that whatever you give them out of the Common way, altho it be ever so much for their good yet it will not go down with them and you will hear nothing but murmurings gainest the man that first invented it, but the Moment they see their Superiors set a value on it, it becomes the finest stuff in the World and the inventor a damn'd honest fellow.

From that time on scurvy was practically unknown on Cook's ships. There were odd incidents, such as on his second voyage when scurvy

broke out on his consort the *Adventure* but this was found to be the fault
of the unhygienic ship's cook who did not obey the captain's orders.

Transit of Mercury Another great advantage which James Cook enjoyed
over his predecessors was that he was able to find his longitude. On the
Endeavour voyage he carried with him the nautical almanac but he also
needed the expertise of the astronomer, Charles Green, who was one of
the few people at that time who knew how to find the longitude from the
position of the Moon. Cook quickly picked up the method and the
astronomer taught the ship's officers how to use the tables and how to
make the calculations. Thus the *Endeavour* has the distinction of
becoming the first ship to be able to calculate her position wherever she
was on the surface of the globe and Cook always knew his position in the
Pacific to within a few nautical miles. Charles Green used other
observations to check his longitude wherever possible. A good example
is the Transit of Venus which was observed at Tahiti. Another example is
a Transit of Mercury observed at Mercury Bay in
New Zealand. Charles Green was able to calculate
an accurate figure for the longitude of Mercury Bay
and Cook used it as a datum to correct the
longitudes on his chart of New Zealand.

*The Sour Krout the men at first
would not eat until I put in
practice a method I never once
knew to fail with seamen, and
this was to have some of it dress'd
every Day for the cabin Table,
and permitted all the Officers
without exception to make use of
it and left it to the option of the
Men either to take as much as
they pleased or none at all...*

The mapping of the world as a grid of
intersecting lines was first suggested in the ancient
world. The Greek astronomer Ptolemy was not the
first to suggest that the earth was a sphere. We must
give him the credit however, for suggesting that the
grid of lines that we know as latitude and longitude
was the best way of mapping a set of points on the
surface of a sphere. Thus the problem faced by the
geographer and the explorer was reduced to the
determination of latitudes and longitudes of points
on the surface of the earth.

Thus distances north and south of the equator could easily be
calculated even before the time of Christ. But what of the east/west
distance, the longitude? The first problem was to establish a zero
meridian to be used as a datum for east and west measurement. There
was no general agreement for this meridian and every country wanted to
use its own capital city as the zero. Distances around the Mediterranean
could be measured with comparative ease simply by pacing out the miles
and sometimes by triangulation. The longitude problem did not become
serious until ships began to explore outside the Mediterranean. In the
ancient world the ships did not stray far from land, but on the land
journeys to the far east the longitudes of places in China and Japan, for
example, were estimated with errors as much as 90° away from the true
values.

Galileo had observed the regular motion of the satellites of the planet
Jupiter and tables were constructed to predict the times when the
satellites entered the shadow of Jupiter – this would allow a navigator to
calculate the time at his zero meridian from anywhere on the Earth.

Galileo designed a special helmet for finding the longitude, with a telescope attached to one of the eyeholes. The satellites of Jupiter could be seen effectively on land, but on the swaying deck of a ship at sea, it was almost impossible to see them. The observation was so difficult that even Galileo had to admit that the pounding of the observer's heart could cause the whole of the planet to jump out of the telescope's field of view.

The French persevered with the method but the English decided to take another approach. The Moon was the most prominent object in the night sky and it moved across 12° of sky in the course of a day. All that was necessary was to produce tables showing the motion of the Moon. By observing the background stars nearest to the Moon its position in the sky could be calculated. The tables in the nautical almanac could then be used to calculate the time at Greenwich and hence the longitude. In daytime, if the Sun and the Moon were both visible in the sky, then all that was required was to measure the angular distance between them.

Jeremiah Horrocks The snag with the lunar method was not the observation, it was the complex motion of the Moon. The orbit of the Moon around the Earth, like the orbits of the planets around the Sun, was an ellipse with the Earth at one focus. But the Moon was also subjected to the gravity of the Sun, the ellipse was only an approximation and the properties of the ellipse varied as the Moon progressed in her orbit. In 1675 John Flamsteed was appointed as England's first Astronomer Royal. One of his main tasks was to measure the position of the Moon so that the constants of the orbit could be calculated. Flamsteed had discovered a text on the lunar motion written by the brilliant young astronomer Jeremiah Horrocks, better known for his observation of the Transit of Venus. He found that Horrocks' theory of the lunar motion was the best available at the time.

THE ROYAL GREENWICH OBSERVATORY

The Royal Greenwich Observatory was founded in 1675 with John Flamsteed as the first Astronomer Royal. The main purpose of the observatory was to solve the problem of finding the longitude at sea. The problem was so difficult that it taxed the minds of astronomers and mathematicians for generations. It was nearly a century before it was solved.

Thus the Royal Greenwich Observatory was established in 1675 and Flamsteed was given the job of making lunar observations. The great mathematician Isaac Newton tried to work out a better theory for the motion of the Moon, based on his inverse square law of gravitation. Newton failed as the problem involved the motion of three bodies, the Sun, the Earth and the Moon and it did not have a unique solution.

John Flamsteed was still working on the problem of the Moon at the time of his death. He was followed by Edmund Halley as Astronomer Royal. Halley was a brilliant astronomer but he did not see eye to eye with Flamsteed. He had spent many months at sea as captain of the *Paramour*. He explored the Atlantic Ocean and he produced navigational charts of the South Atlantic. When he returned to England Halley could swear as fluently as any seaman and this, together with his atheism, was too much for the devout and Puritanical Flamsteed.

As the eighteenth century progressed the longitude problem still remained unsolved, but in the 1750s a major advance was made by the

German mathematician Tobias Mayer who produced a more accurate theory. Eventually, in the 1760s, the first nautical almanac was published with instructions for finding longitude from the position of the Moon in the sky.

Board of Longitude At the same time as the astronomers were working on the final stages of the lunar motion, one man was devoting his life to solving the longitude problem by another method. The Board of Longitude offered a prize of £20,000, a fortune in the eighteenth century, to anybody who could build a clock to keep good time at sea or who could find the longitude by any suitable method. In 1693 at Foulby in Yorkshire a child called John Harrison was born. His father was a carpenter and the family moved to live at Barrow on Humber in Lincolnshire. As a child, young John was brought up to work in wood, and he was so precise with his woodwork that before the age of twenty he had built a working clock made almost entirely from wooden pieces.

When John Harrison heard about the Board of Longitude prize he devoted his whole life towards winning it. He travelled to London where he managed to get an audience with George Graham, the premier scientific instrument maker of the times. At first Graham thought Harrison to be some kind of crank, but soon he realized that the younger man had many ideas in his head for the new timekeeper and that he knew how to solve the problems involved. Graham ended up being so impressed that he gave Harrison a generous loan with instructions to repay the money as and when his finances allowed.

The first problem to be solved was to find a new regulating device. The pendulum was simple and accurate but it could not cope with the swaying of a ship at sea. Harrison devised a movement with oscillating brass weights and springs that worked on the moving deck of a ship. He knew that higher temperatures caused a clock to run more slowly because of the expansion of the metal parts. He experimented using a balance wheel made from a bi-metallic strip of brass and steel, cleverly arranged to retain the same radius when the temperature changed.

> **THE BOARD OF LONGITUDE PRIZE**
> On 22 October 1707 Sir Cloudesly Shovell was lost at sea in a great Atlantic storm with his fleet of five men-of-war. He took his flotilla to the west with no idea of their longitude. Four of the five ships were lost on the Scilly Isles and only two men survived from the four crews. Shipwrecks like these showed the necessity of improving navigation skills and seven years later the Longitude Act was passed, offering a prize of £10,000 for a method of finding the longitude to within one degree, £15,000 for a method to within two-thirds of a degree and £20,000 for a method accurate to half a degree.

Jealousy Harrison built four timekeepers in all. His first piece (H-1) was tested in May 1741 on a six week voyage to Lisbon and back. The outward voyage was made on the *Centurion*, which later became the flagship for Anson's voyage. The official certificate disclosed that on the return journey Harrison correctly located the Lizard when the official navigator, Roger Willis, believed the ship to be at Start Point, twenty-six miles to the east. The inventor was not offered the prize, the main reason being jealousy on the part of Neville Maskelyn who wanted to win the prize with his own method of lunars. The Board of Longitude was sufficiently interested to provide subsidies to Harrison and he persevered

*William Harrison declared that
according to the chronometer they
would sight the island of
Madeira the following day.
Captain Digges disagreed,
according to his traditional
method of dead reckoning
Madeira was still several days
sail away. He was willing to lay
a bet on his opinion.*

with his ideas for more than twenty years. He produced a second chronometer (H-2) in 1741 but for some reason it was never tested at sea.

It took Harrison until 1759 to produce his third chronometer (H-3). The reason why it took him so long was that he kept encountering new ideas and improvements as he was working on it. Consequently Harrison's fourth chronometer (H-4) was completed only a year later in 1760. The Board of Longitude decided to test the two chronometers together.

After a lengthy delay the chronometer H-4 was taken on board HMS *Deptford* and the third chronometer H-3 was removed from the running. Everything depended on H-4. The *Deptford* set sail for Jamaica under Captain Dudley Digges with William Harrison, son of John Harrison, as curator of the chronometer. When they were well out in the Atlantic there was a major crisis when the beer was found to be unfit for human consumption. To the dismay of the sailors the beer had to be thrown overboard and they were reduced to drinking water. William Harrison declared that according to the chronometer they would sight the island of Madeira the following day. Captain Digges disagreed, according to his traditional method of dead reckoning Madeira was still several days sail away. He was willing to lay a bet on his opinion.

The next morning Madeira was sighted. Digges was a good loser. He was very impressed and he offered to buy the next chronometer made by the Harrisons. He wrote to John Harrison with the news:

> *Dear Sir,*
> *I have just time to acquaint you with the great perfection of your watch in making the island on the Meridian; According to our log we were one degree 27 minutes to the Eastward, this I made by a French map which lays down the longitude in Teneriffe, therefore I think your watch must be right.*
> *Adieu.*

Prizewinner Harrison's fourth chronometer led to an error of only one mile in the test voyage to Jamaica – easily close enough to win the prize. On a second voyage to Barbados three years later the watch did not perform quite as well but the error was still less than ten miles. In 1765 Harrison was paid only half the £20,000 reward but, although he had clearly met the requirements, he did not receive the other half until after a protracted legal wrangle that was settled by a private Act in 1773. Even then it needed the intervention of the king before Harrison could be paid. The problem was that the Board of Longitude was mainly comprised of jealous astronomers and mathematicians who thought that their own method of lunars was the solution to the problem.

An exact duplicate of Harrison's fourth chronometer was made by Larcum Kendall for the Admiralty at a cost of £450. The cost of

The H4 chronometer. This is Harrison's prize-winning longitude watch. Harrison had been working on improving watches as a sideline to his development of the much larger H3. In 1753 a pocket watch was made to Harrison's design by watchmaker John Jefferys. This went so well that Harrison began to realize that it pointed to the longitude solution - not in H3 but in smaller watches. Work began on H4 in 1755 and, with its very stable, high frequency balance, it proved to be the successful design.

manufacturing the chronometers came down quickly and a few years later Earnshaw, the inventor of a modified design, was producing chronometers for less than a tenth of Kendall's price.

When James Cook embarked on his second voyage with two ships and two astronomers he carried Larcum Kendall's chronometer with him. He also carried a chronometer by John Arnold made along similar lines but different principles. At first Cook did not trust his chronometers but by the time he had reached Cape Town he realized that they were in fact very reliable and that they were both keeping excellent time. From that time onwards the ship's chronometer became the most accurate and simplest method of finding longitude at sea; the only problem with them was the high cost and the difficulty of manufacture.

THE FIRST FLEET
ARRIVES AT BOTANY BAY

THE CREATION OF A PENAL COLONY IN AUSTRALIA

1788

'It is a very pretty spot and will speedily improve in appearance as the land is cleared.
There is no very elevated land around this port, but it is sufficiently diversified by
green hills and valleys to give it a highly picturesque and pleasing aspect.
The more I see of the harbour, the better I am satisfied and delighted with it...'

LETTERS FROM PORT ESSINGTON 1838. WRITTEN BY SIR GORDON BREMER FROM HMS ALLIGATOR

One of the many problems created by the American War of Independence was that the British could no longer conveniently dispose of their unwanted convicts to the American colonies. They looked around for an alternative place to send them.

It was very fortunate that James Cook had discovered and charted the east coast of Australia, to which he had given the name New South Wales for although it meant making a journey halfway round the world it did provide a solution to the problem. A decision was taken to send out a fleet of ships to create a convict settlement at Botany Bay, the place where Cook's ship the *Endeavour* had landed in 1770. It was the largest fleet ever assembled to create a new colony from scratch on the other side of the world.

The British government provisioned nine ships to carry 759 convicts, of which about 160 were women. Two escort ships, the *Syrius* and the *Supply*, were provided for defence and navigation. In addition to the convicts there were about 250 free men and women on the voyage. Some of these were marines who would be responsible for the convicts when they arrived, but a handful of the passengers were families who had signed on for the voyage hoping to make a new life in the new country.

The eleven vessels arrived at Portsmouth on 16 March 1787. The ships were loaded and inspected and they were made ready to take to sea for the long voyage ahead. The passengers waited on board for the arrival of Captain Arthur Phillip who was to go out as governor of the new colony. The First Fleet left England on 13 May 1787 for what they called the 'lands beyond the seas'. The fleet stopped at Tenerife, then it crossed the Atlantic to Rio de Janeiro. It looked at this point as though they intended to enter the Pacific by the traditional route around Cape Horn, but next we find them at Cape Town taking on provisions for the last leg of the voyage. The fleet became spread out a little with the leaders two days ahead of the stragglers but they arrived at Botany Bay between 18 and 20 January 1788. Twenty-three lives were lost on the voyage from England, but this was seen as a low death rate compared to some of the later voyages.

James Cook had identified Botany Bay as a suitable place to make a settlement but the site was found to be far from ideal. When the First Fleet arrived they found the area was much too open to the sea, there was no suitable supply of fresh water and the land was not the best for agriculture. Whilst they were debating amongst themselves about what to do next a surprising event occurred. Two large ships appeared in Botany Bay flying the French flag.

French Claim Thwarted The French ships were under the command of Jean-François de Galoup, better known as the Comte de La Pérouse. His ships were called the *Astrolabe* and the *Boussole* and they were both 500 tons. They were fitted out in the grand style and manned by 114 sailors plus several scientists, a physicist, three draftsmen, three naturalists, several clergymen and a mathematician. La Pérouse was a French explorer and a naval officer who had served his country against the British in Canada where, in 1785, he had captured two forts on the Hudson Bay. The French king commissioned him to lead an expedition to explore the Pacific Ocean. His mission was to investigate whaling and fur prospects and at the same time to establish French claims in areas where there were no other claimants. The expedition had already made an extensive mapping of the North American west coast from Alaska to Monterey in California, they had also charted some of the Russian coast on the Siberian peninsula of Kamchatka. They had visited the islands of Hawaii. La Pérouse had read the published accounts of Cook's voyages and he greatly admired the Englishman. The *Endeavour* voyage was one reason why, when he came to the southern hemisphere, La Pérouse sought out Botany Bay. The Frenchman was under orders from his superiors to make claim to lands in the Pacific. It was therefore with great trepidation that the British witnessed the untimely arrival of the two well-armed ships bristling with gun power superior to their own.

The fears of the British were unfounded. There was to be no confrontation. Le Comte de La Pérouse was a gentleman. He accepted that he had arrived at Botany Bay just five days too late to make his claim. Governor Arthur Phillip entertained the French on his own ship and the hospitality was reciprocated. Then La Pérouse sailed off into the Pacific with his two ships. He disappeared over the horizon and he was never seen again!

Sydney Harbour The British settlers explored the land around Botany Bay. They decided to move a few miles from Botany Bay to Port Jackson – better known as Sydney Harbour. The latter seemed to have better land and it certainly had a far superior natural harbour than Botany Bay. In fact Sydney Harbour was one of the finest harbours in the world but on his *Endeavour* voyage Cook had failed to discover it. An improved site had been found for the new settlement, but, from the start, the new venture was beset with problems. Few of the convicts knew anything at all about farming and when they tried to grow crops, the soil around Port Jackson was not found to be significantly more fertile than that at Botany Bay. Everyone, from the convicts to Governer Phillip, was on rationed food. In July the nine carrier ships returned to England leaving the settlement with just the two naval vessels *Syrius* and *Supply* to support them. These two ships were sorely needed.

The Australian aboriginals were wary of the new settlers and they kept their distance. They feared that it was only a matter of time before the newcomers took over all the inhabitable land and, in this, they were soon justified. The aboriginals subsisted on local plants and fish, but the settlers did not think much to these local delicacies. The settlers were poor fishermen and poor farmers, most of the food therefore had to come from the supplies brought with them on the ships. Dogs, crows, an occasional kangaroo and sometimes the rats were to be used to supplement the food. It was a very limited supply. Shelter was also a problem. They had very little in the way of building materials; the government had provided a supply of tools but these were not of high quality. There were plenty of eucalyptus trees for felling but they were huge and old, the tools were soon blunted and broken when trying to cut the hard wood. There was little in the way of extra clothing. It was hard to see how the colony was going to survive.

In October the *Syrius* was despatched to Cape Town to buy more provisions for the colony. It was May 1789 before she returned and in February the following year she had to sail all the way to China on another mission to bring more supplies.

Then came another crisis. On 19 February 1790 the *Syrius* was wrecked off Norfolk Island and the colony was left with just one ship. Everything now depended on the *Supply*. This time it was decided that she should sail to Batavia to get more food and supplies. The situation was becoming desperate, and there was only enough of the staple foods to last three more months. On 17 April the *Supply* set sail, leaving behind a few hundred very anxious settlers. It was a very difficult time – the first settlement in Australia was in danger of failing through starvation.

But things were not as bad as they seemed and soon there came a very welcome development. A ship called the *Lady Juliana* arrived carrying 225 women to join the male-dominated colony. Seventeen days later came a second ship, the *Justinian*, loaded with much-wanted food and supplies.

The problems were not over, but after more than two years of isolation and near starvation, the colony at Sydney Cove in Port Jackson at last began to expand. The settlement survived, it soon became self-supporting and with the help of the new arrivals the first children were born and the population began to grow. It was the first settlement in Australia and partly because of that it also became the largest.

In the early days of the settlement the south coast of Australia was still largely unknown. Ships heading for Port Jackson sailed at high latitudes to clear Tasmania before heading north to Sydney Harbour. It was not until 1795 that two Lincolnshire men, Matthew Flinders and George Bass first explored the seas to the north of Tasmania in Flinders' ship, the *Investigator*. Together with his famous cat, Trim, he mapped the south east coast of Australia and circumnavigated Tasmania. The two men discovered that Tasmania was separated from the Australian mainland by a strait that became known as the Bass Strait. The discovery of this sea passage cut several days off the time taken to reach Sydney.

Flinders sailed again from England for Australia in 1801. He surveyed the entire southern coast, from Cape Leeuwin in the south west to the Bass Strait. Then on 22 July, 1802 he sailed north from Sydney and charted the east coast of Australia, around Cape York and into the Gulf of Carpentaria on the north coast. Continuing westward and southward, he circumnavigated Australia and reached Port Jackson again on 9 June, 1803. In October, on the voyage back to England, the condition of his ship

MATTHEW FLINDERS

Matthew Flinders was born at Donnington in Lincolnshire. He entered the Royal Navy in 1789 and in 1795 he sailed to Australia, where he explored and charted the south east coast and circumnavigated the island of Tasmania. In 1801, as commander of the *Investigator*, he again sailed from England to Australia. On this visit he surveyed the entire southern coast, from Cape Leeuwin, in the south west to the Bass Strait, which runs between mainland Australia and Tasmania. In July 1802 he sailed from Port Jackson in Sydney; he charted the east coast of Australia and the Gulf of Carpentaria on the north coast. Continuing westward and southward, he circumnavigated Australia and reached Port Jackson again on 9 June, 1803.

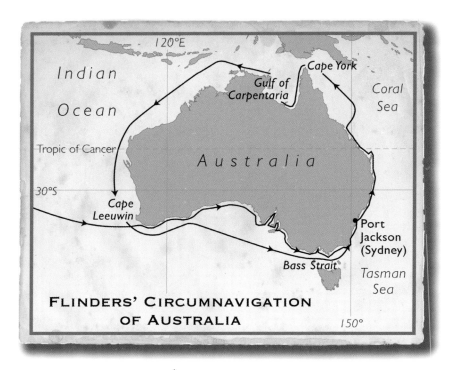

**FLINDERS' CIRCUMNAVIGATION
OF AUSTRALIA**

required him to stop at the Île de France (now Mauritius) in the western Indian Ocean. There he was interned by the French authorities for seven years and he was not allowed to leave for England until 1810.

Flinders is credited with calling the new land Australia where New Holland and New South Wales had always been used before his time. After the voyages of Matthew Flinders the whole coastline of Australia was known for the first time. Flinders' other great contribution to navigation was the introduction of the 'Flinders' Bar'. Ships were being built using more and more metal in their construction and he realized that the metal tended to affect the compass needle so that it gave spurious readings. His solution was to introduce a small magnet set near the compass needle and positioned to counterbalance the magnetic effects of the ship.

The story of the First Fleet to Botany Bay cannot be concluded without a reference to the fate of the expedition of La Pérouse. When the French found that their ships were missing they sent out a search party to follow their last known movements. Bruni d'Entrecasteaux made an extensive search in the neighbourhood of the Solomon Islands, but he could find no sign of La Pérouse or his ships. Further searches were made in the area but the two ships seemed to have disappeared completely and for nearly forty years their fate remained a mystery. Then, in 1827, an English captain and adventurer called Peter Dillon found evidence from the local people in Santa Cruz that the *Boussole* and the *Astrolabe* had both been seen near Vanikoro, one of the Santa Cruz Islands which are now included as part of the Solomon Islands. The French went to see for themselves and in the following year the French explorer Dumont d'Urville discovered the wreckage of two ships. Sure enough they were the missing expedition of La Pérouse. There were still a few elderly people on Vanikoro who remembered what had happened there forty years earlier. It was not a happy story; d'Urville learnt from the islanders that about thirty men from the ships had been massacred as they stepped on shore. He discovered that others who were better armed had managed to escape to one of the other islands. It seemed they had not survived. Nothing more was known about them.

Enterprising People The settlement at Sydney grew from strength to strength. Penal settlements were made in other places such as Queensland, Van Dieman's Land (i.e. Tasmania), Western Australia and Victoria but in all these places the number of free emigrants quickly exceeded the convicts. By 1847 the convict population of Sydney was about 3.2 per cent and opportunities in the new country were plentiful and enterprising people were making their fortune through sheep farming and agriculture.

Farmers and graziers began to fill out an arc of 200 miles radius around Sydney; in 1829 this area was designated as the Nineteen Counties. Following the discovery of Bass Strait new settlements were established in southern Australia in order to secure the southern waterways. In January 1827 Edmund Lockyear began a permanent settlement at Albany, Western Australia. By this time Britain had extended its possession over the whole of the continent, but they were still fearful of French or even American intervention. Lockyear's instructions stated that at this time Britain claimed all of Australia. Transportation was abolished in 1853 and the Australian Federation was created in 1901.

It was not a happy story; d'Urville learnt from the islanders that about thirty men from the ships had been massacred as they stepped on shore. He discovered that others who were better armed had managed to escape to one of the other islands. It seemed they had not survived.

CHARLES DARWIN AND THE VOYAGE OF THE *BEAGLE*

THE EXPEDITION THAT LED TO THE THEORY OF EVOLUTION

1831

'Wherever the European has trod, death seems to pursue the aboriginal.
We may look to the wide extent of the Americas, Polynesia,
the Cape of Good Hope and Australia, and we find the same result.'

CHARLES DARWIN, 1836, *THE VOYAGE OF THE BEAGLE*

*We have crossed the equator, and I
have undergone the disagreeable
operation of being shaved.* About nine
o'clock this morning we poor 'griffins', two
and thirty in number, were put together on
the lower deck.

*The hatchways were battened down, so we
were in the dark and very hot. Presently, four
of Neptune's constables came to us and one by
one led us on deck. I was the first and escaped
easily: I nevertheless found this watery ordeal
very disagreeable. Before coming up the
constable blindfolded me and, thus led along,
buckets of water were thundered all around. I
was then placed on a plank, which could be
easily tilted up into a large bath of water. Then they lathered my face and mouth
with pitch and paint, and scraped some of it off with a roughened iron hoop. A signal
being given, I was tilted head over heels into the water, where two men received me and
ducked me. At last, glad enough, I escaped. Most of the others were treated much
worse, dirty mixture being put in their mouths and rubbed on their faces. The whole
ship was a shower bath, and water was flying about in every direction. Of course not
one person, even the Captain, got clear of being wet through...*

The writer was Charles Darwin. The location was a point on the Equator
in the Atlantic Ocean. The ship was the *Beagle*. The captain was Robert
Fitzroy.

Flora and Fauna The expedition which set sail in 1831 was bound for
Tierra del Fuego, from there to Patagonia and afterwards to the
Galapagos Islands. The British Admiralty wanted an accurate survey of
the islands around Cape Horn and although Fitzroy had carried one out
only a few years previously he had been given instructions to return
again and to make a more detailed report. After much deliberation, the
Admiralty had agreed to allow a naturalist to sail on the expedition. His
mission was to study the flora and fauna of South America and in
particular that of Patagonia.

On his previous visit to Tierra del Fuego one of Fitzroy's boats had
been stolen and he had taken a group of Fuegians as hostage to try and
recover it. He was a deeply religious man and he ended up by taking the
hostages back to England with a view to educating them and giving them
religious instruction at his own expense. Thus, on board the *Beagle* were
three Fuegians with the curious names of York Minster, Jemmy Button
and Fuegia Basket. The first was named after the Cape where he was
found and, although this seems to put a very low value on human life,
the other two were named after the items of merchandise for which they
were traded. The Fuegians had been torn out of their natural
environment, but they had picked up a good understanding of English
and had been well-treated by Robert Fitzroy who was determined to take
them back and return them to their home and family. The *Beagle* also
carried on board a missionary, a Mr Matthews by name, who was to
remain on Tierra del Fuego, to set up a mission and to spread the gospel.
Fitzroy was a competent captain, but as the voyage progressed he
became aware that his naturalist Charles Darwin held some very
unconventional views. Frictions sometimes surfaced between them:

Fitzroy's character was a singular one, with many very noble features; he was devoted to his duty, generous to a fault, bold, determined and indomitably energetic, and an ardent friend to all under his sway. He would undertake any sort of trouble to assist those whom he thought deserved assistance. He was a handsome man, strikingly like a gentlemen with highly courteous manners, which resembled those of his old uncle the famous Lord Castlereagh… (but…) Fitzroy's temper was a most unfortunate one, and was shown not only by passion, but by fits of long continued moroseness against those who had offended him. His temper was usually worst in the early morning, and with his eagle eye he could generally detect something amiss about the ship, and was then unsparing in his blame. The junior officers when they relieved each other in the forenoon used to ask whether 'much hot coffee had been served out this morning?' which meant 'how was the captain's temper?'

Charles Darwin spent seven years of his twenties sailing round the world in the BEAGLE. *He returned home and developed an incredible scientific theory which changed the way the world was perceived.*

Charles Darwin was aged twenty-two at the start of the voyage. Two of his shipmates, the lieutenants John Wickham and James Sulivan, were of a similar age and in the small confines of the *Beagle* the three formed a firm friendship. 'Wickham is a glorious fellow', wrote Darwin, 'By far the most conversible person on board. I do not mean [he] talks most, for in that respect Sulivan quite bears away the palm.' Wickham loved to rag Darwin, he called him the 'philosopher' and sometimes the 'fly catcher' and he good-naturedly complained of the way the ship was always littered with bugs, beetles and biological specimens belonging to his shipmate.

New Life Forms

The *Beagle* called at Rio de Janeiro and later at Montevideo. Darwin was in his element at every landing as he studied the natural history and discovered new life forms. The ship arrived offshore from Patagonia and then proceeded to Tierra del Fuego. Then came the main object of the expedition began – the mapping and charting of the complex group of islands around Cape Horn and of the southern coastline of South America, both Atlantic and Pacific. It was not long before Cape Horn was rounded and nearby the explorers discovered a sea passage that became known as the 'Beagle Passage'; it was a long straight channel with glorious scenery and rugged mountains on all sides.

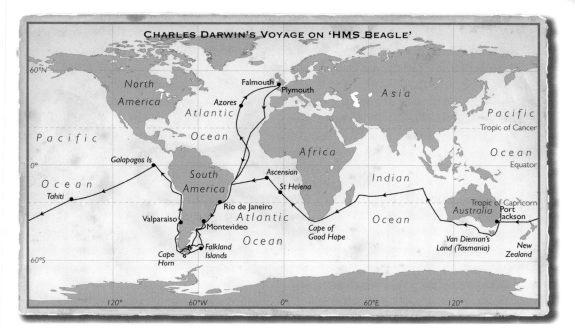

It offered an alternative but slower route from the Atlantic to the Pacific. On shore a lot of time was spent with the Fuegians. Communication was good as Jemmy Button and York Minster quickly proved their worth as interpreters. The Fuegians were an ugly race however, and they made themselves even less attractive by their habit of smearing their bodies with evil smelling oils and their practice of resorting to cannibalism when food supplies were short:

They are excellent mimics: as often as we coughed or yawned, or made any odd motion, they immediately imitated us. Some of our party began to squint and look awry; but one of the young Fuegians (whose face was painted black, excepting a white band across his eyes) succeeded in making far more hideous grimaces. They could repeat with perfect correctness every word in any sentence we addressed them, and they remembered such words for some time...

The missionary was given a primitive house in one of the coves where he was to set about his thankless task of converting the heathen. It was just as well that the *Beagle* returned a few days later to find out how he fared in what was an impossible task. The Fuegians were completely unable to comprehend Mr Matthews or the message he was trying to put across to them. They gave him no respect at all, they had stolen all they could of his possessions and left him to his own resources. He would certainly have suffered a terrible fate had he not been rescued in time.

Fossil Finds The survey work took the best part of a year but Darwin was not concerned. He was happy to explore the islands and the mountains with his companions, always studying the plant and animal life. He was interested too in the geology and he studied the volcanic rock formations intently. He climbed the mountains and he was particularly fascinated by his fossil finds at high altitude in the Andes. He wondered at how the fossils of sea creatures could appear thousands of feet above sea level. His head was full of strange thoughts about the origins of life. New ideas were always formulating and fermenting in his mind.

During the voyage the *Beagle* made two visits to the Falkland Islands. The ship spent more time at the southern tip of America than any ship before her and she seemed to make light of the stormiest seas in the world, but at last in June 1834 she rounded Cape Horn for the last time and sailed northwards along the coast of Patagonia and Chile. There was still a lot of surveying to be done. There was a stop at Valparaiso but again Darwin was able to explore and to collect specimens. He was very taken with a humming bird of the *Trochilus Gigas* genus.

I never saw any other bird, where the force of its wings appeared (as in a butterfly) so powerful in proportion to the weight of its body. When hovering by a flower, its tail is constantly expanded and shut like a fan, the body being kept in a nearly vertical position. This action appears to steady and support the bird, between the slow movements of its wings. Although flying from flower to flower in search of food, its stomach generally contained abundant remains of insects, which I suspect are much more the object of its search than the honey. The note of this species, like that of nearly the whole family, is extremely shrill.

Chilean Earthquake On 20 February 1835 Darwin witnessed what was claimed to be the largest earthquake ever recorded in Chile. He was on the beach at the time and he felt the ground rocking for a full two minutes. The shaking of the ground was so intense that he could not stand upright until the tremor stopped. He took a boat to the village of Talcahuano and from there he rode to another village called Conception. Both villages were utterly destroyed by the earthquake, there were nearly a hundred dead and all the houses had collapsed into ruins. 'It is the most awful spectacle I have ever beheld', he wrote to his sister Caroline. 'The town of Conception is now nothing more than piles and lines of bricks, tiles and timbers. It is absolutely true that there is not one house left habitable; some little hovels built of sticks and reeds in the outskirts of the town have not been shaken down, and these are now hired by the richest people.' Several aftershocks followed, and then he saw a great wave out at sea rapidly approaching the bay. It was a tsunami with a vertical wall of water measuring twenty-three feet. The ship must have been some distance out to sea and it had managed to survive the tsunami. Darwin and his party stayed to render what help they could to the local people but they could not stay long before the *Beagle* was on her way again.

Soon the ship was approaching the next object of the survey – the archipelago of Galapagos. Here Charles Darwin immediately came into his element. With wonder and fascination he studied the terrifyingly ugly but docile iguanas – the scaly black lizards that climbed on the rocky basaltic outcrops. He looked with wonder at the giant tortoises, which marched in file along the well-worn tracks through the foliage of the island to get to the fresh water supplies. He sketched the finches as they prised open seedpods with their beaks. His sketches identified thirteen species of finch and four sub species.

As I was walking along I met two large tortoises each of which must have weighed at least two hundred pounds. One was eating a piece of cactus, and as I approached, it stared at me and slowly stalked away; the other gave a deep hiss, and drew in its head. These huge reptiles surrounded by the black lava, the leafless shrubs, and large cacti, seemed to my fancy like some antediluvian animals. The few dull coloured birds cared no more for me, than they did for the great tortoises.

THE GALAPAGOS ISLANDS

The Galapagos Islands are volcanic and they are changing very rapidly in geological terms. Charles Darwin was easily able to recognize variations of the same species on the different islands. This gave him the idea that each species could evolve to suit its own environment but he progressed to the much greater idea of the evolution of species through natural selection.

Giant Tortoises The party was well entertained by the governor of the Galapagos Islands. The vice-governor of the islands, Mr Lawson, explained how the giant tortoises varied between islands. He described how the shape of the shell differed and the length of the neck and limbs. He claimed that he could tell from the shell which tortoises came from which island. This was one of the key pieces of information that helped Darwin to formulate his theory. The tortoises, although they lived so near to each other, were unable to cross between islands to interbreed. On some of the islands they had to reach high to obtain their food. On other islands they had no need to crane their necks and they adapted differently to the local environment. The result was that the tortoises from different islands evolved with different shapes of shell.

Then he studied the finches again. They could fly, but only rarely and under exceptional conditions did they cross to neighbouring islands. The food supplies differed slightly on each island and the beaks of the finches had adapted to the island on which they lived. Every creature seemed to have adapted to suit its own specific environment. Charles Darwin began to wonder about the origins of life on the planet:

'Hence, both in space and time, we seem to be brought somewhat near to that great act – that mystery of mysteries – the first appearance of new beings on this earth...'

The archipelago is a little world within itself, or rather a satellite attached to America, when it has derived a few stray colonists, and had received the general character of its indigenous productions. Considering the small size of these islands, we feel the more astonished at the number of their aboriginal beings, and at their confined range. Seeing every height crowned with its crater, and the boundaries of most of the lava streams still distinct, we are led to believe that within a period, geologically recent, the unbroken ocean was here spread out. Hence, both in space and time, we seem to be brought somewhat near to that great act – that mystery of mysteries – the first appearance of new beings on this earth...

Mystery of mysteries – the first appearance of life on earth. The light was dawning in the mind of Charles Darwin! He knew that he had been lucky enough to uncover one of the great secrets of nature. The multitude of life

He started to write his great book THE ORIGIN OF SPECIES *but he was some years away from publication when he received a letter from another naturalist, Alfred Russel Wallace, who set out his own ideas very precisely – Wallace had independently come to the same conclusions as Darwin.*

forms evolved with their environment. Minor changes, if they were beneficial, were passed on to subsequent generations. Evolution was driven by a process of natural selection, those creatures best adapted to their environment were more likely to survive and therefore their offspring, with the same inherited characteristics, were also more likely to survive.

The *Beagle* stayed only thirty-five days at the Galapagos Islands. Then she sailed for Tahiti. She stopped at New Zealand and also at Port Jackson in Australia. Then she sailed to Cape Town and from there the long haul across the Atlantic back to the British Isles. All the way back home Charles Darwin was thinking and developing his ideas, applying his theory of natural selection to all the data he had collected and to all the species he could think of. The story was there in the fossils, the insects, the reptiles, the sea creatures, the mammals and the primates. The whole panorama of life fitted together into a stupendous family tree. The big question in his mind was that if the different species had evolved by the process of natural selection, then where did man fit onto the evolutionary tree? There could be no doubt that man too had evolved in the same way as all the other species. But the answer to the question would rock nineteenth-century beliefs to their very foundations. There could be no doubt in Darwin's theory that the ancestors of modern man were the apes!

But Charles Darwin knew that the world was not ready for such a momentous theory. It would destroy the very foundations of the Bible and it would shake the fabric of Victorian society. For years and years he developed his ideas. He found more and more evidence to support his theory and communicated his findings to a few close friends. He started to write his great book, *The Origin of Species,* but he was some years away from publication when he received a letter from another naturalist, Alfred Russel Wallace, who set out his own ideas very precisely – Wallace had independently come to the same conclusions as Darwin. The two men came to an agreement to publish a joint paper on the subject.

It was in 1860 at the British Association for the Advancment of Science meeting in Oxford that Darwin's ideas were fully debated by the scientific community – Thomas Henry Huxley was prominent in the defence of Darwin's theory of evolution. The angry reaction from the established Church was exactly as Darwin had predicted. The cartoonists had a field day and they represented Darwin as the ape which he claimed was his ancestor.

Did the voyage of the *Beagle* change the world? In many senses it changed the world more than any other in history. The voyage of the *Beagle* and its earth-shattering findings will be remembered for all time.

ISAMBARD KINGDOM BRUNEL AND THE RACE ACROSS THE ATLANTIC

THE FIRST GREAT STEAMSHIPS COMPETE TO REACH NEW YORK

1830 – 1865

'Why not make it longer, and have a steamboat go from

In 1819 a curious vessel arrived in the River Mersey. Her name was the *Savannah* and she had crossed the Atlantic from the port of that name in the United States of America. Her lines were those of the classical three-master, but they were broken by a pair of paddle wheels and a black boiler with a curious bent smokestack protruding from it.

The *Savannah*, the Americans claimed, was the first ship to cross the Atlantic powered by steam. It was obvious to all who saw her that she could have crossed the Atlantic without even lighting the boiler. On further investigation the captain admitted that the crossing took twenty-seven days and that the paddles had been in use for only eighty-five hours in that time.

It was not until the 1830s that the British first became interested in the idea of crossing the Atlantic under steam. The main instigator was the charismatic engineer Isambard Kingdom Brunel. At a meeting of the Great Western Railway he suggested that the railway could be effectively continued across the Atlantic by building a steamship that could carry sufficient coal to power the ship from Bristol to New York. Brunel had little problem finding backers for his scheme.

Brunel's ship was called the *Great Western*. She was built in Bristol at Patterson's Dock on the Floating Harbour and the launching ceremony took place on 19 July 1837. She left Bristol on 18 August and proceeded by tugboat and sail around Land's End, along the English Channel and into the Thames at Blackwall where her engines were to be fitted. The Londoners flocked to see her, they admired her great length of 236 feet, her four masts, her paddle wheels which were nearly thirty feet in diameter, her seventy-five-foot-long grand saloon, and her lavish décor. On her bow was a gilded figure of Neptune with a dolphin on each side.

The Race is On There were some however, who were not so pleased to see this great ship being fitted out on the Thames. If Brunel was planning to make the first Atlantic crossing under steam then why should Bristol have the honour of being first when London could just as easily claim the honour? There were others further north who had similar thoughts and, soon afterwards, Liverpool too began to consider making an attempt to claim the prize. Soon there was a race on between the three leading British ports for the honour of the first steam-powered Atlantic crossing.

The Londoners began work on a ship called the *British Queen* and the keel was laid down at Limehouse. In Liverpool the steamship *Liverpool* of 1150 tons was purchased. It was under construction but it was still far from completion. Both London and Liverpool realized that the *Great Western* had a head start on them and they hurriedly had to change their plans to get back into the race. The Londoners abandoned the *British Queen* and chartered the *Sirius* from the St George's Steam Packet Company; she was little over half the size of Brunel's ship but she could be made ready to tackle the Atlantic in a very short time. The Liverpudlians also knew that their ship could not be finished on time and they chartered the *Royal William* from the City of Dublin Steam Packet Company.

The Bristol contingent were very concerned about the attempts by their rival ports to steal their glory. Work was progressing well on the *Great Western* but she had to get back from the Thames to Bristol before the final preparations could be made for her maiden voyage across the Atlantic. The *Sirius* however, set sail from the Thames on Wednesday 28 March 1838 with a crew of thirty-five and with forty passengers on board. She had to stop on the Irish coast for refuelling but she still had several days' start.

The *Great Western* left her moorings at six in the morning of 31 March, three days later than the *Sirius*. Everything seemed to be going well until 8.15 a.m. when suddenly flames appeared from the engine room and clouds of dense black smoke were emitted. There was obviously a serious problem and Brunel described the scene in the log for the day:

Captain Claxton was below deck playing a hosepipe on the flames when a heavy object fell on him from above. He realized that the object was a body and the next thing he saw was a man lying on the boiler room floor. The man was Isambard Brunel who had fallen eighteen feet when a rung had collapsed under his feet.

The fore stoke-hole and engine room soon became enveloped in dense smoke, and the upper part in flames. Thinking it possible the ship might be saved, and that it was important to save the boilers, I crawled down, after a strong inhalation of fresh air, and succeeded in putting on a plunger and opening all the boiler feed cocks, suffering the engines to work to pump them up, as the steam was generating fast from the flames round the upper part of the boilers.

The damage was not serious and it looked far worse than it actually was, but the lagging around the boiler had caught fire and was burning fiercely. Captain Claxton was below deck playing a hosepipe on the flames when a heavy object fell on him from above. He realized that the object was a body and the next thing he saw was a man lying on the boiler room floor. The man was Isambard Brunel who had fallen eighteen feet when a rung had collapsed under his feet. Claxton had fortuitously saved his friend's life by breaking his fall. Brunel was laid on a sail and taken by boat to Canvey Island where he took several weeks to recover. The accident wasted about twelve hours, but the *Great Western* was quickly underway again, and she arrived at Kingroad on the River Severn two days later. Bad news carried quickly, and the rumour that the *Great Western* had been destroyed by fire had travelled faster than she had. It was therefore a surprised and delighted reception committee that greeted the ship in Bristol. Apart from the disaster with the boiler lagging the ship behaved impeccably, but the re-coaling and the re-victualling took several days and it was not until 8 April that the ship left Bristol for New York. The *Sirius* had left Cork on the 4th so there was little hope of catching her.

Historic Crossing At 703 tons the *Sirius* was barely more than half the weight of the *Great Western* but on 22 April when she docked in New York she had made the historic crossing with fifteen tons of coal to spare. She had been nineteen days at sea, four barrels of resin had been taken

THE BLUE RIBAND

The Blue Riband has traditionally been awarded to the passenger ship attaining the fastest crossing of the Atlantic. The eighteen days taken by the *Sirius* was reduced to less than four days by the middle of the twentieth century. Some notable holders of the Blue Riband are:

SHIP	YEAR	TIME		
		Days	Hours	Minutes
Sirius	1838	18	14	22
Great Western	1838	15	12	0
City of Paris	1889	5	19	18
Lucania	1894	5	8	38
Lusitania	1907	4	19	52
Mauritania	1909	4	10	51
Normandie	1935	4	3	2
Queen Mary	1936	4	0	27
United States	1952	3	12	12

from the cargo to fuel the boilers but there had been no need to burn the cabin furniture as some false reports suggested. She presented a fine sight when she arrived in New York with her two tall masts and a dazzling white figurehead of a canine beast holding the Dog Star Sirius between its paws. The Americans turned out in force to give the gallant little ship a richly deserved reception.

But the day was not over for the New Yorkers, and if there had been a Blue Riband to present then the *Sirius* held it for only a few hours. In the afternoon a second plume of smoke appeared in the distance and soon the superstructure of Brunel's new ship became visible on the horizon – both ships are shown on the wood engraving arriving in New York on page 179. The *Great Western* glided in and docked in the harbour after only fifteen and a half days at sea. The New York *Morning Herald* described the event in graphic detail:

The approach of the GREAT WESTERN *to the harbour, and in front of the Battery, was most magnificent. It was about four o'clock yesterday afternoon. The sky was clear – the crowds immense. The Battery was filled with the human multitude, one half of whom were females, their faces covered with smiles, and their delicate persons with the gayest attire. Below, on the broad blue water, appeared this huge thing of life, with four mast, and emitting volumes of smoke. She looked black and blackguard... rakish, cool, reckless, fierce, and forbidding in sombre colours to an extreme. As she neared the* SIRIUS, *she slackened her movements, and took a sweep round, forming a sort of half circle. At this moment the whole battery set forth a tumultuous shout of delight, at the revelation of her magnificent proportions. After making another turn towards Staten Island, she made another sweep, and swept towards East River with extraordinary speed. The vast multitude rent the air with their shouts again, waving handkerchiefs, hats, hurrahing!*

It was a famous day and a very significant event, yet the result was full of paradoxes. Honours were even, the Londoners won the race but the Bristolians had the best ship. The Liverpool entry, the *Royal William*, came in an ignominious third. She did not arrive in New York until July but her time of just under nineteen days was very respectable, and she made the return trip from New York to Liverpool in under fifteen days. On her return she was given a great reception. 'When in Bootle Bay she threw up blue lights and fired guns', reported the *Liverpool Mercury*. 'Soon afterwards she passed Clarence [Dock] and Prince's Pier amidst loud cheering and cast anchor off George's Pier where the passengers landed.'

The Liverpudlians were not dismayed by this failure and in 1840 the paddle steamer *Britannia* was launched on the Clyde, quickly followed by the *Acadia*, the *Caledonia* and the *Columbia*. These four ships became the mainstay of the famous Cunard Line, they carried the transatlantic passenger trade and they also gained the lucrative American mail contract. Liverpool was the port that won the glamorous passenger traffic of the late nineteenth and early twentieth centuries. Thus all three ports were losers but all three ports were winners.

Cosmopolitan Mixture Between 1819 and 1859 an estimated five million emigrants sailed to America and about two-thirds of these sailed from Liverpool. When the American writer Herman Melville arrived at Liverpool in the 1840s he found the dockside was a cosmopolitan mixture of many races:

In the evening, especially when the sailors are gathered in large numbers, these streets present a most singular spectacle, the entire population of the vicinity being turned into them. Hand organs, fiddles and cymbals plied by strolling musicians, mix the songs of the seaman, the babble of women and children, and the groaning and whining of the beggars. From the various boarding houses, each distinguished by gilded emblems outside – an anchor, a crown a ship, a windlass or a dolphin – proceeds the noise of revelry and dancing; and from the open casements lean young girls and old women, chattering and laughing with the crowds in the middle of the street. Every moment strange greetings are exchanged between old sailors who chance to stumble on a ship-mate, last seen in Calcutta or Savannah, and the invariable courtesy that takes place upon these occasions is to go to the next spirit vault and drink each other's health.

Before they could find a berth on their ship the emigrants had to find their way through a maze of officialdom and they had to run the gauntlet of the many swindlers and conmen claiming to be officials. They were lost, sitting on their humble box of belongings, in a strange and busy sea port. They were pestered by orange sellers, toffee sellers, vendors of ribbons and lace, nuts, gingerbread and sweetmeats until the moment of departure. When at last they had found their berths and stacked their worldly belongings into the ship the wind and tide took them across the Mersey Bar and on the way to America.

EMIGRATION
The Atlantic migration from Europe to the USA and Canada was the greatest in history. An estimated thirty-seven million crossed between 1820 and 1980. Seventeen million of these crossed in the peak years 1880 to 1910.

The emigrants came from all parts of Europe and much further afield, even the Chinese had to find their way to Liverpool to get to America. For several weeks the passengers shared the same small world between the decks and they often befriended each other. They talked of their homelands, the towns and villages they had left behind. Sometimes they made their own music: a German would tell a folk tale from the Black Forest, a Swiss shepherd would sing a song from his alpine valley, an Irish family would dance a jig on the swaying and creaking decks.

At last, after several weeks cooped up on the ship, the coast of the New World was sighted to the west. They approached the disembarking point at Ellis Island. Their problems were still not over, but they were no longer emigrants, they were immigrants arriving in a hopeful new world.

A Commercial Success Brunel had grand ideas for developing his steamships and his next venture was the magnificent *Great Britain*. At 3270 tons she was the largest and most luxurious passenger liner of

At last, after several weeks cooped up on the ship, the coast of the new world was sighted to the west. They approached the disembarking point at Ellis Island. Their problems were still not over, but they were no longer emigrants, they were immigrants arriving in a hopeful new world.

the times. In spite of the fact that Brunel changed his design from paddle wheels to screw propeller in the middle of the construction, his ship was launched in 1844. The ship was the biggest ever built in Bristol. It was both too long and too wide for the lock gates leading to the River Avon, a fact of which Brunel was fully aware. The *Great Britain* was too huge to negotiate the River Avon safely. She operated from Liverpool and in the first twenty-three years of her life she made thirty-two voyages to Australia and back. She was therefore a commercial success and the voyages themselves did something to change the world by making the antipodes more easily accessible. The ship itself certainly did much to influence the design of the luxury passenger liners of the future. Already, as the *Great Britain* started on her maiden voyage, Brunel's thoughts were turning to something far larger and grander.

The riverside was a mass of timbers, chains, winding drums and lifting tackle to get the massive iron plates into position. The sightseers still came, even though the Thames was little more than an open sewer at that time and one of the most unhealthy places in England. When Queen Victoria came to view the works her nose never left her nosegay.

Isambard Brunel's next venture was to design and build a ship that could sail to Australia without having to refuel. It needed to carry 8000 tons of coal to achieve this target. He then thought about a ship that could sail round the world without refuelling and estimated that 15,000 tons of coal would be required. The size of a ship to meet this requirement worked out at 660 feet in length, 83 in the beam and 30 feet depth.

He managed to obtain support for his design and in 1852 the keel was laid down at Millwall on the River Thames in the shipyard of John Scott Russell. There were many problems. Some of them were technical and Brunel was in his element solving them. Many were financial and Brunel suspected that John Scott Russell was embezzling the funds. But gradually the great ship began to take shape on the bank of the Thames and sightseers flocked from afar to see it. Brunel decided to call it the *Great Eastern* for it was designed to open up trade with the Far East, but it became known colloquially as the Great Leviathan. The ship was to be powered both by paddle wheels and a screw propeller, as well as the usual array of masts that the steamships still carried with them in case of engine problems. The massive hull took shape, it was shored up by wooden blocks and scaffolding. The riverside was a mass of timbers, chains, winding drums and lifting tackle to get the vast iron plates into position. The sightseers still came, even though the Thames was little more than an open sewer at that time and one of the most unhealthy places in England. When Queen Victoria came to view the works her nose never left her nosegay.

As the time of the launch grew near the public were very eager to support the event. Much against Brunel's wishes it was decided to make a public spectacle out of the launching. When the great day arrived the whole thing was a disaster. The ship would not move; she refused to leave her birthplace. The crowd went away disappointed and the credibility of the project was badly undermined.

But Brunel persevered against all odds. He found that the only way to move his ship was by the use of hydraulic rams. Moving a few inches a day at first, but increasing to a few feet every day, the great ship was edged sideways into the Thames. By February 1859 she was afloat at last but the mental strain on Brunel was very great. By the time the *Great Eastern* was ready for her maiden voyage poor Brunel was bedridden and he was not well enough to travel with her. There were many wealthy people aboard when the *Great Eastern* made her maiden voyage down the Thames, and they enjoyed the superb grand saloon with great mirrors camouflaging the smokestack. Victorian luxury such as this had seldom been equalled. The great ship made her way out of the Thames, around the Kentish coast and into the English Channel. Then came a tragic accident.

A Terrible Disaster *The Times* correspondent was on the deck when there was a mighty explosion with steam hissing from all over. The forward part of the deck appeared to explode like a mine with such power that it threw the huge funnel into the air. There was a great rush of steam and glass, then giltware, ornaments and broken pieces of wood rained down on the deck. Worst of all the scalded bodies of some of the crew were thrown out from the bowels of the ship onto the deck. It was discovered that one of the steam safety valves had been accidentally shut off and the pressure of steam had been building up and up inside the cylinders until they could take no more and a tremendous explosion had occurred. The *Great Eastern*'s maiden voyage had turned into a terrible disaster.

When the news of the disaster and the loss of life reached Brunel it proved too much for him. He lived only a few more days and died from a stroke on 15 September.

All this was too difficult for the world to comprehend. Everybody remembered the disaster of the launching and the myth was born that the *Great Eastern* was an unlucky ship. It was unfortunate that the great ship should have started off with such a bad name, as in her subsequent career she became the greatest luxury liner on the seas and she should be remembered for her later achievements rather than her early problems. She made several voyages which changed the world and one in particular.

The Electric Telegraph By the time the *Great Eastern* was launched the race to carry passengers across the Atlantic was well under way, but it took nearly three weeks for news as well as people to cross the Atlantic. The invention and patenting of the electric telegraph in the 1830s had changed the world and messages could be transmitted along a wire at the speed of light. A cable across the Atlantic Ocean would greatly speed up the time for news to cross between the Old World and the New. The first cable to be laid across the Atlantic was only partly successful. It sent 732 messages but it was too frail for the Atlantic conditions and it only

---

BRUNEL'S SHIPS

Brunel was a great innovator and he built three steamships in all, which were all revolutionary in one way or another:

1838 **The *Great Western***
1,340 tons
Paddle wheels

1844 **The *Great Britain***
3,000 tons
Screw propeller
The largest ship in the world

1859 **The *Great Eastern***
17,000 tons
Paddle wheels and screw propeller
The largest ship in the world
for a generation

The breaking of the Atlantic telegraph cable aboard the GREAT EASTERN, *2 August 1865.*

The transatlantic cable is fed from the ship's hold by the wheel in the foreground. The artist depicts the moment when the cable snapped. The grappling gear could not locate the cable but it was eventually recovered when the second cable was laid.

survived for two months. A new and more robust cable was required and in 1865 the Telegraph Construction Company chartered the *Great Eastern* for the nominal sum of £50,000. She was the only ship in the world large enough to carry a cable that would stretch all the way from Europe to America.

With her cable tanks installed, the *Great Eastern* set off from Valencia in Ireland paying out the precious cable as she sailed. In charge of the project was Daniel Gooch, formerly a locomotive engineer under Brunel on the Great Western Railway. All went well for the first part of the journey, but with a thousand miles still to go the cable snapped. No amount of blind searching and grappling on the sea bed could find it again. The curse of the *Great Eastern* had struck again and the attempt was a failure.

At 1.30 p.m. (wrote Gooch) the cable broke a few yards from the ship and all our labour and anxiety is lost. We are now dragging to see if we can by chance recover it, but of this I have no hope, nor have I heart to wish. I shall be glad if I can sleep and for a few hours forget I live. This is indeed a sad and bitter disappointment. A couple more days and we would have been safe. God's will be done. This one thing, upon which I had set my heart more than any other work I was ever engaged on, is dead, and all has to begin again, because it must be done and, availing ourselves of the experience of this, we will succeed.

The following year the great ship left Ireland again; this time she sailed from the neighbouring port of Bantry Bay. She paid out the cable as before and carried greatly improved grappling gear in case the same misfortune happened again. The new gear was not needed. This time the Newfoundland coast was reached without mishap.

When the great ship arrived there was a rapturous welcome at Content Bay in Newfoundland. The end of the cable was taken ashore amid scenes of great enthusiasm. One cable man held up the end of the cable and danced around with it in his mouth. Daniel Gooch sent a message back to Ireland through the cable. 'Gooch. Heart's content to Glass, Valencia, July 27th 6 p.m.: Our shore-end has just been laid and a most perfect cable, under God's blessing, has completed telegraphic communication between England and the Continent of America.'

There was even better news to come. On the following day the new grappling gear did prove itself to be useful and found the end of the earlier cable – soon afterwards there were two cables connecting the Old and the New World, both of them laid by the *Great Eastern*. The ship went on to lay a cable from France to America, then from Bombay to Aden and up the Red Sea. She went on like a great spider laying a web of cables around the world. Every voyage brought parts of the world closer together. The great ship changed the world for the better.

Scott, Amundsen and Shackleton travel to the ends of the Earth

The expeditions of the legendary Polar explorers

1840 – 1916

'Five weather-beaten, frost-bitten fists they were that grasped the pole, raised the waving flag in the air, and planted it at the first Geographical South Pole.'

ROALD AMUNDSEN, *ARRIVAL AT THE POLE*

The nineteenth century was an important century in the history of discovery, but most of the great expeditions of the time were not made by sea. They were made overland in America, in Africa, in the Arctic and the Antarctic.

The mapping of the world was almost complete before 1800; practically every island had been discovered and every scrap of coastline, except for the most inhospitable parts of the world, had been charted. Towards the middle of the century however, there was yet another renaissance in the idea of the northern passages to Asia. The hope of finding a North East and a North West Passage to the Pacific Ocean had never completely gone away. In a sense the geographers were right. It was indeed possible to get from Europe to the Pacific over the north of Asia and also from the Atlantic to the Pacific over the north of America. It had been noted that after a very mild winter followed by a warm summer the ice melted and passages which had been bound by ice for decades or even centuries could sometimes open again for a short time.

All through the eighteenth century and well into the nineteenth the British, in particular, never let go of the concept of the North West Passage. The Hudson Bay Company, set up by Charles II to trade in furs and minerals, explored the whole of Hudson Bay and before 1700 they had shown that there was no passage to the west leading out of it. In 1719 the company sponsored an expedition under the leadership of James Knight to explore to the north, but Knight did not return and it was not until fifty years later that the macabre remains of his ship were found. Another attempt was made by Christopher Middleton in 1741 with two ships, the *Furnace* and the *Discovery* but again the expedition was a failure. Russian discoveries in the north Pacific showed the existence of the Bering Straits between America and Asia. This gave rise to a lot of speculation because it quite rightly implied that the western exit from the North West Passage had been discovered.

Exploration continued fitfully and in 1766 Samuel Hearn sailed north from Fort Churchill in Hudson Bay to a latitude of 71° – but even at this far north he did not find a passage to the west. In 1773 an expedition penetrated to 80° north, only 10° from the North Pole. The ships were the *Racehorse* and the *Carcass* and the expedition was distinguished by the presence of a young man of sixteen who was one of its junior members. His name was Horatio Nelson. In the eighteenth century the last serious attempt to find the passage was James Cook's abortive expedition of 1778 when he successfully passed through the Bering Straits only to be foiled by a wall of ice in the Beaufort Sea.

Sir John Franklin In the nineteenth century explorations were made by land along the north coast of Alaska. Thus by this means the western end of the North West Passage became better known and it was correctly surmised that in a very mild year the ice might relent enough to allow a ship to pass through. A passage called Lancaster Sound had been discovered near Baffin Island at a latitude of 74°. It was only a few

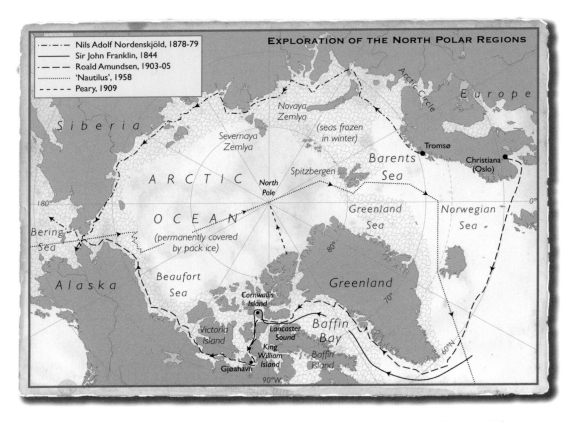

hundred miles from Lancaster Sound to the Beaufort Sea, and if a way could be found through the ice and the islands in between, then the North West Passage would be conquered at last.

In 1844 the British planned their next expedition. It was to be led by Sir John Franklin, an experienced explorer who had been to Alaska and who had sailed on the Beaufort Sea. He was very keen to make the voyage in spite of the fact that he was nearly sixty years of age. Franklin entered the Royal Navy at the age of fourteen, and sailed under Matthew Flinders in 1801 and 1803 on an exploratory voyage to Australia. He fought under Horatio Nelson at the battle of Trafalgar in 1805 and he also saw action at New Orleans in 1814. Franklin and his men were very confident that they would succeed where so many had failed. They had two fine ships called the *Erebus* and the *Terror*. The ships were wind powered although they carried a steam engine on board whose purpose was obscure. They took a supply of canned food and were well stocked with all the modern comforts that early Victorian society could supply for the voyage.

The expedition started well – the ships passed through Lancaster Sound without incident. They wintered at Beechey Island, then they passed southwards along the western side of Cornwallis Island, continued through Peel Sound and into what became Franklin Strait. Then they became frozen fast in the ice of Victoria Strait off King William Island, about midway between the Atlantic and Pacific oceans. Three young sailors died and were buried at Beechey Island. Years later it was discovered that they had suffered from lead poisoning contracted from the canned food.

Horrific Disaster From there on the voyage turned into a terrible and horrific disaster. The ice did not melt in the spring and the ships failed to become free. They were trapped in the ice for eighteen months as they slowly ran out of food and supplies. John Franklin died in June 1847. The ships, still gripped by ice, were finally deserted on 22 April 1848, and the 105 survivors tried to head south across the North American mainland to the Back River. They had little food with them and they found no food supplies along the way. The men hauled their boats across the wilds of northern Canada in the fragile hope of finding a route to survival. The local Inuit (Eskimos) witnessed them as grey starving men pulling their boats across the land and begging for food that the Inuit could not afford to give them. An old Inuit woman, many years later, told of how she saw the men falling down and dying as they walked. The whole of the party perished in a tragedy of even greater proportions than Scott's ill-fated expedition to the South Pole two generations later.

The dreadful fate of Sir John Franklin and his crew prevented any further exploration to the north for many years. Towards the end of the nineteenth century the initiative passed to the Norwegians who were interested in both of the northern passages. It was the North East Passage which was discovered first. The Swedish explorer Nils Adolf Nordenskjöld started out from Tromsø in Norway in the spring of 1878. He had the great advantage of steam power and his ship, the *Vega*, sailed through the Novaya Zemlya Archipelago and navigated along the northern coast of Siberia until it became locked in the ice when he was still some distance away from the Bering Straits. Nordenskjöld survived. He endured the cold Arctic winter and when the thaw came in the spring his ship was free again. He completed his voyage and successfully entered into the Pacific.

It was not until a generation later, in 1915, that the first ship navigated through the North East Passage in the opposite direction, from east to west. But once the weather conditions allowed it and the route became known, the North East Passage became a practical trade route for ice breakers and powered ships.

Roald Amundsen One young man who showed a great interest in the voyage of Nordenskjöld was Roald Amundsen who was born in 1872 at Borge in Norway. From his childhood days Amundsen decided that he wanted to become an explorer. His parents, however, thought otherwise and sent him to study medicine – but he spent most of his time devouring all the literature he could acquire on polar exploration. At the age of twenty-one, when both his parents had died, Amundsen sold off all his medical textbooks, packed away his medical instruments, and announced his intention of becoming an explorer. He decided that what a successful polar explorer needed was good discipline and inspired leadership. Applying a systematic approach he decided to study for his

At the age of twenty-one, when both his parents had died, Amundsen sold off all his medical textbooks, packed away his medical instruments, and announced his intention of becoming an explorer. He decided that what a successful polar explorer needed was good discipline and inspired leadership.

master's ticket, and in 1894 at the age of twenty-two he went to sea as one of the crew of a sealing vessel.

Three years later he was appointed first mate on board the *Belgica*, a ship sailing on a Belgian-financed Antarctic expedition led by the polar explorer Adrien de Gerlache de Gomery. The expedition almost ended in disaster when the ship became trapped in the ice near the Island of Peter the First. Thirteen months of anxious isolation followed with the *Belgica* unable to move. The winter months were very arduous. Virtually all the expedition members contracted scurvy and when the captain fell ill it was Roald Amundsen who took over the command. He quickly rose to the situation – he put the crew to work catching penguins and seals for food and to making warm clothes out of woollen blankets. The *Belgica* was still under Amundsen's command in March 1899 when the spring came and she finally broke out of the ice. This voyage was noteworthy as the first expedition ever to survive a winter in the severe cold of the Antarctic.

THE ANTARCTIC

The first ship to enter the Antarctic Circle was Captain Cook's ship the *Resolution* in 1773. Cook circumnavigated Antarctica as closely as he could within the limits of the ice and his sailing ship. The following year he reached a latitude of 71° 10' south. This was the occasion when he declared that he had 'Ambition not only to go farther than any one had gone before, but as far as it was possible for man to go...'

Magnetic North Pole Amundsen was inspired rather than dismayed by his Antarctic experiences. He obtained his captain's ticket and set about planning his own Arctic expedition, this time in search of the North West Passage. He realized that to obtain financial backing he must have a scientific goal and he decided that the determination of the magnetic North Pole would be a suitable subject. He left for Hamburg where he signed on for a course to study earth magnetism, but all the time he studied magnetism he was also making detailed plans for his next expedition.

The vessel selected by Amundsen for his voyage was called the *Gjøa*. It was a secondhand ship, a sloop about seventy feet long with a displacement of only forty-seven tons. He set out from Christiania (now Oslo) in the summer of 1903 with a crew of six. The *Gjøa* crossed the North Atlantic, then hugged the west coast of Greenland before crossing to the northern end of Baffin Island. The voyage continued into Lancaster Sound where the *Gjøa* started to thread her way through the labyrinth of islands off the north west coast of Canada. These were treacherous waters with many dangers from ice floes, fog and shallow water, and Amundsen was well aware that he was close to the place where Franklin's expedition had floundered. Towards the end of the summer Amundsen and his crew had found a natural harbour on King William Island, north west of Hudson Bay, they called their port Gjøahavn after their ship. Instead of pressing on to the west Amundsen decided to remain there with his crew for two years. His plan was to learn as much as he could about the environment and how to survive it. His companions built observatories to take magnetic observations using high precision instruments.

Their studies established the position of the magnetic North Pole and included observations of such precision that they provided the experts on polar magnetism with sufficient data to last them for twenty years. This was a mere sideline to Amundsen's real objective. He befriended the Inuit, studied their way of life and how they survived in the cold. He taught himself and his men how to drive the dog teams. He carefully observed the clothes the Inuit wore and he realized that they provided better protection from the Arctic winds than his own garments. He studied their customs and, most importantly, the food they ate and how they procured it. He even slept with them in an igloo and he noted how the walls, built from blocks of ice, retained all the heat inside. He stored all this information in his retentive memory. If he ever became trapped in the polar regions he wanted to know how to survive, how to find food and how to cross the ice and snow with the dog teams to reach civilization.

The North West Passage Conquered In August 1905 the scientific work was completed and the *Gjøa* resumed its westerly course through the ice and the fog. The channel was very shallow so that at one point the vessel had barely an inch of water beneath its keel. The *Gjøa* moved slowly along its perilous course but Amundsen and his crew knew that if they could make sufficient progress to the west they would soon be in waters that were known and had been charted by navigators moving eastwards from Alaska. Barring accidents they could complete the final stage of their journey through the North West Passage. After three more weeks of steadily working to the west there came a historic moment when the expedition sighted a whaling ship out of San Francisco. It was a great moment for the small party as they knew with certainty that their ship had successfully navigated the North West Passage, the passage that had defeated so many seamen for many centuries before them. The *Gjøa* was the first vessel to get so far but the voyage was not over and shortly after sighting the whaler Amundsen's ship became trapped in the ice. It was stuck fast and it remained immobile all through the winter.

Amundsen was anxious to tell the world about the achievements of his expedition. This was one situation where his training and experience were put to use. In October he set off with a dog team and one of his crew. The two men had to travel five hundred miles and climb across mountains 2700 metres high, but on 5 December the men arrived with their dog team at Eagle City in Alaska. There was a telegraph connection at Eagle City and Amundsen was therefore able to relay his news to the rest of the world. He still had to travel through the last reaches of the North West Passage and he had to wait for the thaw before he could get back to his ship and take it further. The *Gjøa* passed through the Bering Straits in 1906, and only then could Roald Amundsen claim to be the first to navigate the North West Passage.

He befriended the Inuit, studied their way of life and how they survived in the cold. He taught himself and his men how to drive the dog teams. He carefully observed the clothes the Inuit wore and he realized that they provided better protection from the Arctic winds than his own garments. He studied their customs and, most importantly, the food they ate and how they procured it. He even slept with them in an igloo and he noted how the walls, built from blocks of ice, retained all the heat inside.

A member of the expedition led by Roald Amundsen.

Where Scott used ponies to pull the sleds Amundsen used dog teams on his expedition to the South Pole. This was one of the main reasons why Amundsen won the race, but the downside was that the dogs were eaten for fresh meat.

The North West Passage never became a commercial route for regular traffic. It was not until 1940-42 that it was navigated again, this time by Henry Larsen of the Royal Canadian Mounted Police. In 1954 the first passage by a deep-draught vessel was made by HMCS *Labrador*, a Canadian naval icebreaker. In 1969 the *Manhattan*, the largest and most powerful commercial ship ever built in the United States at that time, smashed through 650 miles of ice between Baffin Bay and Point Barrow in Alaska to assess the commercial feasibility of the passage. The *Manhattan* made the passage, but the future of the North West Passage as a regular commercial route is still not, and probably never will be, a viable proposition.

A Secret Destination Amundsen was far from finished as an explorer. His next venture was to try and reach the North Pole. His plans were thwarted when he heard that the American Robert E. Peary had got there before him. Undaunted, he continued his preparations and secretly changed his venue from the North Pole to the South Pole. When Amundsen left Norway in June 1910 nobody except his brother knew that he was heading for the South Pole instead of the North. He sailed his ship the *Fram* directly from the Madeira Islands to the Bay of Whales, to Antarctica and along the Ross Sea. The base he set up there was sixty miles closer to the Pole than the Antarctic base of the English explorer Captain Robert Scott, who was heading a British expedition at the same time with the same goal. Amundsen prepared for the coming journey in his usual meticulous fashion, making a preliminary trip to deposit food supplies along the first part of his route to the Pole and back. To transport his supplies, he used sled dogs, while Scott depended on Siberian ponies. Amundsen set out with four companions, fifty-two dogs and four sledges on 19 October 1911 and, after encountering good weather, he arrived at the South Pole on 14 December. The dogs were seen as part of his food supplies. Scott reached the South Pole on 17 January, but he had left it too late in the season and on the difficult return journey he and all his party perished.

Ernest Shackleton The British explorer Ernest Shackleton had accompanied Scott on one of his earlier Polar expeditions and in 1914 he set off on his own expedition to Antarctica. His plan was to land on the coast of the Weddell Sea and make his way to the South Pole. From there he planned to return by another route to the Ross Sea, thereby achieving the first crossing of the Antarctic continent.

The Great War broke out just before Shackleton set sail from London. His ship the *Endurance* and his whole company were offered to the government for service against the enemy, but the government refused the offer and allowed the ship to proceed on its journey. Shackleton had bad luck right from the start of his enterprise. In January 1915 his ship became trapped and frozen in the ice of the Weddell Sea (see opening photograph on page 188) and he and his crew were forced to spend the whole of the seventy-nine days of the Antarctic winter with no sight of the sun, huddled in the close confines of their ship. They were confident that the ship could be freed in the spring when the ice melted and when there came a great crack in the ice it gave them hope. It was not to be. The ice floes closed in on the ship, putting her under tremendous pressure. The crew were forced to abandon the *Endurance* before she was crushed by the ice and they now faced an extraordinary journey back to civilization.

They had saved a large quantity of food and gear, as well as their three boats, but the men were adrift on the ice at the mercy of the wind and the currents. For three months the ice floes took them

Sometimes huge grampuses charged up from below, smashing ice a yard or more in thickness, and sought to attack them. On several occasions a sea leopard mounted the ice to assail them, but each time it was shot and eaten. The fish contained in its stomach proved one of the most delicious meals of the ordeal.

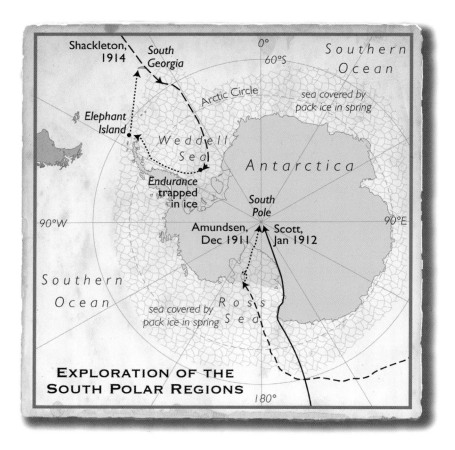

Shackleton,
1914

South
Georgia

0°

60°S

Southern

Ocean

Arctic Circle

sea covered by
pack ice in spring

Elephant
Island

Weddell
Sea

Antarctica

Endurance
trapped
in ice

South
Pole

90°W

90°E

Amundsen,
Dec 1911

Scott,
Jan 1912

Southern

Ocean

R o s s
S e a

sea covered by
pack ice in spring

EXPLORATION OF THE
SOUTH POLAR REGIONS

180°

further to the north. They had just enough food to maintain life, for they
caught seals and ate the flesh, they drank the oil from the blubber; and
eventually they killed and ate their beloved companions, the dogs. All
but the most indispensable property was thrown away. The men kept
photographs and letters of loved ones but there is a story that they
emptied their pockets of sovereigns, half-sovereigns and silver and
threw the money into the snow. From time to time the ice cracked and
broke up – on one occasion this happened in the middle of the night
beneath a tent – carrying away a man in his sleeping bag. Sometimes
huge grampuses charged up from below, smashing ice a yard or more
in thickness, and sought to attack them. On several occasions a sea
leopard mounted the ice to assail them, but each time it was shot and
eaten. The fish contained in their stomachs proved to be some of the
most delicious meals of the ordeal.

Water had to be obtained by melting ice in the cookers, but when the
oil began to run out men put chips of ice in tobacco tins and slept with
these next to their bodies so as to give them a little drink of water in the
morning. The ice floe they encamped on split in two, then it repeatedly
split due to the warmer climate until it was dangerous to stay on it any
longer. At last the boats were launched. Finally they had some control of
their destiny but when they left the floe there was no ice and therefore no
drinking supply. Mouths swelled, lips split, food became uneatable, and
the men suffered tortures of thirst with 40° and 50° of frost around them.

Elephant Island At last they reached an uninhabited island known as
Elephant Island. The three boats landed with difficulty and the men
quenched their thirst by sucking the ice to their hearts' content. Here the
party was split up. Frank Wild, second-in-command of the expedition,
was left in charge of twenty-one men on a small desolate sandy bay open
to gales and snowstorms, with only two upturned boats for refuge. He
had only the barest food supply to keep his men in health and spirits
until Shackleton could bring help to rescue them.

Shackleton, with five chosen staunch rowers, made a momentous
boat voyage, horrible in its details of agony and privation, through
appalling weather, tempestuous seas, ice, gales, enduring bitter cold, wet
that soaked everything from clothes to food and covered the sufferers
with sea boils, to reach the distant island of South Georgia 650 nautical
miles away. A landfall was made but the only habitation, a whaling
station, was situated on the far side of the island. Shackleton and two of
his four men had to climb the jagged and icy mountains and without the
aid of any maps, they had to find the whaling station on the east coast. At
last, to the astonishment of the whalers, he made contact with
civilization. He had difficulty finding a boat to rescue his men but he
succeeded in chartering a steamship called the *Yelcho*. On 30 August 1916
Shackleton managed to return to Elephant Island and amid great emotion
he picked up his remaining twenty-two stranded men.

It was one of the most amazing voyages in history and it says much
for Shackleton's inspired leadership in the most severe conditions in the
world that he was able to take his men so far in the most terrible
conditions on the planet - yet he returned them eventually to civilization.

Voyages under the sea

Advances in submarine warfare and scientific discovery

1776 – 1960s

*'What is it that the coming of the submarine really means?
It means that the whole foundation of our traditional naval strategy,
which served us so well in the past, has been broken down!'*

Memorandum in papers of British Admiral Jellicoe, 1912

Exploration on the surface of the sea was usually undertaken for the purpose of finding land or sometimes to find a sea passage. The primary reasons for wanting to travel beneath the surface were those of warfare, but later these journeys were undertaken in the interest of the scientific study of the waters below, the marine life and the seabed.

The earliest attempt to use a submarine in warfare can be dated to 1776, the year celebrated by America for the Declaration of Independence. David Bushnell, a brilliant American inventor, actually designed and built a submersible craft and launched it against the British in the hope of sinking HMS *Eagle*, a man-of-war.

His craft, the *Turtle*, looked very like the creature of its name; it consisted of two six-foot shells with a conning tower where the turtle's head would be but it progressed in a vertical rather than a horizontal orientation. A single sailor served as the captain, the navigator, the steersman and the power supply for the vessel. Bushnell had to crank a screw to propel the craft forward, he had a valve to let in water to submerge the craft and a handle with which to pump out the water when he wanted to resurface. As if this was not enough, he also had to work the tiller and to navigate with a compass and a water gauge. When he reached his target Bushnell had to attach a 150-pound keg of gunpowder to his prey, which had a time fuse of half an hour. In that half hour he had to crank furiously to get his submersible away from the explosion, but in fact this proved unnecessary for HMS *Eagle* resisted the assault without even trying. Bushnell was unable to drill through the copper plating around the hull of the ship and he was forced to retreat without setting the charge.

Robert Fulton Bushnell's effort was not the last American attempt to built a submersible craft and in 1800 Robert Fulton, better known for his experimental steam vessels, built a cigar-shaped shell of iron about 21 feet long, designed to travel beneath the water. Again it was propelled by hand but the prototype raised many problems and it was not successful. Very few other attempts to build submersible craft were made in the nineteenth century.

When World War One broke out in 1914, however, the submarine came into its own. The Germans launched their U-boats which were very effective submarines and because they were invisible from the surface they were able to play havoc with Allied shipping. In World War Two a very similar situation developed with the Battle of the North Atlantic when, early in the war, the Germans had the capability to sink the Allied merchant shipping almost at will. A sonar system was developed to detect the U-boats but it was only partly successful. The Allies then used aircraft to detect the German submarines which proved much more effective. Many U-boats were destroyed but the end result was a very closely fought conquest.

After World War Two the submarine came into its own as a vehicle of exploration. Nuclear powered submarines were developed by the USA.

Bushnell's Turtle was built during the American War of Independence. The single seaman had to provide power, navigation, diving and surfacing. He had to lay the charge and set it, and then he had to escape from the scene of the explosion.

They were able to travel many miles without refuelling and could carry sufficient food, air and water to stay underwater for thousands of miles. In 1954 the submarine *Nautilus* was launched, named after Robert Fulton's craft from many years earlier. On 23 July 1958 the *Nautilus* departed from Pearl Harbor in Hawaii and headed for the Bering Straits. Here she submerged and sought a place to enter beneath the polar ice cap. Having got beneath the ice she was able to travel in a dead straight line to the North Pole where she arrived on 3 August. 'For the world, our country, and the Navy', announced Commander William Anderson. There were 116 men on board.

The *Nautilus* then continued into the Atlantic seas east of Greenland and continued south until she reached Portsmouth harbour at Kittery in Maine, having travelled 1,830 miles beneath the sea. It was a very different voyage from the explorations of old, but it was certainly a significant voyage and the first of its kind. The success of the *Nautilus* generated interest in other areas of submarine development, and vessels were designed to explore the deepest of the ocean trenches.

THE NUCLEAR SUBMARINE

The application of nuclear power to the submarine created a great advance over the traditional submarine. The nuclear submarine could stay under water for many months at a time, it could travel at maximum speed for as long as required without consuming oxygen supplies. It carried nuclear warheads and it became a major part of the nuclear deterrent programme. The Falklands conflict in 1982 was the only time the nuclear submarine was used in anger, when HMS *Conqueror* sank the Argentine cruiser *General Belgrano* although it used non-nuclear torpedoes.

Mariana Trench The first bathyscaph, as the vessels were called, was built in Belgium between 1946 and 1948 but it was damaged during trials in the Cape Verde Islands. The bathyscaph was rebuilt and greatly improved, and was renamed FNRS 3. In 1954 it carried out a series of dives including one of 4,000 metres (13,000 feet) into the Atlantic off Dakar in Senegal. A second, improved, bathyscaph, called the *Trieste*, was launched on 1 August 1953, and dived to a depth of 3,150 metres (10,300 feet) in the same year. It is depicted in the picture on page 198 in a late 1950s artwork showing it operating on the deep ocean floor. The *Trieste* was subsequently acquired by the United States Navy, taken to California and redesigned to enable it to reach the seabed of the great Pacific trenches. Several dives were made by Jacques Piccard, the son of the designer Auguste Piccard, and on 23 January 1960, accompanied by Lieutenant Don Walsh of the US Navy, the *Trieste* dived to a record 10,916 metres in the Pacific's Mariana Trench.

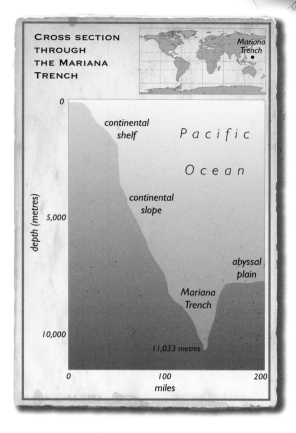

CROSS SECTION THROUGH THE MARIANA TRENCH

This depth represented the limit of underwater exploration in the 1960s. Many new life forms were discovered which had adapted to the conditions very deep in the ocean. It was soon recognized however, that life support systems were a great price to pay for the research when it was obvious that very sophisticated automated systems could be developed. Thus in the twenty-first century a remotely operated bathyscaph reached a record depth of 11,000 metres in the Mariana Trench and it was able to collect samples from the wall of the trench. Single celled organisms were collected and returned for examination. They threw light on the origins of life on the planet Earth. Whilst submarine development will never challenge surface travel for commercial purposes it has many applications in construction, scientific research and maintenance of underwater facilities.

Great Age of Exploration In the third millennium, as scientists and technologists push ever further out into space to discover more about the solar system, the exploration of the Earth appears to be complete. Yet the capes and headlands, the sea passages, the winds and currents discovered in the great age of exploration will always be with us. At Cape Horn are the ghosts of Magellan, Drake and Dampier. On the American continent

Yet the capes and headlands, the sea passages, the winds and currents discovered in the great age of exploration will always be with us. At Cape Horn are the ghosts of Magellan, Drake and Dampier. On the American continent Thanksgiving is celebrated every year. In the remote Antarctic Ocean is the place where Cook at last turned his ship the RESOLUTION, *covered in ice and with sails as stiff as boards, at the furthest south that it was possible to go.*

Thanksgiving is celebrated every year. In the remote Antarctic Ocean is the place where Cook at last turned his ship the *Resolution*, covered in ice and with sails as stiff as boards, at the furthest south that it was possible to go. As they set the sails to turn the ship a young midshipman called George Vancouver scrambled out along the jib and waved his hat at his comrades, he wanted to boast that he had been further south than any man before him. In the wintry north of Canada are reminders of Hudson, James and Franklin. The Pacific Islands owe much to Torres, Tasman, Cook and Bougainville. The Galapagos Islands will always remember the visit of the young Charles Darwin. Such is the spirit of the great voyages of exploration.

INDEX

Entries referring to illustrations and maps are in bold

Quercus Publishing plc
21 Bloomsbury Square
London
WC1A 2NS

First published 2007

A catalogue record of this book is available from the British Library.

ISBN	Cloth case edition	1 84724 004 6
		978 1 84724 004 0
	Printed case edition	1 84724 146 8
		978 1 84724 146 7
	Paperback	1 84724 208 1
		978 1 84724 208 2

Printed and bound in China

Edited and typeset by Windrush Publishing Services,
12 Adlestrop, Moreton in Marsh, Gloucestershire GL56 0YN
Picture research by Victoria Huxley
Maps by John Taylor